CU00648175

Land Rover Discovery
Series 1 and 2

Land Rover Discovery
Series 1 and 2

Ralph Hosier

THE CROWOOD PRESS

First published in 2014 by
The Crowood Press Ltd
Ramsbury, Marlborough
Wiltshire SN8 2HR

www.crowood.com

British Library Cataloguing-in-Publication Data
A catalogue record for this book is available from the British Library.

ISBN 978 1 84797 826 4

Disclaimer
Safety is of the utmost importance in every aspect of an automotive workshop. The practical
procedures and the tools and equipment used in automotive workshops are potentially
dangerous. Tools should be used in strict accordance with the manufacturer's recommended
procedures and current health and safety regulations. The author and publisher cannot accept
responsibility for any accident or injury caused by following the advice given in this book.

Acknowledgements
The following people allowed me to photograph, and in some cases disassemble, their cars:
Nick, Franc, Diana, Jill, Ranen and Rebecca. Thank you all very much. The biggest thank you
goes to Diana, for support and inspiration in all things.

Typeset by Jean Cussons Typesetting, Diss, Norfolk

Printed and bound in India by Replika Press Pvt Ltd

contents

The Discovery's proportions were very carefully engineered to make it look smaller than it was. Note how much the rear door slopes forward at the top.

1 introduction

The Land Rover Discovery is a fantastic go-anywhere vehicle, unless it's broken down on your driveway. If that happens then chances are it is because of poor maintenance. The Discovery 1 is based on the Range Rover Classic, which first went on sale in 1970, so some parts are from an age where extensive maintenance was simply routine, and whilst the Discovery 2 didn't need its distributor cap replacing every year, its added complexity brings with it a few more jobs to do.

A Discovery and the Range Rover that inspired it, undaunted by rough roads and poor conditions.

Good maintenance makes these superb vehicles a joy to own; poor maintenance makes them a nightmare. Knowing what to look for is the key to keeping your car working, but sadly the usual workshop guides miss a few things out. This book is written largely from personal experience and some lessons I learned the hard way so hopefully you don't have to.

I have been enjoying these cars since they first appeared, having owned four Series 1 and two Series 2 Discoverys and worked on a great many more. I've used them for everyday commuting, the school run, moving building materials (750kg pallet of bricks does just fit in the back of a 200 with the back seat out!), towing my race cars all over the country and off-roading trips through mountainous valleys, rivers, deep mud and glaciers. My Discoverys have rescued people from floods, shipped families to weddings, carried furniture home and also been used for pure entertainment at 'pay and play' off-road days. And that's why I think they are brilliant.

I have always done all the maintenance, and a few modifications too, myself. That way I know the job was done the way I wanted it, plus when working on my own car I learn more about its condition, which sometimes helps to stop problems developing. One such problem is the scourge of fake parts, which can make a mockery of home maintenance and lead to dire consequences. So please read the section at the end of this book about where to buy parts and tools from to avoid any nasty surprises.

That's me, your author, clearly pleased with my day's 'work' with my '94 Discovery 1 V8.

I have also included a glossary at the end of the book, which hopefully should explain any technical jargon that's crept into the book.

With the right knowledge, tools and quality parts, maintaining these great cars is very rewarding. Being able to fix things yourself is very liberating, plus it saves a ton of money on labour costs.

WARNING

However, before you read on I must give you a word of warning: working on your own car can be dangerous. Many parts are sharp or heavy and could very easily injure you, but also if you make a mistake then you could turn the car into a death trap. Making mistakes on things like suspension or brakes could lead to loss of control and a potentially fatal accident.

So please ensure you have the right skills to do the job before you start. If in doubt, get professional help. You can also learn the necessary skills at one of the great classes run by local colleges, with the added advantage that you will meet other like-minded enthusiasts who might just be persuaded to come round and help with the tricky bits.

Even if you have prior knowledge it is often worth retraining and expanding your skills. I am a professional automotive engineer with decades of experience, and I still constantly study and undergo training. Never stop learning.

I have made every effort to ensure everything in this book is correct, but no one is perfect. If you spot an error then let me know. Please do not take this book to be superior to the official workshop manuals.

Where I show a technique that worked on my car there is no guarantee that it will work so well on your car. Land Rover changed detail specifications on a regular basis and made some variants that were poorly documented, particularly those for some specific foreign markets, and of course anything made by the Specialist Vehicle division.

It is amazing just how much can be done by the home mechanic. Here I'm checking and setting suspension geometry.

It is remarkable to think that the Discovery was launched way back in 1989, designed with real purpose in mind: to bring active families to the scene of their adventure. Capability was the key, being equally as good as a family estate car as it was an off-road work horse. The interior was brilliantly appointed by Conran Design and the exterior was styled to make it look smaller than its big brother, the Range Rover, even though it was built on a near identical chassis. In fact, not only is the chassis borrowed from the Range Rover Classic (RRC), a design first launched in 1970, but the front bulkhead, windscreen, door frames and the complete engine and transmission system was too. Other parts came from the Rover parts bin, including Sherpa headlights, Metro indicator stalks and Montego van rear lights, which all helped to bring production costs down.

The visual trick of making it look smaller was done by making the back door stop short of the rear bumper and sloping it forwards. It's not obvious but it actually slopes quite a lot. All this was done to combat the effect of the higher rear roof, designed to make it easy to get bicycles and other 'adventure' equipment in. It is also quite useful as a work horse: with the rear seats out I have been able to forklift a full-size industrial pallet into the back carrying three-quarters of a ton of bricks. Safety was important in the new design: the body shell had a welded-on steel roof and big rear pillars, giving much better rollover protection than either the Range Rover or Defender, and a welded-in steel rear floor pan, which all adds up to a much stronger shell. The downside is that all that extra steel, about 200kg of it, adds weight when compared to a Range Rover of that era and most of it is quite high up. For that reason early Discos tend to roll more in corners, which soon lead to the introduction of anti-roll bars.

On arrival the Discovery had the 200Tdi diesel and 3.5 V8 petrol engine (initially with twin SU carburettors, then subsequently Lucas fuel injection), the LT77 five-speed manual gearbox and LT230 transfer box and the two-door body. The four-door version was launched in 1990 and subsequent years saw the specification gradually improve to include things like electric windows, central locking/alarm/immobiliser, ABS and the ZF4HP22 four-speed automatic. I think those very first cars had a beautiful simplicity to them, but they are getting very rare now and becoming quite collectable.

The Sherpa headlights have a slightly unfair reputation. If kept in good condition and with quality modern bulbs they are perfectly adequate.

Some enthusiasts were concerned that the introduction of anti-roll bars would limit axle articulation. Here my long suffering '94 model suggests there is nothing to worry about.

The face-lifted Discovery Series 1 became known as the 300, after the 300Tdi engine that was introduced at the same time.

In 1993 Land Rover introduced the 4-cylinder petrol 2.0Mpi engine because some countries such as Italy had severe taxes on vehicles over 2 litres. Also the Discovery Commercial was introduced that year – a very useful two-door car with no rear side windows and a slightly different floor pan at the back with more usable space.

The V8 was enlarged to 3.9 litres in 1994 and had anti-roll bars fitted front and rear, which reduced roll in corners very noticeably. Some earlier cars had the anti-roll bar mountings on the chassis but no bars were fitted, so these cars can be upgraded fairly easily.

In 1994 the 300 Series facelift arrived and the diesel engine was revised for better refinement. Named 300Tdi, it was now attached to a new, stronger R380 manual gearbox. The rear indicators, side and brake lights were moved to the bumpers to comply with new regulations that required the lights to be visible when the rear door was open, but the original side and brake lights were retained in the clusters too, giving double the number of lights. The headlights were enlarged from the original Sherpa units and were significantly brighter.

The interior was revised, the dashboard became clearer, and the heater became a dual-zone unit with rotary controls that were easier to use and more reliable.

Camel Trophy special editions were made from 1990 to 1997. All were used in the competition and have had a hard life, but all were refurbished before being sold on and have a strong following, which has boosted values. The cars had a full roll cage, large roof rack, front winch and underbody protection as well as many detail changes. Honda made Discoverys for sale in Japan, called the Honda Crossroad.

The last year of production for the Series 1 was 1998, with the Safari and 50th Anniversary models introduced as a final flourish. By then the old Range Rover chassis was beginning to show its age and so a new project began to completely redesign the Discovery, and although the Discovery 2 looked very similar to the original it was almost completely different. The only body panel carried over was the back door and even that had different electrics and trim.

The body was extended at the rear behind the axle to provide a much bigger boot space and to allow for the forward-facing third-row seats, which also benefited from proper three-point seat belts.

Every aspect of the Discovery 2 had been adjusted in some way, making it essentially a completely different car to the Discovery 1. The road-holding was significantly improved with the option of Active Cornering Enhancement (ACE), which controlled body roll with hydraulic rams, while revised rear suspension with trailing arms (similar to the front axle but facing the other way) and a Watts link gave much better lateral location and made the car more stable at speed.

The V8 was heavily revised with larger bearings and a new intake system, and the diesel was now the mighty TD5 5-cylinder unit with electronic diesel injection. Gearboxes were similar to older models, the ZF auto now having electronic control.

A huge amount of engineering work went into the Discovery Series 2, where almost everything is different except the back door. The body is stretched behind the rear wheels to allow forward-facing third-row seating.

Refinement was improved, noise reduced and comfort refined, but all this was at the expense of weight and complexity. The Discovery 2 weighs approximately 300kg more than its Series 1 counterpart and has a vast array of electronic modules that all interact with each other, making some DIY operations a little more challenging.

The increased capability of the Discovery 2 was quickly noticed by the racing community and was raced in cross-country rallies and extreme off-road events all over the world. Perhaps the ultimate incarnation of the Discovery 2 was the Bowler Wildcat, an out-and-out off-road race car that had a plastic body resembling a Defender but used Discovery 2 axles, drive shafts, gearbox, engine, dashboard instruments and a raft of other components.

Production came to an end in 2005 with just over 514,000 Series 1 and 2 vehicles made. Its replacement, the Discovery 3, was a completely different car with independent suspension and shared no parts with the Discovery 1 and 2 at all, but it capitalized on the image and reputation that the magnificent Series 1 and 2 cars had carved out and kept the engineering philosophy of practicality and capability.

Discovery 2 back seats are more supporting and safer than Series 1 items, with fold-down head restraints and three-point seat belts, plus headphone sockets and drinks holders, making it ideal for the little ones.

using the Discovery

This may sound like a silly idea for a chapter, but I have found a few things that make the Discovery that little bit more useful and reliable.

Washing the car First of all a note about cleaning: pressure washers can cause problems. They are fine if you stand a few metres away and use them to remove mud from the body panels, but that's about all.

The trouble is that the very high water pressures cause damage if used close up. They force water into electrical connectors, through rubber seals and can even get into the rubber itself, causing damage to tyres, air springs and hoses. Never use a pressure washer in the engine bay for these reasons.

Problems may appear over time – water in electrical connectors will induce corrosion and it may be a few months after cleaning that you start to get intermittent electrical faults. Water in the tyres may unbalance them, which will get worse over time, and if there is a danger of frost the water may freeze inside the tyre wall or tread and start to weaken it.

Never pressure-wash oil leaks from gasket joints, as if the oil can get out, then high pressure water can get in!

After washing the car, take it for a drive to spin the water away from the brake discs, or they will start corroding quite quickly.

Wading Before going into deep water always test the depth using a long stick. If the water is flowing then avoid it – just 1 foot of fast-flowing water can knock you off your feet, and 3 feet of fast-flowing water will sweep the Discovery away too.

If the water isn't a raging torrent but likely to be at or above headlight height, make sure your headlights are

turned off for a minute before going in, or the cold water hitting the hot glass of the headlight may crack it.

Also keep the revs down to prevent the viscous fan turning into a propeller and becoming damaged.

Seizing levers and switches If you don't drive off-road very often, you may find that the transfer case levers seize up. It's usually nothing serious, just a build up of road grime on the links, so it's worth dropping it into low range and diff lock every so often. You don't need to move the car, just move the levers. Then it will be ready and working should you ever need to use it.

It's a similar story with switches: if a switch is rarely used the contacts can start to tarnish, as can relays. A common failure is the hazard warning switch, which often only gets used at the yearly MOT test. Switching it on and off several times usually brings it back to life. Operate all circuits once in a while to keep them working.

Big loads If you need to move a large object in a Discovery, such as a wardrobe, it is fairly easy to unbolt the rear seats to give full access to the rear of the car. The bolts protrude through the floor and the lower part of the bolt thread corrodes, so if it has not been done before then it's worth getting a small wire brush on them and using a good dose of penetrating oil before trying to take them out. I found this out when I sheared one off trying to get it out. Subsequently I replaced the bolts with stainless steel items to prevent it happening again.

Child seats All Discoverys are great for transporting the family, but as the rear wheel arch intrudes into the corner of the rear seat, some child seats don't fit. Just check the dimensions of the seat base before buying.

Avoiding rocks The lowest points on a Discovery are the differentials, so when negotiating rocks or other obstacles it's handy to know where they are. On right-hand-drive Discoverys the diffs are in line with the driver's left leg, so as long as you line the car up to avoid boulders going under your left leg you'll stand a better chance of getting through. If your car is left-hand drive, you are less fortunate although you could entertain your passenger by asking them to direct you!

Towing When towing heavy trailers it is all too easy to make the car less stable. The most important factor in keeping the whole rig stable is keeping the back axle under control. The back axle has far more influence on stability than the front axle. So if you tow big stuff then pay particular attention to the rear tyre condition and inflation pressures (see below under *Tyres*) and make sure all the bushes and links are in good order. I found it to be most stable when the tow hitch was loaded at near its maximum recommended

The standard Discovery can safely wade half a metre of standing water, but post wading maintenance is essential on older cars to deal with leaking seals.

Rated for a 3.5-ton trailer with overrun brakes, the Discovery is a superb tow car. Stability is excellent as long as the car is well maintained.

load. In a car without load levelling this results in the vehicle being slightly nose up. Never exceed the recommended maximums though.

Hitching up a heavy trailer with a car that has load levelling rear suspension (seven-seater Discovery 2) is made a bit easier by setting the suspension on low, reversing up to the hitch and then raising the suspension to hook up. Also with long flat-bed trailers, loading and unloading can sometimes be easier if the rear suspension is on maximum height, thus tilting the trailer down at the back.

Turbo wind down After driving a Tdi hard, allow the engine to idle for a few minuets to allow the turbo bearing to cool down before turning it off. This prevents the oil in the bearing from cooking.

Tyres Tyre pressures make a huge difference to the way the Discovery handles, and tyre technology has moved on a long way since 1989, so some of the original tyre-pressure advice given then may be questioned. When fitting new tyres ask for the tyre manufacturer's advice on pressures. For instance, depending on brand I usually run mine at around 40psi for most road work and up to 50psi when loaded near the maximum. Compared with the significantly lower pressures in the original handbook these gave me greater stability, even tread wear and slightly better fuel economy. For deep mud and off-road work I drop them to a lower pressure, maybe 30psi for green lanes and as low as 20psi for short runs through very deep mud. But don't copy me blindly; ask for the tyre manufacturer's recommendations.

Lay up and recommissioning Many of these cars will be left standing unused for long periods, which can seriously increase corrosion rates. Over long periods the oil film will completely drain from engine parts, gears and differentials,

exposing metal to moist air. Many of these parts have a very thin surface hardening and when corrosion takes hold this layer can be ruined very easily, leading to rapid wear next time the car is used.

For this reason a car must be driven, even if it is for a short distance, regularly during the lay-up period. When a cold engine is started water condenses out of the exhaust gasses and pools in the exhaust system. As the exhaust pipe heats up eventually it gets hot enough for the water to evaporate, resulting in a temporary increase in the amount of white vapour coming out of the tailpipe. It's important to keep the engine running until this phase has finished because stopping the engine before the pooled water has been driven out will rapidly increase exhaust corrosion. If it is not possible to run the engine during the lay-up period then you could put a few drops of oil in the cylinder bores, which should be dispelled by cranking over with the spark/glow plugs out when recommissioning. There are lay-up oils and additives that drain less readily for engine and gear parts, but this should be replaced with normal oils when recommissioning.

Brake pads can slowly bond onto the discs and the handbrake shoes can bond onto the drum. This results in the brakes appearing to be on but they will suddenly free off when pulling away. Unfortunately in so doing they will have lost some of their integrity and may fail soon afterwards. So always chock the wheels and leave the handbrake off.

Moisture will condense on metal panels every day as the temperature rises and falls; in normal use driving will draw air through the car but during lay up it will accumulate in cavities and floor mats. To prevent this ensure the storage area has some air flow through and is protected from rain. Avoid storing cars on grass or dirt, which generates huge amounts of moisture and will rot the underside of a car very rapidly.

When you pick up a new project car it is well worth taking the wheels off and carefully inspecting all the common problem areas.

common problems and solutions

There is no reason why a well-maintained Discovery shouldn't be as reliable as any other make of car. Older Land Rovers had a reputation of poor reliability, but this was largely due to poor maintenance and miss-diagnosis of faults.

Faults should not reoccur – once a fault has been fixed it should stay fixed for a long time – if a fault keeps com-

Although the first cars arrived in 1989 they are stronger than some modern cars. This unfortunate example was rolled several times without collapsing, and amazingly still drove.

ing back then it was never really fixed in the first place, just masked. Even experts can make the wrong diagnosis sometimes. Second opinions on complex problems can often help, and a genuine expert will welcome a good second opinion, not fear it. Finding and fixing the root cause is vital, for instance if your car keeps flattening batteries then changing the battery won't fix the electrical fault that's causing the problem.

Luckily some of these faults have relatively simple fixes, so in this chapter you will find some of the most common problems and a few simple solutions. The solutions are briefly described in this chapter so you can decide if you want to fix it yourself or take it to a garage. If you want to fix it yourself then some of the fixes are described in more detail in later chapters; the rest are described in the usual workshop manuals.

ENGINES

Land Rover engines are generally low powered so they can cope with heavy use for extended periods and with poorer specification fuels found in far-off lands. However, that robustness does depend heavily on good maintenance, something often neglected.

Head gasket failure – all engines Head gasket failure can happen to any engine, and it always has a cause that must

Even later engines, all dressed in plastic covers, are fundamentally traditional and simple units. No variable cam timing or multi-path compound turbo systems here.

be addressed before changing the gasket. If it has failed between a coolant gallery and an oil feed then oil will be forced into the coolant, forming a film in the header tank. If it fails between the coolant gallery and an oil drain hole then coolant will get into the sump, forming a mayonnaise-like emulsion in the rocker cover and a light grey sludge in the oil. If it fails between the combustion chamber and the coolant gallery then there will be clouds of white smoke (actually water vapour) when starting from cold, and it may blow coolant out of the pressure cap when hot. Temperature gauges are only a rough guide to engine temperature.

If the failure was caused by overheating then the culprit may be a stuck thermostat, clogged cooling system or defective fan. If all that checks out correctly then it may be due to liner sinking, particularly on later V8s, or it may be due to a poor rebuild where inferior gaskets were used or the head bolts were not correctly torqued down. Whatever the reason, sort that out first before changing the gasket.

Groaning noise from front of engine Sometimes the steering pump (and ACE pump on Discovery 2 models) can make a bit of noise due to fluid cavitation. Using PAS

It was found that the outer row of head bolts on V8s cause the head to tilt on the gasket and increase the likelihood of failure. That is why the torque setting for those bolts was reduced, and eventually they were deleted altogether.

Do not use ordinary ATF or the ACE pump will start groaning; use PAS fluid of the right specification.

The seller of this V8 swore it ran fine despite a ticking sound, but two bent push rods left it running on just six cylinders! The V8s keep going even when poorly maintained, which is why many are sadly neglected.

Water pumps leak from worn bearings, eroded gaskets and corrosion under the hose connections.

fluid with the right additives is important, but some owners top up a leaky system with the cheapest fluid, which can cause a noise problem. To get rid of the noise, drain and flush the steering or ACE system with the correct fluid before refilling.

Petrol engines

The Rover V8 in 3.5-litre form, as fitted to the very first Discoverys, was almost indestructible. It may leak oil from the valley gasket, rocker covers and sump, but that's fairly normal. It does need regular oil changes, however. Many cars are neglected and driven far too long on old oil, leading to tar build-up and possible big-end bearing failure, cam wear, tappet collapse, rocker shaft wear and worn bores. You must check an engine by starting from cold, and when you view a car open the bonnet and check the engine has not been warmed up before you start it. Often engines are driven for years with less than the full eight cylinders working. Even when working badly these tough little engines still work enough to drive the car, and that's the beauty of not being too highly tuned.

Coolant loss from water pump Water pump bearings wear, particularly if the car has ever lost coolant in its life; look for telltale coolant traces on the back of the pump pulley or a tendency to squeak from cold.

The solution is to replace it, unless you have a good workshop press in which case you might be able to fit a new bearing and seal.

SU carbs can be made to run very nicely if kept clean and well maintained. If regular adjustments are needed then something is wearing out and should be investigated. Dashpot oil should be replaced if it starts going sticky.

Changing the head gasket on any Discovery engine is reasonably straightforward, but before getting to this stage find out what caused the failure. Maybe the cooling system is struggling. Even thermostats have a service life.

Blowing coolant out or contaminating oil When the bore was stretched for the 3.9 V8 the cylinder liner was not held quite so well as in the 3.5 engine. It has a tendency to creep down, which in turn compromises the cylinder head gasket clamping and gasket leaks are then common. Engines with this fault are expensive to fix properly, although it has to be said the fault can usually be 'lived with' if it's not too severe.

The results of this problem are a tendency to blow coolant out, resulting in overheating, and in some cases a tendency to burn a bit more oil than usual, but if the coolant gets into the oil then the engine will quickly destroy itself. The same problem occurs on the Discovery 2 V8 engine – if the liners have sunk and caused the head gasket to fail then skimming the heads will NOT fix the problem. Either new liners have to be fitted or a replacement engine block found.

Carburettors, poor running (very early Discovery 1) Carburettors on the very first Discoverys can suffer from old fuel clogging the small bores and also gaskets leaking. If the engine runs rough, it may be worth stripping the carburettors down, cleaning them out and rebuilding them with new seals and gaskets – this can transform an old engine. Moving parts wear, so items like the main barrel in an SU should be replaced if it exceeds tolerance; the same goes for needles and jets.

Idle quality and initial pull away are governed by idle fuelling, the throttle stop and by ignition advance. If the idle is a problem, check the ignition first, then adjust the idle fuelling and throttle stop to get it precise.

Check ducts are secure. To preserve the screw head, use a small socket on hose clamps and not a screwdriver.

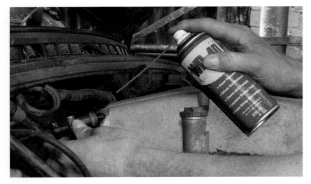

Idle valves should be periodically removed for cleaning. Before refitting apply a drop of thread sealant (not thread lock) to prevent air leaks.

You can see from the soot pattern where this exhaust gasket was leaking. The gas passing the hole draws air into the exhaust system and makes the lambda sensor read too lean, causing the engine to run too rich in an attempt to compensate.

Fuel injection system, poor running and misfires The most common cause of faults on injection systems is electrical, particularly poor earth connections. A problem on high-mileage or old engines is injector wear, and they can clog up over time giving a poor spray pattern or reduced flow. If the seat is pitted, the injector may leak, resulting in black smoke and a misfire. Removing the injectors and sending them off for ultrasonic cleaning can help in most cases, although sometimes the injector is so far gone it will need replacing.

Air leaks between the air meter and engine will cause problems, so make sure all the hoses and small pipes are secure and not cracked.

Stalling and poor idle control Engines with the 14cux control system have an idle-speed control valve that can become clogged. The solution is to undo it and wash the end out with WD40 or similar, and extract the gunge from the housing. It may take a couple of attempts before it properly clears.

Higher-than-normal fuel consumption, poor emissions and noise from the exhaust If the engine uses lambda sensors then make sure there are no exhaust leaks on the exhaust manifold. If there are then change the gaskets. A leaking manifold on these variants reduces miles per gallon and idle quality, and can coke up the combustion chambers and foul the spark plugs.

Oil-pressure light stays on There are two possible causes. A common fault is that the oil-pressure switch has relaxed and comes on even at normal oil pressure. The fix is to fit a new switch, which is easy and cheap. If the oil pressure is genuinely slow to pick up then the main and big-end bearings may be worn. It's a substantial job to change them but can be done at home if you know how. Whether you do it yourself or get help, change them before the engine starts rumbling and suffering real damage.

It is just about possible to change the main and big-end bearings with the engine in situ, but it is far better to take the engine out and do it properly.

Wear on this cam lobe has reduced lift and as a result ruined performance. The follower has worn in sympathy and followers must always be replaced when fitting a new cam.

This essential tool is ideal for gently clearing carbon deposits from old distributor caps and rotor arms without cutting into the soft metal too much. Every tool kit should have one.

Low power The camshaft is one of the first things to wear if the oil has been neglected. Symptoms include reduced top-end power but still reasonable low-speed pull, almost like having a restriction in the inlet, and a rattle on start-up as the hydraulic tappets pump up to compensate for the wear. These engines can run with only half the cylinders working properly, so often cam wear goes unnoticed for years. With fuel consumption becoming ever more important, if you are changing the cam then it may be worth using an improved profile. Using a milder cam (duration of 220 degrees or less) or retarding the cam a fraction can improve low-end torque and miles per gallon at the expense of top-end power.

Changing the cam can be done at home but requires the removal of the radiator, sump, front-end belts, intake manifold and the front engine cover, so it's not a small job. *See the Repair chapter for details.*

Engine runs but starts misfiring under load and will not rev After first checking the fuel system, the next possible culprit is the ignition system. If the coil is not charging up fully after each spark then it limits speed and power. This could be because the coil is damaged internally or the driver unit is malfunctioning. Check the earth wire from the driver unit on Discovery 1 models, as it tends to corrode where it's attached to the inner wing.

A very common cause of ignition faults is the earthing. Check the earth studs for corrosion as well as the straps on the coil and also on the back of the cylinder head.

Rough idle and stalling Discovery 1 V8 distributors are very sensitive to degradation of the distributor cap terminals and rotor arm. Once these go the engine struggles to idle cleanly and then it starts to foul up the spark plugs and will stall when slowing down to stop. The distributor cap tends to foul up the terminals with a hard white deposit, which can cause the engine to lose power and stall at idle. If this happens when out in the wilds then simply scrape the deposits off with the edge of a coin. Dressing the terminals with a small grinding tool will restore them briefly, but as the corrosion eats into the terminals and widens the spark gap the cap will eventually need to be replaced. It is the same with the rotor arm, with hard black deposits forming on the trailing edge. Again these can be scraped off as a temporary fix, but eventually it will need replacing. I have also seen some new distributor caps loose their spring-loaded centre electrode, so check this is not loose or missing when buying a new cap.

2.0-litre Mpi The 2.0-litre Mpi petrol engine used briefly in the Discovery was taken directly out of the Rover road cars. It is a simple and usually reliable engine although performance is limited. A worn engine will make telltale rattling or tapping noises.

Make sure the cam belt is changed when due; it's quite easy compared to other engines.

Diesel engines

Runaway – engine revs even with the ignition off (all diesels) Diesel runaway is the name given to an engine running on its own oil, which can be caused by excessive bore wear or worn piston rings that result in oily crank case gases being pumped into the intake through the crankcase vent system. A warm diesel engine will run quite readily on this oil-rich gas and even turning the ignition off will not stop it. If left to its own devices, a runaway engine will continue revving until it destroys itself or runs out of oil. Any make or model of diesel engine can suffer from this if sufficiently worn. If this happens, the only way to shut the engine down is to stall it. This can be a very frightening experience and has the potential to be very dangerous.

The crankcase vent system takes gas from the block into the intake via an oil separator. If the drain becomes blocked, oil will be burnt in the engine and could lead to harmful deposits in the combustion chamber or runaway.

Stalling is best done in a high gear. If the car is in motion then leave it in whichever gear it is currently in, because as soon as you dip the clutch the engine will rev up very quickly and may destroy the crankshaft and block. When safe to do so simply apply the brakes as hard as possible and bring the car to a halt in gear, this must be done as quickly as possible to avoid overheating the brakes, which could otherwise start to fade. If the car is already parked and in neutral then dip the clutch, put it in top gear, put your foot as hard as possible on the brakes and let the clutch out very quickly. Don't let the clutch out gradually as it will simply overheat and slip. Obviously this will not work on automatic gearbox models.

The other way to stop a runaway is to collapse the air intake by squashing one of the air ducts, or pull off the breather tube to prevent oil going into the intake. This can be very dangerous as the engine could explode whilst you are working in the engine bay, so I really would not recommend it.

A slightly safer version is to use a CO_2 extinguisher discharged into the air intake, which will remove most of the oxygen. Never use a foam or water extinguisher as any liquid breathed into the engine will cause it to fail catastrophically.

Smoke when cornering, due to oil in the intercooler (all diesels)

All models have intercoolers and one of the common complaints is that of the intercooler filling up with oil. The result is that if you accelerate while cornering, for

The intercooler by its very nature causes oil mist to condense into liquid oil, which could be drawn into the engine at high loads. Taking it out and cleaning it removes the danger.

This TD5 is leaking oil from the ducts, which indicates two things: there is oil in the intake and the hoses are leaking very slightly. This might be okay but should be investigated to be sure.

This 300Tdi oil separator is essential to prevent oil entering the intake; check the drain is clear and the connections secure. The plastic hardens and can crack, so do not over-tighten the fixing bolt.

instance exiting a roundabout, the combination of side force and higher intake air flow draws the oil out of the intercooler and into the engine, resulting in a cloud of black or blue smoke and potentially a severe misfire.

The oil deposit is caused by gas from the crankcase vent system condensing in the cold intercooler. That is not really a fault in itself, but if the oil level builds up too far than it can cause problems.

The solution is to remove the intercooler, maybe once a year or so, and clean it out, ensuring no cleaning agent is left inside when you refit it. If it fills quickly then this may indicate excessive crankcase vent gas flow, which may mean worn piston rings or cylinder bores. This should be investigated immediately as very high blow-by can lead to the engine inhaling enough oil to run on, causing it to rev up out of control (*see* last section).

Smoke and loss of performance due to duct faults (all diesels) If your diesel engine has reduced power but doesn't emit huge amounts of smoke and, other than the lack of power, seems to work, then it might be a problem with an air duct. The ducts between the turbo and the intercooler, and between the intercooler and the intake manifold, can fail, in which case you will loose boost and performance.

If the retaining clip weakens or corrodes through then the boost pressure can cause the duct to be blown off, resulting in increased turbo whistle. The obvious solution is to pop it back on with a new clip.

On older engines the rubber ducts will have become harder and prone to cracks – the bigger the crack, the more boost is lost. In this case it's worth replacing all the rubber ducts, because if one has failed then the others will not be far behind.

If there is a large air leak after the turbo then the turbo could over-speed and go into 'turbo surge'. In severe cases this can make a banging sound and terminally damage the turbo, so deal with leaks promptly. The TD5 uses a bit of software that detects surge and reduces engine power to save the turbo. The symptoms are that when you accelerate hard it picks up as normal then suddenly reduces power, almost as if you had released the accelerator pedal completely. If that happens then check your air ducts.

Turbo wear and oil leaks (all diesels) The turbo will whistle quietly in operation. It shouldn't really be audible to bystanders but if it is then it may be because a hose has split, letting the air and sound out, or it may be because the turbo has become unbalanced due to wear. Never run a turbo without an air filter – the slightest bit of grit will damage it as it spins at over 120,000rpm.

Turbo bearing failure is usually caused by over-speeding (leaking duct or boost set too high) or by oil-feed problems. One of the main causes of oil-feed problems is fuel diluting the oil due to a cracked cylinder head. If caught early enough, the bearing can be replaced and new seals fitted, which is considerably cheaper than a new turbo, but if the engine has run for a while with a worn turbo, the impeller blades may have contacted the compressor housing and be beyond economic recovery.

If you replace the turbo but don't fix the cause of the failure, then you will probably need another new turbo in a few thousand miles.

EGR valve stuck (all diesels) Exhaust Gas Recirculation (EGR) has a slightly unfair reputation. The idea is that as exhaust gas is inert, introducing a small amount into the intake, up to 10%, slightly cools combustion and improves thermal efficiency. What that means is that fuel consumption is improved by up to 5% and emissions of nitrogen oxides are drastically reduced.

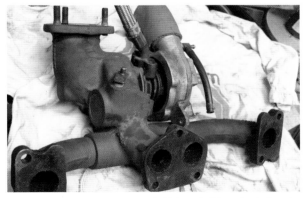

With the inlet duct removed you can hold the end of the turbo shaft and check for play. You should be able to move it a millimetre but no more. If there is no play then it is seized; if there is a lot then it is worn out. The impeller should not touch the compressor housing.

This EGR valve has been blocked off permanently and the tubes removed because it became faulty and jammed open.

The valve is controlled to give peak efficiency at part load but is shut off when you put your foot down to give maximum power. The trouble is that the valve has to cope with very hot gas containing soot and corrosives, and it really has a hard life. That is why it can jam up, which results in recirculation at full load causing excessive exhaust smoke and, ironically, poor economy.

It can sometimes be brought back to life by removing it and cleaning all the gunge and carbon out with WD40 or petrol, but if it's very clogged then it might need replac-

ing. Another solution is to remove it permanently and fit a blanking plate instead – although this reduces efficiency slightly compared to a fully working system, it improves things compared to a faulty one.

Difficulty starting on cold days (all diesels) Poor starting on any of the diesels can be due to either the starter not spinning fast enough (check battery and connections before getting the starter checked), low compression (which will also make the engine smokey on load), but it

Soot leaking from the joint here prompted the owner to unplug the connector to disable the EGR valve.

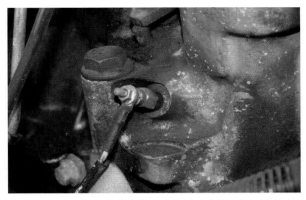

The glow plug at the front is easy to get at to check it is getting 12v when the glow plug light comes on.

That thin band of rubber holds the outer part of the crank pulley onto the inner part. When it fails, the pulley will squeak on gear changes and when the engine stops.

is most often due to faulty glow plugs, a problem that worsens in the winter. If the plugs are weak then you can try giving them two burns by turning on the ignition, wait for the glow plug light to go out, turn the ignition off and on again and wait for the glow plug light to go out a second time, and then start the engine.

Usually glow plugs fail by burning out the element and going electrically open circuit, so they can be tested by using a multimeter. To test them individually you have to undo the wire first. Replacing them is a simple matter of unscrewing the old one and fitting a new one, but they can corrode in place, so let them soak in penetrating oil for a day or two first.

Engine squeaks when turned off due to crank damper wear (all diesels) Although designs vary between models they all have a Torsional Vibration (TV) damper in the crank pulley, which is simply a rubber collar between the inner and outer pulley. The outer pulley serves as a mass to absorb vibration from the crank, making the

engine smoother and reducing peak stresses on the crank shaft. It seems simple but is vital for the longevity of the engine.

As with all rubber parts this ages and, depending on use, will start to weaken at about ten years or 100,000 miles. Eventually the bond to the pulley will fail and allow it to slip and wobble. It's that slip that makes a squeaking noise when you suddenly change the engine speed, such as when it's switched off or you change gear swiftly. The solution is to fit a new pulley. They are not cheap, but it's one of those important things where it's worth buying a good one.

200Tdi general The 200Tdi was the first diesel engine with decent performance produced by Land Rover. It has proved very reliable if correctly maintained and can provide loyal service for a standard Land Rover, although it can be a bit noisy. Regular oil changes are essential to keep the turbo bearings in good order, and cam belt changes involve a large amount of work and so are frequently overlooked.

The Bosch VE fuel injection system is used on a huge variety of vehicles, making parts and information readily available. They are very reliable, so check timing and fuel supply before suspecting the pump.

300Tdi general The 300Tdi replaced the 200Tdi in around 1994. It is basically the same engine but with a large number of detail changes to make it more appealing. First, it was quieter, with revised combustion chambers and fuel-injection equipment. Second, it was easier to work on, and the cam belt change requires much less work than on a 200Tdi. The 300Tdi engine initially had a reputation for misaligned timing-belt followers, but all these will have been replaced when the belt was changed.

Brake fault due to loss of vacuum (200 and 300Tdi) If the brakes become unusually hard then it might be that the vacuum pump is leaking. It is held together with rivets that eventually weaken and allow the seal to fail. They can be rebuilt or replaced. *See* the Repair chapter.

Hose and pipe damage leading to leaks Some of the hoses on the 300Tdi are very close to the fan belt and pulleys, so lift the covers off and check for chafing and leaks. Any hoses that have nicks taken out of them should be replaced, but when you do that take a bit of time to adjust the brackets and clips to make sure the hoses can't rub again.

200 and 300Tdi cam (timing) belts Regular cam belt changes are essential on both the 200 and 300Tdi. If there is no documented evidence that it has had one recently then budget for changing it as a precaution. They are not expensive and don't take very long to do. Cam belt failure can occur around 40,000 miles and can destroy the engine. Luckily the engine uses push rods, which can bend if the valve nudges the piston at low speed and may save the engine. There is a revised idler design that extends belt life – *see* later chapters for servicing and repair information.

TD5-specific issues

The TD5 diesel was the first and only product from a new Rover modular engine design. The tooling was intended to produce 4-, 5- and 6-cylinder engines, but its launch coincided with the acquisition of Land Rover by BMW who already had a 2-litre 4-cylinder and a 3-litre 6-cylinder diesel engine. So only the TD5 was ever produced, although the names TD4 and TD6 were later used on vehicles with BMW engines.

The TD5 was another big step forward in technology. Totally electronically controlled fuelling allowed the injec-

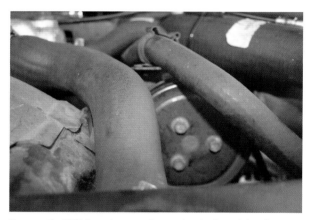

Hoses on the 300Tdi get close to pulleys, so the plastic retaining clips are a vital component.

The Tdi cam belt kit should come with idler and tensioner pulleys. If converting to the later 300Tdi system, there should also be the flanged crank pulley.

This vacuum pump has had the rivets replaced with bolts to prevent leakage at the joint, improving reliability.

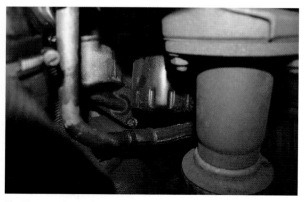

The TD5 cartridge oil filter is behind the exhaust; the centrifugal one is to the left and up a bit, accessed from the top.

tors to be switched off on overrun to save fuel, which is why the engine gets suddenly quieter when you back off the accelerator. It has more complex oil filtering to extend oil change intervals and to improve oil quality for the more sensitive components. There is a conventional paper cartridge filter plus an additional centrifugal filter with a central element that is spun at great speed by oil pressure – you can often hear it running down after you switch the engine off.

There is an ECU chip for the TD5 available from Land Rover dealers to increase torque at low revs. Check the service record to see if it's been done.

Oil leak on the front of the engine The TD5 camshaft front oil seal has a tendency to perish, resulting in oil covering the front of the engine and spreading down all over the sump. The seal consists of a large plastic plug with an O-ring and is a simple push fit. Unfortunately the O-ring gradually becomes squashed and hardens, resulting in a fairly loose fit. In fact if it wasn't for the cable held in front of it by two P-clips the plug would probably fall out eventually.

The solution is simple: remove the plug and fit a new O-ring. Remember to clean away the dirt from the area before removing the plug, as grit falling into the engine would be harmful. Do not use a pressure washer as this could blast the dirt in past the perished seal.

Oil in the ECU connector causing a misfire One curious feature of the TD5 was that oil leaking near the fuel injector wiring loom will wick up the wires into the ECU, eventually causing electrical problems and a misfire at low rpm. The best solution is to fit a new injector loom (*see* Repair chapter).

TD5 oil pump Some TD5 engines suffer from oil pump failure, which can result in a completely destroyed engine if it happens when the engine is at speed. The problem is caused by the bolt securing the drive sprocket coming loose, or else the bolt stays tight and the thin sprocket deteriorates at the drive face such that it just spins on the oil pump drive shaft without driving the pump.

TD5 cylinder head TD5 cylinder-head failure was common in early-life engines, and by 2007 cracked cylinder heads were becoming so common that the supply of replacement heads dried up. Most of the engines that were going to fail will have done so by now, and if one does go then replacement heads are readily available once again.

Check for oil in coolant or loss of coolant, but also check the oil level regularly. Rising oil level can be caused by a cracked head leaking fuel from the high-pressure fuel rail. This can lead to severe damage and even runaway. The only fix is a new head.

Fuel problems The in-tank fuel pumps can wear if any dirt gets into the tank, which results in the motor making a whining noise. However, this noise can also be caused by cavitation due to the mesh filter below the pump becoming clogged, so it's worth checking and cleaning before you spend money on a new pump.

The plastic fuel pipes between the tank and the fuel filter in the rear wheel arch are prone to damage from rubbing against the chassis. Check the filter and housing and for damp patches around the connectors, and check the filter connections in case they are loose.

Check the fuel pressure regulator, bolted to the head on the right side, as they are known to leak. If diesel is leaking out, then air can leak in.

This innocent plastic disc is probably the cause of the oil spread around this TD5.

Check the red connector of the TD5 ECU for oil contamination. Oil wicks up the wiring loom from the fuel injectors and eventually causes misfires.

The TD5 has a fuel filter in the rear wheel arch. It should have a drain tap at the bottom to let water out, which should be checked occasionally.

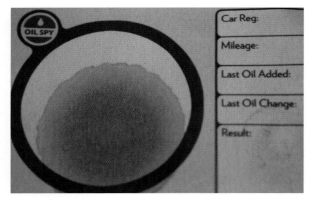

Just a drip of oil on blotting paper will reveal if there is contamination: water, oil, fuel and carbon disperse at different rates, so the rings on the blotting paper indicate the oil condition.

Fuel leaking into the oil from injector seals If the injector seals leak, then fuel will be blown out of the cylinder and into the head, eventually ending up in the sump. This is doubly dangerous as not only do you contaminate the oil but it also increases crankcase pressure and the amount of crankcase gas being drawn into the intake, both contributing to runaway. New seals are reasonable cheap, but you will need a special puller to get the injectors out. *See* Repair chapter.

TD5 exhaust manifold leaks Exhaust manifold studs shear because the exhaust manifold warps. The manifold can be refaced and new studs fitted. The manifold should have done all the warping it is likely to do, so it shouldn't do it again.

Fuel cooler leaks coolant The fuel cooler coolant pipes have O-ring seals on, which become deformed over time and start to leak. The solution is to simply unbolt the connections, fit new Viton O-rings and refit.

Cooling

Often overlooked, the cooling system also needs regular maintenance.

The cooling system is sadly often forgotten until a fault develops. Check pump, hoses and radiator fins and make sure the cowl is secure and intact – it makes a big difference to fan efficiency.

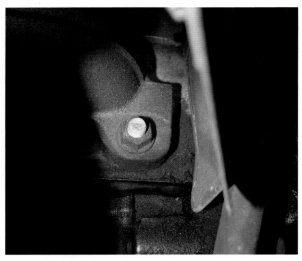

As the engine warms up the expansion can cause the exhaust manifold studs to break, resulting in exhaust leaks.

Overheating Cooling problems can be caused by the radiator front face being blocked with debris. This, combined with corrosion from road salt, can cause the delicate fins to become detached from the core tubes. This ruins its ability to transfer engine heat to the cooling air flow and must be repaired immediately.

Overheating on petrol engines can also be caused by retarded ignition or lean running, so before taking drastic action just check the fuel and ignition settings.

Engine overheats or over cools Thermostats have been known to jam, so check any prospective purchase reaches normal operating temperature readily and doesn't overheat on a test drive. The thermostat can fail in two ways: if it is shut, the engine overheats very rapidly; if it is open, it never warms up. They can fail with age and there are also some very poor fake parts in circulation. Another cause of thermostat failure is overheating, caused by some other fault that can overstress the wax capsule. So if the thermostat has failed, check the rest of the system, including the fan and head gaskets, just in case.

Soft or oily hoses Because most engines are prone to oil leaks, coolant hoses can start to soften and rupture due to a coating of oil. These have to be replaced, as they are weakened and could rupture without warning.

Excessive fan noise, over- or under cooling The viscous fans fitted to most models become stiff when cold as they age, so check the fan rotates easily with a cold engine. Stiff or seized fans rob power and economy.

Viscous fans are notorious for either seizing, causing the fan to be engaged fully all the time, making a substantial whooshing noise and wasting fuel, or failing so that the fan never engages and the car overheats in traffic. Removing one needs a very slim spanner. Specially made tools are inexpensive and save a lot of hard work. The water pump pulley should be held stationary by clamping the belt or by holding a steadying bar such as a long square-edged screwdriver against the pulley bolt heads.

Typical radiator damage. It is best to stop any corrosion as soon as it starts by applying a spot of paint. Left alone the corrosion will spread until the radiator suddenly fails. Early radiators can be replaced by later alloy/ plastic ones.

Early cars used ethylene glycol; later ones used OAT. Some coolant types do not mix, so check the labels. You can now get universal coolant that will work with either system.

Coolant Check the coolant level. A low level could be caused by a corroded radiator, a fractured heater matrix, leaking pipes or even a leaking head gasket.

Check the coolant has antifreeze in. Dip a clean white rag or paper into the header tank and it should come out showing some colour (most coolants are blue, green or red). If it shows clear water then the chances are the car regularly loses coolant and has been topped up with neat water.

There is a choice of coolant now. The Discovery 2 switched over from ethylene glycol to OAT (Organic Acid Technology), which lasts significantly longer than the glycol type. The coolant is dyed so you can tell which sort it is: blue and green are generally glycol and orange is OAT.

Ageing, leaking and poor cooling performance Most of these cars are well over ten years old now, and the cooling system suffers from age quite badly. All the rubber parts perish, and it's best to replace them every ten years, but also the hose clips corrode and should be renewed at the same time.

The coolant becomes acidic over time and should be replaced every three years, and the water it is mixed with should be mineral free rather than just tap water.

Magic leak-fix bottles If the system starts to leak, some people put in a chemical cooling system sealer, just poured from the bottle into the header tank. While this does stop the leak, it also coats the inner galleries of the cylinder head, radiator and heater matrix, and in the worst cases causes engine overheating or a cold-running interior heater. So if the radiator or heater matrix is leaking, then take it out and get it properly repaired or better still re-cored.

Core plugs The engine core plugs also corrode over time and can fail suddenly. If one has blown out then a new one can simply be tapped in, but often they will start leaking but still stay firmly in place. To remove them a small hole can be drilled and a screw driven in so that the plug can be pulled out. Another method is to tap one side in forcing the plug sideways and allowing it to be pulled out with pliers. Before driving the new plug in, the hole should be cleaned up so that the plug seals against a smooth surface – the plug must be driven in straight otherwise it may leak.

TRANSMISSION

Manual gearbox The LT77 5-speed manual suffers from wear in the input shaft bearing, resulting in rumble when the clutch is pressed and vibration, and oil may leak out of the bell housing and eventually the bearing may collapse. Gear changes can be a bit slow, but that is normal. This was heavily revised in the R380 version fitted to 300-style Series 1 cars and Series 2 cars, and although it uses the same casing it is entirely different inside. It is more robust but suffers from loss of synchro in second and a tendency not to allow swift changes up to fourth. On diesel cars the vibration causes excessive wear on the gearbox output shaft, resulting in a delay when engaging drive and a thud as the slack is taken up. There is a replacement Land Rover part available to fix this problem.

Vibration when changing gear This is a particular problem on diesels: vibration wears the splines on the input shaft so that when the clutch is dipped it all gets a bit slack. The solution is to fit a new input shaft, which is a big job and it might be cheaper to fit a second-hand gearbox instead.

These R380 gearbox output shaft splines were about to fail. Replacement parts are available with improved oil supply to prevent it happening again.

If you replace the clutch disc before it is completely worn out you only need a new disc, but leave it too late and it wears down the pressure plate and flywheel too.

Don't ignore the problem though. When it finally wears through the splines you suddenly get no drive at all, usually when you are pulling out of a busy junction in the rain at rush hour.

Clutch pedal moves down of its own accord If you find that on long journeys the clutch pedal sometimes travels down on its own, making gear changes awkward, but pumps up again quite easily then chances are there is an internal fault in the master cylinder. A very small number of these appear to be prone to this behaviour and the best course of action is to fit a new one.

Clutch lever Both LT77 and R380 clutch release levers have a weakness in that the pivot ball can punch through the lever. Reinforced levers are available and well worth fitting to older cars next time you change the clutch.

Automatic gearbox

The ZF 4HP22 hydraulic gearbox was fitted in Series 1 cars and the electronically controlled 4HP22E version was used in Series 2 cars. Both should be very smooth in operation. The oil should be red, but if it has turned brown then it has been overheated, indicating heavy wear and possible imminent failure.

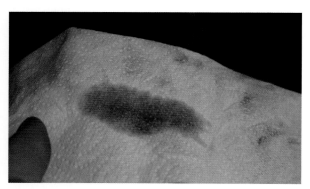

Check the level and also the colour of the automatic transmission fluid: red is good, brown is bad. And remember to put the dipstick back securely. Later models did away with the dipstick and just had a level plug in the sump.

Oil leaks The ZF 4HP22 gearbox is a remarkably reliable unit, as long as it has oil. The only common issue is losing drive due to oil leaking out of the cooler hoses, or if you are very unlucky off-road and manage to bash the gearbox sump enough for it to leak. If the fluid loss is gradual then you will find it jumping into neutral when going round corners at first, which is caused by the oil sloshing away from the central pick-up inside the gearbox, but eventually you will have no drive at all, even from standstill.

If you have a gearbox sump leak, check for sump damage and get a replacement if needed. Changing the gasket should be coupled with changing the gearbox oil filter too.

If the hoses have perished then replace all of them; if one has gone, the others are not far behind. But if the hose is leaking due to damage then just that one hose can be replaced.

To be safe I check the gearbox oil every time I check the engine oil.

Won't pull away in D A few high-mileage units may have a rear clutch failure, which means they won't pull away in D but will work normally in 1,2,3. The clutch is available from specialists, but unless you fancy stripping the whole gearbox down at home then it will be an expensive repair and it may work out cheaper to fit a second-hand gearbox.

Transfer box

The LT230 has three shaft seals, four large gaskets, two lever seals and a few washers, and is thus prone to leak. Check the breather on top of the range selector is clear and intact. Clean grit and mud from the link rods to keep them working.

The LT230 transfer box has served in both Series 1 and 2 Discoverys. It is a tough old unit even though it often leaks oil, but as long as the level is topped up they seem to go on forever.

Unable to select low range The low-range selector lever seldom gets used by most owners, so it is quite common for it to seize up, but this can usually be fixed fairly easily by wiggling it vigorously.

Oil on the handbrake If the rear oil seal leaks then oil spreads into the handbrake drum, which obviously reduces handbrake efficiency. Oil dripping from the brake drum gets flung all over the underside and coats the right-hand chassis rail and exhaust, which is less than ideal. *See* the Repair chapter for seal change details.

If you are unfamiliar with the 'other' gearstick, remember to move it occasionally. Read the handbook and try using it – low ratio is great for pulling out unwanted shrubs.

I heard the wheel bearing rumbling but kept driving. It did not end well. The rollers in the wheel bearing eventually jammed and spun the inner race against the hub, destroying both and locking the wheel.

Axles

The early units used half shafts with ten splines where they joined the differential, which were fine for normal use but if frequently put under extreme load could break. In 1993 a slightly more robust twenty-four-spline system was introduced. Earlier units can be exchanged for these later 'fine spline' axles if needed.

ABS faults The introduction of ABS brakes in 1990 required a revised swivel pin bearing on Series 1 cars to reduce 'noise' in the system, so if you change them then make sure you get the right sort.

Axle noise or a clonk when moving from forward to reverse If you get a droning noise at speed, try gently easing off the accelerator; if the noise gets quieter then it is related to how much load (torque) the engine is putting into the axle and the chances are the differential is worn. If the droning noise stays the same at a given speed no matter how much load you give it then the chances are it is tyre noise, possibly due to under inflation or a very knobbly tread design.

You can check for differential wear with one wheel raised on a suitable jack and the car safely chocked. The wheel can be rotated back and forth, and there will be some move-ment before the propshaft moves. However, more than about 45 degrees indicates a heavily worn differential. The differential can be rebuilt, but often it is more cost effective to buy a good second-hand unit.

Noise that gets louder when cornering If noise from the axle gets louder when cornering then it may be hub bearings. Discovery 1 bearings can break up if worn, or if the grease gets contaminated due to a leaking seal they make a droning noise that gets louder at speed and can make a clicking sound at low speed and when parking. Eventually the cage will fail and the bearing can seize, causing the inner race to spin on the stub axle and weld itself on, causing the wheel to skid.

Replace the bearings before the noise gets loud; if the race has seized then you will also need a new stub axle.

The Discovery 2 had significantly revised axles; they were wider and in some ways easier to service. The hub bearings are now sealed units, and whilst very easy to replace they are quite expensive and come with the ABS sensor pre-fitted.

Oil leaking from the swivels Discovery 1 front hub swivels have a seal, which is ground down by fine particles of grit in mud and road grime. This inevitably leads to them failing and letting in moisture, which ruins the bearings. There

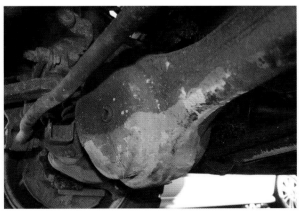

Sadly leaks are common, but if oil can get out then water can get in. Ensure the axle breather is in good order to prevent pressure build up or water ingress.

This swivel is clean and polished, which is good. But the seal is old and hard, letting oil seep out. Simply replacing the seal should be all this one needs, but it is worth checking the top and bottom swivel bearings while you are there.

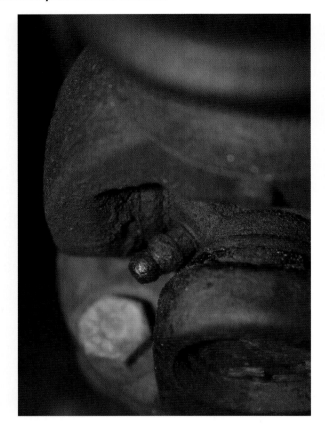

Grease this, now! Remove all the dirt before you start, or you will pump grit into the bearing.

Later Discovery 2 front propshafts have a rather nice double universal joint (also known as double Cardan or double Hookes). There is no grease nipple on some shafts and joints, and a bung has to be removed and a grease nipple screwed in for the operation.

have been a number of detail changes to hubs over the years with varying levels of success. The front hub swivel seals should be replaced before they let oil out or mud in, and heavy mud-plugging reduces their service life. The later 'one shot' grease can be retrofitted to older cars once the old oil has been drained and has the advantage that it doesn't leak out.

Instability at speed Worn swivel bearings are another thing that can cause steering vagueness and make the car wander at speed. To test them raise a wheel and get a strong assistant to rock it (holding it at top and bottom) while you feel for knocking at the swivels. Replacing them is basically a matter of bolting new ones in.

Vibration above 50mph Propshaft universal joint bearings wear if not regularly greased, resulting in speed-related vibration, typically worst between 50 and 60mph. To replace them, remove the propshaft and undo the C-clip holding the bearings in. It is a fairly simple fix.

BRAKES

Brakes are generally simple, with discs all round for all models. Old pads, particularly if the car has been wading, can perish such that the friction material splits from the backing, so check when they were last changed. The brake fluid

There is no point going half way. If you are going to change the brakes, do all the pads and discs at once, and be safe. Remember to use new fluid and pump it right through the system.

needs changing regularly on any car. Look at the reservoir and the fluid should be clear or very light tan with most types of fluid; dark or grey fluid needs changing immediately.

When fitting new brake discs it is vital to make sure the mating surface between the disc and hub is completely clean and free of any flakes of paint, old grease, rust or road grime. Even a tiny speck of grit will eventually cause brake vibration, but it is very easy to clean them up. Sadly many garages do not do this and so about 2,000 miles later the brakes will start vibrating again.

Instability when braking One of the problems I have found with non-ABS Discoverys is the car veering to one side when braking hard. This can be a complicated problem, but it usually comes down to the pistons in the callipers on one side sticking. This is often caused by corrosion or dirt on the piston surface when the brake pads are low, then when nice new pads are fitted and the pistons are pushed back into the calliper the corrosion or dirt rips up the rubber seals. There are two seals on each piston, an inner seal, which stops the brake fluid leaking out, and an outer seal, which is designed to stop dirt getting into the inner seal. It is often the outer dust seal that gets all mashed up and can impede the movement of the piston, leading to uneven pad and disc wear. Once the area in the calliper between the inner and outer seal gets rubbish in it then the clearance between the piston and calliper disappears. Often it starts with a small patch, which causes the piston to jam at a small angle when the brakes are applied.

So depending on which problem you have, the car may pull to one side under light breaking but be fine under heavy breaking, or vice versa, or indeed pull to one side under light braking and to the opposite side under heavy braking. Either way the brakes will need a complete overhaul. One solution is replacement callipers, which make the job a lot quicker. However, piston and seal kits are available and are cheaper than a new calliper, but to get the calliper bores properly clean can be tricky if they are corroded.

Discovery 2 ABS fault lights on A very common fault on the Discovery 2 is for the ABS to throw up a fault resulting in three warning lights (ABS, TC and HDC, known as the 'three amigos') and three chimes from the dash sounder. This usually happens when you brake hard, but it can occur on light braking or even as soon as you start the engine in severe cases.

The fault often disappears when you turn the ignition off and on (obviously never do this when the car is moving). The fault results in the ABS function not working, so you still have full braking power but no anti-lock function and the car could skid under heavy braking.

There are several possible causes, including a faulty wheel sensor and corroded connections, but the top two causes are the shuttle valve connections in the ABS unit and, oddly enough, the wheel bearings. When the wheel bearings become worn the sensor ring on the hub wobbles about a bit and sends an inconsistent signal to the ABS computer. Genuine replacement Discovery 2 hub units come with the ABS sensor already installed and correctly set, but be aware that some cars may have had a replacement sensor fitted at the dealer with the connector situated right up near the ABS unit, so hang on to the old sensor just in case you need to splice the old wire onto the new sensor.

However, the number one cause of the 'three amigos' is a poor connection inside the ABS unit. Early units fitted to 1999 and 2000 model cars seem to suffer more, and the problem is usually the connection inside between the shuttle valve switches and the solenoid head, and as luck would have it Land Rover produce a replacement shuttle valve switch unit. Unluckily the problem is often the two small solder joints on the circuit board where the switch connector plugs in. The more intrepid enthusiasts cut the plastic back and resolder these joints, but you need to be competent at soldering and very careful when cutting the plastic back so as not to accidentally cut through the tracks on the board. A less elegant but more achievable solution is to bring the wires from the switch pack out through the plastic panel and wire them directly into the wiring harness. *See* Repair chapter for details.

Judder or sudden deceleration at speed If the car occasionally judders when you get up to speed as if the handbrake had mysteriously come on then there is a fair chance it has. The handbrake shoes have been known to break

Look for signs of corrosion or fluid leak around the pistons. Also look for uneven wear; if one side has less wear then it is doing less braking.

If the TC, ABS and HDC warning lights come on together and the dash chimes three times then you have the 'three amigos'. Either a wheel sensor or the ABS modulator shuttle valve needs fixing.

up into small chunks, which rattle around the drum. At low speeds they just skid across the surface but as speed increases eventually they start bouncing around like lottery balls and randomly jam in the mechanism. If this appears when out on an expedition, a temporary fix that some people have employed is to remove the drum, take all the pieces of broken shoe out and refit, making a note not to use the handbrake unless absolutely necessary. However, this is only for emergencies and the shoes must be replaced as soon as possible for safety.

STEERING

Discoverys are renowned for vague steering, but it doesn't have to be that way. If all the links and bearings are in good order then it should steer as well as any other car.

Steering feels vague and wanders at speed It may sound strange but the main cause of poor steering is the rear axle. On Discovery 1 models the trailing link bushes where they meet the chassis are the number one culprits, followed by the trailing link rear bushes, then the A-frame bushes and ball joint. On Discovery 2 models the prime suspect is the Watts link bearings, followed by the trailing link forward bushes. Luckily all these can be replaced. About ten years is a good lifespan for most of these items, so I would consider replacing them as a matter of course on a newly acquired Discovery.

Other causes include too-low tyre pressures, mismatched tyres on an axle (rear axle more sensitive here), slack in the steering and dampers (shock absorbers) being worn.

Slack in the steering There are a number of parts in the system that can wear, and even a small amount of slack in each item can add up to a vague feeling and a tendency to wander.

The first step is to check how much play there is. Follow the workshop guide here, but basically with the car stationary move the steering wheel each way to check the free play; any more than a couple of centimetres at the steering wheel rim and something needs mending.

Depending on model and age, the steering column will have a number of joints on its way down to the steering box. Rubber couplings perish over time and even the universal joints wear. The column can be checked by holding it while an assistant gently moves the steering wheel from side to side; any play and it needs replacing. These units are not easily serviceable but replacements are relatively cheap and easy to fit.

Next in line is the steering box, which wears over time but luckily has an adjustment screw, so some slack can be taken up. *See* servicing chapters.

The rear axle has a large part to play in steering stability. There are many links and joints, all of which need to be sound, and the bushes must be in good condition.

The rim of the steering wheel should not move more than about a centimetre or two without the road wheels starting to move too. Box steering systems will always have some play in them, and that is normal. There is far more play when the engine and power-steering pump are not running.

The lower steering column has rubber isolators that can perish and crack. Its design means it will not fall apart completely but will make the steering more slack as it deteriorates.

Check the links across the front axle are not bent. Crawling over rocks can put a curve into them, which will affect the steering.

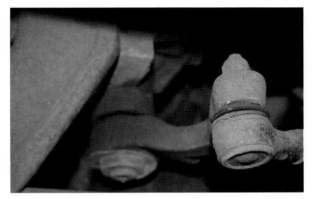

All the ball joints wear and should be replaced as soon as any damage or play is detected.

Look for oil leaks where the steering shaft comes out of the bottom of the steering box. Slight wetting may be okay, but if it is dripping then it needs fixing. Also check the lower nut is tight, as they can work loose.

Drag links and ball joints To test these, have an assistant rocking the steering wheel with the engine running whilst you feel for play at each joint. Replacing the joints is a relatively simple matter of screwing a new one on, but the steering centre point and toe settings must be checked and adjusted afterwards.

Steering box oil leaks The power-steering box has a tendency to leak after a while. Small leaks can be lived with, but if it's dripping then the seals and bearings need to be checked and replaced where needed. Reconditioned boxes are readily available. The power-steering hoses become porous after about ten years. Check that the power-steering pump pipes do not rub against the edges of the sump, which have been known to cut through the hoses. If there is any damage to the hoses they should be replaced.

SUSPENSION

Land Rover suspension is one of the things that makes the Discovery so capable both on and off road. A well maintained car should be stable and predictable, but a poorly maintained car will feel disconnected and quite unpredictable.

Car leans to one side when parked The car should sit level when parked. If it leans then a spring may have cracked or become weak.

Every now and again, when the car is parked on flat ground, just walk back and see if it looks like it is standing straight. Simple checks are very useful tools.

Perished damper bushes allow the damper shaft to rub against the mounting bracket, wearing both out and making it difficult to fit a replacement.

The dampers should be replaced long before they get to this stage. These made the car feel like the steering was faulty and made it swerve when breaking.

Clonking noise when going over bumps The bushes have a hard life. Look at the ones on the radius arms, trailing links and dampers (shock absorbers) and if any are cracked or worn then a replacement is needed.

Sometimes a noise can be due to the axle hitting something that is in the wrong place, such as a drooping exhaust.

Poor stability when cornering Dampers are vital for good handling and safety. If they are failing then you will lose traction as the wheel bounces and continuously loses contact with the road. Check for oil stains, as any oil leaks mean the unit has failed and must be replaced. Grab the roof bars and rock the car from side to side; when you let go it should rock back completely upright straightaway. If it continues rocking for a second or more, the dampers must be investigated.

Poor high speed stability, vague steering The Series 2 rear axle had a Watts link and the Series 1 cars a Panhard rod. The Watts link used a central mounting point attached to the centre line of the axle. The joints can wear and if the mounting bolts were not tightened properly, the holes in the brackets can be eroded making the rear axle less stable. If the rear axle is not controlled well then the steering feels terrible. The Panhard rod was simpler with just two bushes but had much the same effect when worn.

Both Series 1 and 2 cars are sensitive to tyre condition, particularly on the rear axle, which has a large influence on stability. Mismatched tyres are to be avoided, and often problems attributed to steering or suspension are actually down to poor tyres. Check for cracking round the tread block bases and on the side walls. Also check the date code to make sure the tyre is less than about six years old.

Excessive body roll or a clonk when turning into corners From 1994 some models had anti-roll bars and the axles had mounting points welded on. Often the anti-roll bar link ball joints wear, making the car feel less stable as you turn into corners. Luckily they are a simple bolt-on fix.

The Discovery 2 is available with Active Cornering Enhancement (ACE), a very capable option that makes a huge difference to handling. The downside is the added complexity of an electronically controlled hydraulic system. The more there is, the more there is to go wrong. Luckily most of it is fairly easy to fix. *See* the Repair chapter for details.

Another problem that can occur with ACE is failure of the ride-height sensors. Usually just one goes first and the system will detect this and leave the suspension in a fail-safe state. Less commonly a pair of sensors will go and the systems will become disorientated and set the suspension up so the car leans to one side. *See* the section on level sensors below.

One bearing in this Discovery 2 Watts link had worn, making the car feel unstable and making a knocking noise over rough roads.

When the anti-roll bar bushes age the car feels less stable round corners. Also check the condition of the drop links, which have two ball joints each, adding up to a lot of potential play.

Active Cornering Enhancement (ACE) rams leaking If the ACE ram hoses have been removed, new copper washers are needed. If old ones are reused, they will have work hardened, will not seal properly and will leak from the hose connection. Replacement is simple.

The ram seals can become damaged if the rubber boot is ripped and lets grit in. Here a new ram may be needed if the shaft is scored, otherwise it may be possible to rebuild the ram with new seals.

Air suspension goes down overnight The seven-seat Discovery 2s had air springs on the rear axle. These gave a smoother ride for rear passengers and also allowed self-levelling to cope with load changes – after all, seven big passengers could weigh up to three-quarters of a ton.

The system is fairly simple but can become faulty, the most common fault being to find either one or both springs completely deflated in the morning and the car sitting on its bump stops. This is usually due to the air springs becoming porous.

The rear air springs on a Discovery 2 will degrade with age, and just as with any other rubber component they usually need replacing after about ten years. Often the inner edge of the bag that sits over the lower location cone picks up grit and may leak when the car is parked at a certain angle. One day it can be fine and the next it will go down; the following day it might be fine again. Do not rely on the pump bringing it back up to the normal hight all the time. The pump is designed for short running periods, just enough to adjust ride height, and it can wear much faster if it is on for extended periods of time. Replacing the air spring is fairly simple. *See* the Repair chapter for details.

The air lines are a fairly hard plastic and quite durable, but it is possible to damage them if you are unlucky while doing some heavy off-road work. These pipes should not be repaired because repairs usually fail again soon afterwards. Instead, a damaged pipe should be replaced with a new one.

The solenoid valves are very reliable, but they can fail and are simply replaced by bolting in a new one.

A more common failure are the electrical connectors, which can corrode. Often, unplugging and plugging them in again will give a temporary fix (something some unscrupulous garages have charged a lot of money for), but if corrosion has started then the connector pins will need to be replaced, and at the very least the connector should be cleaned out and given a dose of electrical contact grease.

Car does not sit level when parked (air suspension) The system relies on the rear-axle level sensors to work. They give a ride height signal accurate to one millimetre. Again the sensors are fairly robust, but the plastic link rods down to the axle are susceptible to damage. Both the link rod and the sensor are easy to replace, but because the reading from the sensor needs to be calibrated to the car, you have to run a special diagnostic routine to make the system work properly. This involves using accurately made spacer blocks that go between the axle and the bump stops. The diagnostic system will deflate the springs until the car is sitting on these blocks – it then knows that the current read-

If the ram is leaking from the union, first try tightening it. If it keeps working loose then fit new washers.

Just like all the other rubber parts, air springs perish with age. Check for crazing on the surface and tiny cracks where it rolls over.

Clean grit and mud off the air springs. On this one I have supported the chassis to allow the air spring to fully extend before cleaning it.

This small delicate-looking unit, the ride-height sensor on a Discovery 2, makes a big difference to handling. When refitting them the height level has to be set by a dealer diagnostic tool or a similar device.

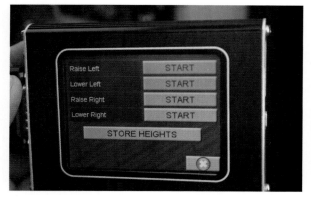

Thankfully there are now affordable diagnostic tools to reset things like ride-height sensors. Here I am using a Nanocom.

Scrapes are inevitable if you use the Discovery in heavy off-road conditions. The radius arm mounts are low points and can get bent like this one.

ing from the level sensors corresponds to the height of the blocks. Aftermarket systems are available to do this, or you could visit your local Land Rover dealer and get them to set the height. If these options are not feasible then the level sensor link rod can be adjusted and measurements taken of the ride height on level ground until it is exactly level on both sides.

CHASSIS

Chassis, all Discoverys The rear cross member traps water where it joins the main chassis rails, so have a good rummage round there. It's hidden by the rear bumper unless you look from underneath.

The backbone of the Discovery, the chassis needs to be totally solid for safety. It weighs less than 10% of the total car weight, yet provides the vast majority of its strength.

The back of the chassis gets the most damage from road salt, grit and water. Unlike the front of the chassis, it is not protected by engine oil leaks.

Check the outriggers that secure the body – there are four main ones with a pair under the front bulkhead and the other pair just in front of the rear wheels. There are also smaller mounts at the front and rear of the body, plus a myriad of smaller brackets.

Look at where the spring hangers are welded to the chassis, as these are high stress areas and prone to corrosion.

Also check for off-road damage – scrapes on the chassis rails can rot through and seriously weaken the car.

Chassis (Discovery 1) When checking out a potential purchase, you have to get down and dirty. Look carefully under the middle of the chassis where the cross member under the back seat holds the top A-frame for the rear axle – this is a prime target for rot. You might not be able to see it, but reach up to the top surface and check for weak metal, but be very careful as there could be sharp, exposed edges there.

> *Old Land Rovers leak oil, fact. This usually means the front half of the chassis is well protected from rust by a thick layer of oil, but the rear half often suffers terribly. Discovery 2 chassis seem to be more prone to rust than Discovery 1 cars. This is partly due to a different paint process but also due to the better gaskets and seals on the later car reducing oil leaks.*

A simple job is to spray the high stress areas to protect them before the rot sets in. This is until you can repaint the area properly.

Typical rot on the back of a back of a Discovery 2 chassis, which seems to be more prone to rust than Discovery 1 items.

The back edge or the rear door on Series 1 cars is exposed to road debris thrown up by the wheel and the paint suffers, exposing the alloy.

Chassis (Discovery 2) The paint protection on these chassis seems to be worse than the Series 1 cars, so check the seams that run the length of the chassis from underneath, and also look at the top seam from the engine bay.

BODY

The door skins, front wings and bonnet are aluminium alloy, the rest is steel. Most of the trouble starts where the two different metals join. Technically the body does not count as a structural part, but rot near seat belts, sills and pillars will massively compromise safety.

Flaking paint and white corrosion Finding white powder round the edges of the doors instead of metal is a common problem. Most of the outer skin is made from an aluminium alloy, which is then crimped round a steel frame, but the dissimilar metals react and corrode much faster, so when the cars were built the joint was made with a sealing compound to help prevent this reaction. However, over time moisture will get into these joints and the reaction starts up, just like pouring the electrolyte into a battery. For instance, on the doors the window seal will gradually harden with age and let a little more rain into the inside of the door, which will then start corroding from the inside out. Often you first notice the problem as the lower corners of the door start to bubble and then the paint falls off, revealing the dreaded white powder. Also the front wheel arches suffer as the paint is chipped by road grit being thrown up by the wheel.

As with any corrosion the area needs to be taken back to what remains of the bare metal before filling (small holes) or welding in new metal (larger holes), and any leaks fixed to prevent the problem reoccurring. *See* the Repair chapter for details.

You may have seen modified Discoverys with alloy tread plates attached to the bottom of the doors. Although this can protect the paintwork underneath from off-road damage, quite often it is there to cover up the holes, something to think about when you are searching for an older Land Rover.

Problems can occur where panels join, particularly if they have been replaced or welded. Check the shut lines, panel gaps and look along the length of the car to see if it all looks straight.

A-pillars rot at the top. This is a Series 2 car with the trim removed.

Here a new rear arch panel has been welded in sometime in the past, but sadly the surrounding area was not fixed too, making it a bit pointless.

The welded joints at the top of the A- and B-pillars seem to be badly painted on some cars, so check for corrosion here as well as the bottom of the A-pillars where they join the floor. Treat any rust or paint loss immediately by wire brushing the loose stuff off and painting with a decent primer. Then leave it to cure and give it a good top coat. If the corrosion has holed the metal it will need welding up.

Corrosion in the engine bay In the engine bay check the inner wings, particularly where they meet the bulkhead and under the battery tray. The jack and wheel chock on a Discovery 1 should be found in the front wing just behind the headlight. They rest on a rubber mat and are secured with a rubber strap. These parts can chafe away at the matting and erode the inner wing metalwork, so it is worth removing them to have a good look at the steel. On a Discovery 2 they sit in a plastic tray behind the battery. Ideally the whole tray and battery should be removed every few years to check for corrosion. If surface rust has started, then clean it back to clean metal and paint it properly. The lower surface gets struck by road grit and the paint struggles here, so tougher paints such as Hammerite can help extend its life.

Discovery 2 cars have a plastic wing liner that significantly extends the life of the metalwork. Make sure it is intact and that all the fixings are present, as they are frequently left off by unscrupulous mechanics.

In the engine bay the area where the bulkhead meets the inner wing tends to accumulate dirt and mud, accelerating rust. Keep it clean and treat any rust immediately.

Damp front carpets The front bulkhead where it meets the sills and footwells can accumulate dirt and moisture, which makes the joint line rust out. Lift carpets and check for dampness and rust. Also check it from underneath, and give the panels a good push and listen for crunching rust.

Sills Sills rust at the rear edge where road grime is thrown up from the rear wheel. The front of the sills may be rotten too, particularly if the front mud flaps are missing. The sills have trim pieces that hide the rot, so look carefully at the surrounding area for signs of spreading rust.

Corroding rear arch On four-door Discovery 1 cars where the rear side doors meet the wheel arch, there can often be trapped mud leading to corrosion. This problem area was redesigned on Discovery 2 models to remove the rot trap, so pay particular attention to the rear seat-belt mounts. Also the boot floor tends to rust due to moisture being trapped under the carpets. This is usually worst at the rear, and lifting the mats up should show the worst of it. If it is damp under there, remove the carpets and let it dry out.

The roof is steel – sunroof leaks can make the upper surface of the headlining wet and cause the roof to rot from the inside.

Rain leaks in The window sealing strips perish, particularly the tight corners on the rear side windows. These cracks let in water, which leads to corrosion in the panels below. These can be cleaned and filled with black silicone sealant (available in most large DIY stores) as a temporary fix until new rubbers are fitted. Where water has leaked in it is a good idea to remove the trim and check for corrosion to the bodywork, and also to any electrical connectors or earth studs, and allow the area to dry out properly.

Excessive wind noise from the front (Discovery 2) On Discovery 2 models there can be excessive wind noise from the top corners of the front windscreen. There is a gap between the screen top seal and the A-pillar trim at the top corner, which can be filled with a blob of silicone sealant. This can be removed easily when the time comes to replace the windscreen.

Window drops, jams or will not go up Window lift mechanisms are prone to failure after about ten years if not serviced every few years. Typical symptoms involve the window jamming and twisting in the frame, suddenly dropping into the door or failing to come up once opened. Sometimes the door card can be removed and the mechanism just put back in place, but sometimes it is best to fit a replacement mechanism. *See* later chapters for more detail.

Rear door will not unlock The rear door lock can seize up due to lack of use, and usually it stays in the up position due to the aluminium corroding and jamming it. There is a very simple fix, detailed in the Repair chapter. In fact all the door latch and lock mechanisms can become a bit stiff, making it difficult to open or lock doors, but all are fairly easily fixed with penetrating oil and gently working the handles back and forth.

Rear door unlocks but is difficult to open or close If your rear door tends to stick and you have to lift it to close it then your hinges have worn. Lubricating them should be part of your maintenance schedule. All the weight of the spare wheel puts a high force on those hinges and without a little helping lubrication they can start to wear and become loose, which means you have to lift them to close them. As more weight is bearing down on the striker plate they become more difficult to open. If the hinges are very worn then it's best to replace them.

Door locks The internal linkages of the door locks contain a mix of metal and plastic parts. As the car ages the plastic parts can become more brittle, and also if the car is not used for long periods the mechanism can become stiff

A really easy fix for a sticking rear door lock: some oil spray and a bit of wiggling. Pop the Land Rover badge out for access.

and put higher forces on the plastic parts. Typical problems include the key turning in the door lock and nothing happening due to the plastic collar at the end of the lock barrel breaking (this requires a replacement part from a new lock barrel).

INTERIOR

The Discovery interior is remarkably well thought out and quite durable. Discovery 1s initially had the option of a soft 'handbag' in the centre console. In use it was secured with a clip on each side, but it could be easily removed so you could take all your papers, CDs and car sweets with you. Most of these have been lost over the years and replacements are getting rare. Later models had a proper cubby box with a lockable lid; if you buy one of these, check there is a key for it.

The usual faults with the interior are cracked plastic on the dash top and instrument binnacle. The edge of the seats wear as people slide in and out. The seat-belt buckle is prone to getting jammed between the door and B-pillar, so treat any paint chips swiftly.

Rear seat latches can dry up, and get stuck with fluff and children's sweets. Clean them out and spray with light oil to keep them working.

Voltage with the engine idling should be 13.5 to 14.5V or thereabouts. If it is higher then the alternator regulator is failing; if it is lower then either the alternator is failing or the belt is slipping.

Subsequent models just have a normal cubby box, which folds back to form a cup holder. Check the hinge has not been pulled out by someone putting excessive load on the lid. If it has, then drill the hinge bracket holes out and fit bigger screws.

Peeling dashboard Some 300-style Discoverys had a problem with parts of the dashboard peeling. Repair kits are available but are getting rarer now, so if your dash is peeling badly then you may want to consider buying a second-hand one.

Rear seats will not latch If the second or third row seats on a Discovery 2 wont latch down, it's usually because the latch under the seat has become stiff due to lack of lubrication. A quick squirt of light oil such as WD40 and operating the mechanism to get it moving usually sorts this out.

ELECTRICAL

Noise from the alternator, poor charging The alternator used on most models is a development of the old Lucas A127 unit, making it fairly simple for a specialist to rebuild. The alternator bearings will wear on high-mileage cars or ones that have seen a lot of mud or wading.

Discoverys with Tdi engines have a speed output on the back of the alternator to drive the rev counter. You can tell when it is not working properly because the rev counter reading becomes erratic.

If one of the diodes fails in a low-resistance state, then it will flatten the battery when left standing for a day: replacing the diode or regulator pack should solve this.

Engine will not crank or stalls, Discovery 1 (200-style) If the engine fails to crank or the ignition fails to come on in a 200-style Discovery 1 then it could be the fusible links in the engine bay. Instead of big fuses these cars had lengths of fuse wire in flame-proof sleeves built into the main power-feed wiring from the battery. The cable is located on the front right wing and if the fault leaves you stranded you can sometimes get the car to start by squeezing the links.

The problem is that the dissimilar metals in the fuse wire and the copper cables cause corrosion and eat the copper away, leaving a green powder. Eventually this results in an open circuit, and that's why sometimes squeezing that area can temporarily restore power.

One solution is to cut out the links and solder in new ones. However, a better long-term solution is to fit a high current fuse box (such as those for 'Megafuse') in its place.

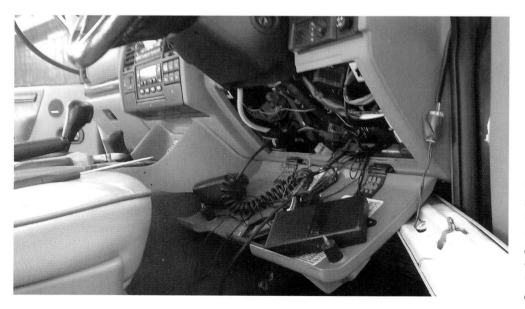

Possibly the single greatest cause of Discovery faults: the wiring. This in-car phone set-up was crudely spliced into the wiring, causing ignition problems.

Replacing some electrical items, such as the integral heater fan switch, means replacing the whole unit. Sometimes a more pragmatic solution is to replace the faulty item with a modern equivalent.

Discovery 1 (200-style) heater fan switch burns out The fan-speed switch suffers from weak contacts, which overheat and burn out. You may find that the fastest speed setting stops working first, or the speed that you most commonly use. On one of my cars the switch got so hot that smoke came out and the knob started to melt.

The switch is part of the heating unit and does not really lend itself to replacement, so I fitted a non-standard switch instead.

Unusually dim lights Typical symptoms include lights that work but are dim, or when the indicator is operated the brake/side light dims in sympathy. This is usually due to poor earthing, or the bulb mounting burning out. Earthing might be by a wire to the car body work, and the common fault is corrosion at the connection point, which can be diagnosed by temporarily fitting a separate earth wire directly from a sound earthing point to the light cluster's earth point, making the unit spring magically back to life. The solution is to clean up the earth points, replace the earth wire if necessary and give it a spot of paint to stop it corroding again.

The rear light clusters use a circuit board to mount the bulbs, and any contamination or corrosion here will cause the tracks to heat up and eventually burn out. If caught early enough, this can be fixed by sanding down the contamination/corrosion. If it has gone too far then a new light unit will be needed.

Discovery 2 auxiliary lights not working The Discovery 2 had a factory option of a pair of driving lights mounted on an A-bar or full front protection bar (bull bar). After about ten years the relay in the control unit can fail, but unfortunately it is a 'potted' sealed unit and trying to dig it out of all that solid compound is nearly impossible. The quickest solution is to replace the control unit, although they are getting harder to find now and prices reflect this. Another solution is to replace the unit with something else. Have a look in Chapter 8.

Engine turns over very slowly This could be a worn starter motor, but before spending a fortune on a new one check the engine earth cable. There are two on most models.

There should be a very thick braided band that goes from the back of the cylinder head to the bulkhead, and there is a thicker cable from the front of the engine to the battery (Discovery 1) or battery earth block (Discovery 2). Because they are often exposed to road grime they have a tendency to rot out, and then a fair chunk of the earth current is borne by other components that connect to the car body such as the accelerator cable, which starts getting very hot. Check the condition of both straps and also pay particular attention to where they attach to the bodywork and the engine – if the fixings work loose they will reduce starting capacity, become hot and corrode faster. Fitting a secondary earth strap is a useful temporary way just to see if the earth strap is the problem, and if it is then clean up the fixings or fit a new cable permanently.

Fuel gauge drops to empty when there is still half a tank left, or becomes intermittent The fuel-level sensor is a variable resistor operated by a float on the end of an arm in the tank. As it is a mechanical device, with the sensor contact sweeping across the resistor as the fuel level changes, it is prone to mechanical wear. Most cars spend most of their lives with less than half a tank of fuel, so the lower end of the scale usually wears out first making that part of the scale faulty. This can be confirmed by testing the voltage at the sensor with a multimeter. The solution is to replace the sensor.

Engine continues running when ignition turned off and heater on recirculation, Discovery 1 (200-style) There is a weird back feed in the wiring on some models such that when the heater fan is on full and the recirculation switch is on, the ignition stays on even when the key is removed. The ignition will turn off and the engine stop when recirculation or the fan is switched off. It doesn't seem to do any harm, but it can catch out the unwary.

Battery will not hold a charge First check it is being charged properly. For the battery to charge up the voltage at the terminals has to be greater than the battery's open-circuit voltage, so a 12V battery needs more than about 13V to charge properly. Most alternators charge at between 13.5 and 14.8V (check the manual for your model)

Batteries do not last forever. If you leave the car for a day after being fully charged, the terminal voltage should still be over 12.4V with the engine off. If it is below 12.0V then the battery may be faulty.

With nothing connected, a fully charged battery should have a slightly higher voltage than its nominal rating. A 12V battery should read 12.5 to 12.8V when charged. If it reads 12.0 then it is a bit low, while 11.5 is very discharged.

Sometimes charging a very discharged battery for a very long time, possibly days, can revive it, so it's always worth a try. But if the open-circuit voltage is very low then it is probably damaged and will never hold a charge for any useful amount of time. Also, batteries age and impurities compromise the plates, so traditional wet plate batteries generally need replacing every five years or so. Modern AGM batteries last a bit longer and although more expensive they can work out cheaper in the long run.

and should charge just as happily at idle as when the revs are higher. If it does not and assuming the belt drive is okay, then it's off to the repairers to have the windings, brushes and regulator checked and fixed.

Alarm system, Discovery 1 The Discovery 1 had a reviver unit that unlocked the doors and enabled the ignition and fuel pump, as well as controlling the flashing LED on the dash. The units have been known to fail internally. New units are hard to find now, so a second-hand unit would be needed. If you need one then make sure you get at least one matching key fob with it, otherwise you will never get it to work. Interestingly, almost 1,500 Discovery 1s were put

off the road in 2002 because an immobiliser part 'Spider Unit' (Land Rover part No ARM 4889) become virtually impossible to obtain.

You can test the Discovery 1 immobiliser system as follows. Start with the ignition off, all doors unlocked and the bonnet closed. Then, within 8 seconds, open the bonnet, turn the ignition on, lock all the doors, turn the ignition off then on again. If it has worked, the horn will beep once and the LED flash.

Now if you open any door, the LED will light. If you close the bonnet, the hazard lights will flash. If you try to start the engine, it should not crank.

Press the key-fob button to test the ultrasonic detection system. If anything moves in the cabin, the LED will flash.

If any one of these tests does not work then you know which bit needs fixing, most often just the bonnet or a door switch. Once you turn the ignition off it will revert to normal mode.

Alarm system, Discovery 2 The Discovery 2 is a sophisticated machine and uses a radio signal to the Body Control Module (BCM) to unlock and disarm the alarm. Then it uses another code between the key and the BCM, read by the ignition barrel, to send a further code to the Engine Control Unit (ECU) to allow the engine to start.

The BCM is behind the passenger glove box, and if the windscreen is prone to leaks then the connectors here can become damp and cause problems. If caught early the connectors can be cleaned up to restore function, but if left then it will eventually damage the BCM, which will require

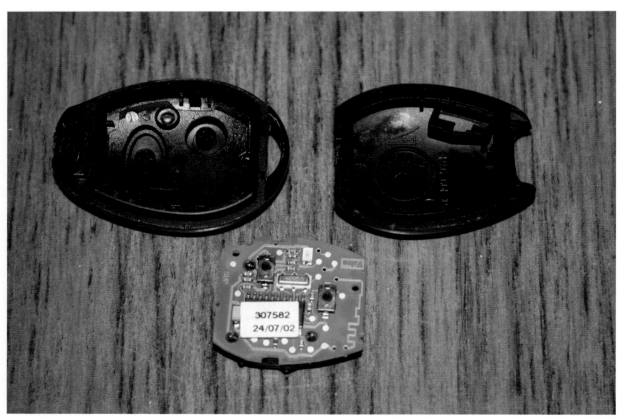

When buying spares make sure you get the correct part. The plastic shell is often described as the 'fob' without the electronics, ideal if your old shell is deteriorated but no use if you want a new spare key.

replacement. Getting a second-hand BCM is easy, but programming all the security codes into it is not. Luckily there are several aftermarket diagnostic systems that can do this such as Nanocom. Ask your local Land Rover club if someone has one you can use.

Another source of alarm faults is the main fuse box under the dashboard, next to the steering column. This is an intelligent unit with a small computer built in and it has a multitude of connector plugs. The problem is usually caused by water leaks corroding the connectors on the reverse side. *See* Repair chapter for details.

Key-fob buttons have no effect If the key-fob buttons have no effect, you can unlock the car using the EKA code (*see* below). There are two possible causes of this sort of failure: either the fob is not working or the radio receiver in the roof has broken, usually due to water ingress from a leaky sunroof. Before doing anything expensive, first check and clean up the remote function actuator (RFA) earth point on the roof.

Key-fob faults A quick check for the key fob is to try the second key fob if you have one. If the fob isn't working then the first check is the fob battery. Depending on your exact model of Discovery the alarm LED on the dash should tell you when the key fob battery is running low – *see* your handbook for details. To be certain of the battery condition you have to open the fob case and extract the battery. Check the battery voltage: it should be above about 75% of its as-new voltage, so a 3.2-volt battery will still work even when the voltage is down to 2.5 volts, although the range will be much reduced. If the voltage is lower than this then replace the battery, close up the case and try using it again.

If it is working, the red LED on the fob should flash when you press any of its buttons. If it does not flash and has a good battery then the circuit has failed and you will need a new one, which will have to be programmed to the car. *See* the Servicing chapter for details.

If you want a new key fob then have a look on Land Rover forums and see which ones other people have used. There are now a number of companies making new replacement units, which work just as well as the originals but at a fraction of the price. But, as ever, beware of cheap copies that could leave you stranded.

Using the EKA code On Discovery 2 vehicles, which have been locked with the key fob but will not unlock, you can unlock and turn the alarm off by using the Emergency Key Access (EKA) code. This is stored in the BCM, so you will need to have written it down beforehand by either reading the BCM with a diagnostic tool or taking the car to a main dealer.

To enter the code, put the key in the driver's door lock and turn to unlock until the flashing alarm light glows steadily and the horn beeps once (if enabled). Then turn the key to unlock repeatedly to enter the first EKA number. Then turn to lock repeatedly to enter the second number. Turn to unlock to enter the third. Finally turn to lock to enter the last EKA number. Then you have to wait about 5 minutes, after which the alarm light will stop flashing and glow steadily.

At this point you have 30 seconds to get in and turn the ignition on. Any longer and the alarm will reset and you will have to start again.

If you have had to do this because the key fob has stopped working, you can carry on using the car by locking and unlocking the car using the key in the door instead of the fob buttons.

IDENTITY

As with most cars there are some that are not what they pretend to be. A stolen car may have its identity changed simply by changing the number plates, so look at the car's documents. In the UK that is a V5, sometimes known as the log book, and check that the car has the right Vehicle Identification Number (VIN) stamped on the VIN plate riveted to the front of the engine bay above the radiator.

However, this itself may have been swapped and so it is vital to also check the VIN stamped into the chassis just in front of the right-hand spring hanger, and the engine number too.

The main VIN plate is riveted on and so is relatively easy to swap. That is why you should not rely on it and must also check the chassis and other body VIN tags, plus the engine number. Note the overspray on the corner of this tag where the car has been resprayed.

Some cars will have had a genuine Land Rover replacement engine, which should have a plate like this bonded very securely on.

The simple stuff only takes a few minutes but can mean life or death to an old car, and to the occupants! Do not take risks with maintenance, do it properly and if in doubt get help.

servicing – simple jobs

Land Rovers are very durable and can keep on running, albeit badly, despite very poor servicing. This unfortunately means that there are quite a few cars out there that are running very badly or in danger of imminent mechanical failure. A full service can transform a car, make the engine and gearbox smoother, reduce vibration and improve fuel economy, plus make the steering safer and improve the handling around corners.

This chapter is not a substitute for the correct workshop manual, but it contains some of the tips and tricks that owners have picked up over the years, and as such it should be considered as an addition to the standard manuals.

ONLINE SERVICE INFORMATION AND MANUALS

Land Rover provide an online technical service. There is a basic free version where you can access owner handbooks and accessory fitting guides, but for a fee you can register and have access to all the service manuals, wiring charts, service schedules and technical bulletins. It does not cover the 200-style Discoverys but it does cover everything from 1995.

At time of writing the site is at: topix.landrover.jlrext.com

If you can't find it then try searching for 'topix landrover'.

AGEING

Many parts age even when not in use, most notably rubber, which reacts with oxygen in the air and becomes hard and brittle. Sunlight speeds up this process and tyres stored in the open will crack within a few years. But even hidden parts such as cooling hoses and fuel pipes made of rubber

These rubber bushes have cracks all round them, and although they are still the right shape and in the right place they are too hard to allow the damper rod to move properly.

After about 1994 the rear propshaft joint was a rubber coupling to improve refinement. This too has a limited shelf life and this one on my Discovery 2 is cracking next to the bolt holes.

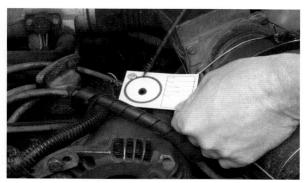

Oil condition can be checked with some blotting paper or an oil test card. Water makes the edge of the blot crinkly and fuel in the oil makes a lighter coloured band around a darker central spot.

Safety-critical parts should always be bought new, particularly brake pads (the bond between pad and backing plate deteriorates) and brake fluid. Even wheel bearings can form small rust spots if left on the shelf for many years.

will perish. Ten years should be considered the maximum life of a rubber component, and six years the maximum life of a tyre regardless of tread depth. Fuel pipes should be replaced for safety well before they show clear signs of perishing.

Engine coolant (antifreeze) gradually becomes acidic and after about three years must be replaced, otherwise it will slowly start eating away at the cooling system and engine from within.

Oils age and so mileage cannot be considered as the only indicator that replacement is necessary. Replace the engine oil every year even if the mileage is minimal. Oils also age while still in the can; additives separate out and can form a jelly-like substance in the bottom of the can, and when this happens the oil is no longer usable.

Even oil ages. Motor oils contain additives that settle out and decompose, which changes their characteristics, and the oil oxidizes slowly meaning it will not protect the engine so well. Avoid 'New Old Stock' bargains.

Brake fluid absorbs moisture. It is sold in sealed containers and as soon as the seal is broken it starts ageing and must be discarded after a time just as if it was in the car.

Fuel ages too, more so with modern complex blends. The lighter parts of petrol evaporate off and leave a thick lacquer, which can jam injectors and fuel pumps. If the car is to be laid up for a long period, there are fuel stabilizer fluids that can be added to the tank.

Brake pads also perish, the bond between the friction material and the metal backing plate can crack and result in the pad failing. Often the pads will work fine until the bond breaks and the friction material falls out completely. The next time the brakes are used the pedal will travel a long way as the calliper piston pushes the bare backing plate into the disc. Then the brake will appear to work again but with a scraping noise from the metal-to-metal contact, but in an emergency stop the car will veer sideways. The next stage is the backing plate is ejected, the piston falls out of the calliper and all braking is lost. For this reason, inspect the bond on the brake pads very carefully and replace them before they perish.

A word of warning: Discovery 2 vehicles with air suspension should not be lifted on two-post ramps or any other means that leaves the axles dangling – this would stretch the air bags and has been known to weaken the rubber. So always ensure the axles' weight is taken by suitable stands when working on a raised vehicle.

The Tdi was fitted in many cars, making spares readily available. But beware, only the core engine was common, the Defender has different shaped exhaust manifold and turbo, hoses, ducts etc.

ENGINES

200/300Tdi

The 200 and 300Tdi engines have drain plugs at the lowest point of the bell housing, and originally the advice was to periodically undo them to drain out any water that may have accumulated in there. Water can get in when wading but also it can accumulate slowly when driving in normal wet conditions.

Land Rover now recommend that the plug is left out for normal driving, to prevent water build-up in the bell housing, but it is essential to refit the plug before wading. Make sure they are stowed in the car securely.

Oil changes are important. Oil in a diesel runs colder than in an equivalent petrol engine and so needs different addi-

Do not forget to drain the water from the fuel filter every few months, and change the filter on time too.

The Tdi bell-housing drain plug should be left out unless wading.

After an oil change the oil pipes will be empty, so to minimize the time after that first start up when there is no oil going round pre-fill the oil filter with new oil before fitting. Be patient when filling, it takes a while for the oil to soak into the element.

tives to cope with the potential for greater fuel and moisture contamination, so always use the right sort of oil for your engine.

Prime the new oil filter by slowly filling it with oil, just so the oil pump is not sucking on air when you next fire it up.

Some of the hose clearances are very small, and some hoses may end up rubbing until they fail. The prime suspects here are the bottom hose rubbing on the steering box and the 300Tdi top heater hose rubbing on the fan belt. If your car has this problem then it may need a new hose, re-orienting the hose or supporting it with wide cable ties.

TD5 oil filters This engine is a little more advanced and uses two oil filters, a conventional one and in series a centrifugal unit that you can often hear winding down after the engine stops. The deposits accumulate in a little disposable pot, which must be replaced every 36,000 miles. The ordinary oil filter change is every 12,000 miles, but as ever if the engine is worked hard or spends a lot of time wading then the intervals should be shorter.

Rover V8 engines

Distributor On Discovery 1 cars check the distributor cap and rotor arm yearly. The distributor cap tends to foul up the terminals with a hard white deposit, which can cause the engine to lose power and stall at idle. The cap can be easily replaced – note there is a notch in the flange so it can only be fitted in only one orientation. When transferring the leads across I put the new cap next to the old and transfer one lead at a time to ensure they are still in the right order.

The TD5 was the last Rover-designed diesel engine, and it is quite a good one if looked after. Key points are oil changes, two oil filters near the turbo, and preventing oil leaking into the injector wiring.

There are many different caps available for the V8, but not all fit. Make sure you get a matching rotor arm too as the height of the cap and rotor changed a few times. If it starts misfiring when you are away from base then scrape the deposits off the terminals with a small coin.

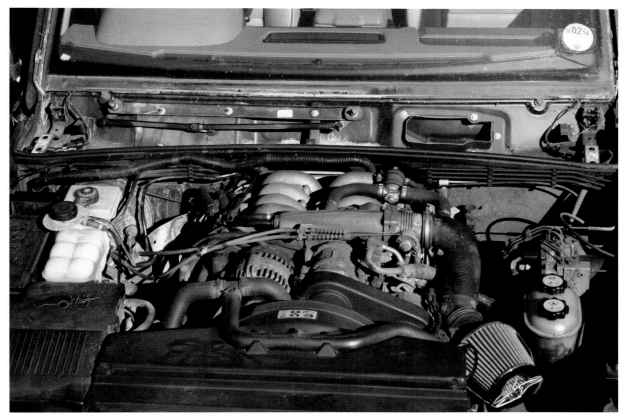

The fuel injection may be almost modern, but the core of the V8 dates back to the 1950s, so more traditional maintenance methods work well.

The rotor arm can become stuck if it has been there for many years, so even if it looks okay, it is still worth removing it to check. And remember to put a few drops of engine oil on the felt pad under the rotor arm. This keeps the mechanism in good order, and without it the advance system may fail.

It is very unlikely the ignition timing will have changed by itself, but it is still worth checking on a new purchase in case the previous user set it incorrectly.

This is simple to do: fit a timing strobe to number 1 spark plug lead and point it at the timing marks on the crank pulley. The timing marks can be difficult to read so I usually clean the area up first and put a little white paint on it, then wipe it gently so the paint stays only in the recesses of the lines and numbers.

If the ignition seems to be jumping about all over the place then most likely the distributor cap is faulty as detailed above, but it could also be a poor-quality earth on the ignition module or a problem with one of the connectors. Occasionally it can be the coil driver or pick-up becoming faulty, so if you have eliminated all the cheap options then you may need a new coil driver or pick-up unit.

Adjust the ignition timing by loosening the distributor clamp bolt and carefully rotating the whole distributor is the required direction.

If you wish to make best use of some of the high-performance modern petrols about these days then you might want to try advancing the ignition to get the best out of it, but if you go too far the engine will suffer from 'knock', which can destroy it quite quickly. The engine will be most prone to knock at mid rpm on full throttle. Seek professional advice on this, but done correctly it can give you a few more miles per gallon.

Oil changes All V8 engines need frequent oil changes, but often this is neglected resulting in tar building up in the oil galleries and clogging the valve gear. Rapid rocker-shaft wear then results and cam followers may fail, which reduces power and makes a heavy tapping noise – there have been plenty of cases of cars being driven in this condition with the owners blissfully unaware of the damage. In more severe cases the oil feed to the main bearings can be compromised and failure becomes inevitable. If you have

Getting a full filter into position is tricky and spillages are likely, so put down some cloth first.

just bought a car and the oil is in poor condition, change it immediately. Then drive the car normally for a few hundred miles to allow the detergents to remove the deposits and then change it again. The oil filter must be changed on both occasions too.

If you empty the sump of oil and also remove the old oil filter then oil will drain out of the pump and oil pick-up tube. If this happens then when you next start the engine after filling with new oil you will get no oil pressure because the pump is sucking on air and will not prime. To avoid this I drain the sump, then fill it with new oil, then replace the oil filter. That way a slug of old oil stays in the pick-up tube and the pump works immediately. I also fill the new filter with new oil before fitting. You have to be patient here as it fills slowly, and fitting a full filter is a bit messy too, but it is worth it.

> *The basic engine design goes back to the 1950s and as such has fairly wide tolerances in the bearings and needs a reasonably thick oil to prevent it flowing out of the bearings too fast. The original oil viscosity was specified as 20/50, but Land Rover gradually reduced the specification to 15/40 in order to reduce drag and improve fuel economy very slightly. I find that reverting to the thicker 20/50 on high-mileage engines reduces rattle on start-up and makes them run a bit smoother when warm.*

Pre-fill the oil filter before fitting, and lubricate the seal so that it can slide in its groove to prevent it riding up when fitting and leaking.

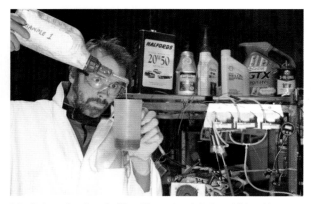

It is all about the oil on the V8s, with good anti-sludge additives. Use any Castrol, Mobil or other top brand, but avoid low viscosity – 15/40 is a minimum for most and 20/50 is good for older high mileage V8s.

The later idle-speed control valve has a plunger that opens or closes off an air channel and tends to get gummed up with oil and tar. If it sticks, the engine may stall at junctions

Choosing the right plug is vital. Buying cheap is false economy, but also some gimmicky multi-electrode plugs are best avoided.

If even after this the engine oil pressure warning light stays on after an oil change then bring the engine speed up to about 2,000rpm immediately to increase pump suction. But if the light stays on for more than a few seconds then turn the engine off immediately and find out what has gone wrong.

The V8 engine on the injected Discovery 1 cars has an idle-speed control valve at the back of the plenum chamber, which can get clogged with oil and tar, resulting in an unstable idle speed and stalling as the valve fights against the blockage.

To prevent this, remove the valve and clean off the gunge with WD40 or similar. There may be deposits stuck inside the valve so it may be necessary to repeat the cleaning process.

Spark plugs The old V8 can be a bit hard on its spark plugs, and if you do a lot of short journeys in cold weather then they will need changing a lot earlier than if the car does mainly long motorway journeys.

> You don't need a 'special' plug for running on liquified petroleum gas (LPG), just a good quality one in good condition. The standard ignition system provides over ten times more spark energy than the minimum required for petrol, to allow for petrol's poor mixture formation. LPG mixes much better than petrol and so needs less overcompensation, even though its minimum energy requirement is higher than petrol.

The plug leads are just as important as the plugs, and often corrosion sets in at the plug boot. There is no need to buy thicker leads, just good quality standard ones.

As the cylinder head is alloy you must be careful not to cross-thread the plugs when fitting them, so always wind them in by hand and use a tool only for the final tightening. A very small amount of copper grease on the thread will make them easier to get out later. If a plug is proving difficult to get out then soak it in penetrating oil for a day before extracting it. You should never need to apply a large force to get them out.

Today there is a very wide choice of plugs available, but I have found platinum single-electrode plugs to give the longest and most reliable service. Avoid multi-electrode plugs as they do not work so well on this sort of combustion chamber and can give cold-start issues.

Cooling (all engines)

Fan belt Belts perish just like any other rubber part, so check the inside edge for cracking. To change the belts on

Use a long bar on the tensioner to make life easier. Unhook the belt from the most accessible pulley first and remember to fit the new belt to that pulley last.

Layouts can be complex and not all are documented. Phone cameras are ideal for getting into tight spaces and photographing the belt layout before you undo it.

Use the right spanner for the viscous fan nut. It needs to be a good fit and very slim. Remember it is a left-hand thread!

early cars, slacken off the appropriate unit (alternator, PAS pump etc.), but on later models there is a spring-loaded tensioner that can be pulled in by putting a spanner on the idler pulley bolt.

Make sure you know the routing of the belt before starting this as some engines have a very complicated layout. There was a huge variety in the layout through the years and not all are covered by the official service manuals. If in doubt, take a picture of it before you start.

In all cases the viscous fan will have to be removed first – remember it's a reverse thread!

Coolant Coolant degrades over time and traditional ethylene-glycol-based coolants should be replaced every two years or so. The Discovery 2 switched over to using OAT (Organic Acid Technology) coolant, which lasts a lot longer but still needs changing after about five years on average. Old coolant not only looses performance but also turns acidic and can eat into the engine and radiator.

The cooling system is far too often neglected until it fails. Check the coolant level regularly and if it goes down, find the leak and fix it. Pressure caps wear out just like any other part and are often forgotten.

The cooling system passages are complex and prone to airlocks, so bleeding out any air is important. Be gentle with these fragile plastic caps and do not over-tighten or the rubber thread will rip out – you should not need tools.

Coolant leaks like this should be cured by replacing the failing part, not by adding stuff to the coolant.

The coolant needs to be a mix of water and glycol/OAT because water is the better heat carrier. If the concentration is too strong, there will not be enough water and under extreme circumstances it may overheat. Conversely if it is too weak then it may boil prematurely and allow cylinder-head damage as well as accelerated corrosion. Generally a 50/50 mix is best, going a little stronger in extremely cold climates. Although advice is given in the Discovery handbook, it is worth reading the coolant manufacturer's guidelines as the technology moves forward.

When adding new coolant, avoid using tap water as it may contain a high concentration of minerals, and just like a kettle element the engine will scale up over time, resulting in overheating problems. Instead, use demineralized (deionized) water. It may seem expensive, but do not think of it as water, think of it as a vital component of your car. Of course, you could make it at home using a kettle and a suitable condenser.

Radiator and avoiding overheating The fine fin spacing on the radiator can make it prone to trapping mud and dirt, which will reduce air flow through it and ruin cooling ability. To make things worse some radiator packs may consist of several elements including a gearbox cooler and an air-conditioning condenser, which can trap debris between the radiators.

If you enjoy off-road driving through mud, things will get worse much quicker, and sand can be terrible for clogging the radiator air ways.

The solution is to hose them out, but you must never use a pressure washer as this will bend or destroy the delicate fins. The secret is to remove the front grille and the fan and shroud, and then soak the radiators with water until all the grime is soft. Then hose it out with minimal pressure. For cars with multiple radiators it is worth removing the top brackets so you can get a bit more space between them to clean them effectively. I use a garden hose with my thumb over the end, no fancy spray heads or jets.

Once it has been washed down, inspect the fins for damage, very gently straighten any bent fins and then clean up and paint any areas where corrosion has started.

Leaking hoses Old cars leak and it can be tempting to 'cure' a small coolant leak by pouring in a bottle of 'stop leak' or similar substance. Whilst this will bung up small leaks it may also coat the upper cylinder head and interior heater coolant passages with a thin layer that reduces heat transfer. In bad cases this can lead to warped cylinder heads or a heater that only blows cold. I never use a liquid leak fix – it is always better to find the leak and fix it.

MANUAL GEARBOX

The manual gearbox needs very little servicing although

An early Discovery V8 radiator shows typical corrosion. These fins are easily damaged or clogged and need to be cleaned gently. Never use a pressure washer on the radiator.

The manual gearbox fill port is up on the side, so you need a long spout on your oil bottle to fill it. This is an R380 unit.

it is vital to check the oil every year or so. Do this by undoing the oil-level plug on the side of the box when the car is level. Ideally a little oil should just dribble out. If nothing comes out then add oil using a small oil bottle with a long spout, most ½-litre ATF (Automatic Transmission Fluid) bottles have one. Put the spout in the level hole and slowly add oil until it just starts to dribble out, then put the plug back in.

If a lot of fluid comes out, or if the fluid is grey and contaminated, then it needs changing. To do this simply undo the drain plug underneath (and the one on the extension housing on LT77 models), drain the oil, clean off the drain plug and refit it. Then fill with fluid as above.

Both the LT77 and R380 gearboxes use ATF. Early manuals recommended ordinary gear oil, but this results in poor gear changes.

AUTOMATIC GEARBOX

ATF change The official manuals say the ZF automatic gearbox is sealed for life and does not require oil changes. That was based on how cars lived in the 1980s, and it works if your desired life is only about 120,000 miles or ten years maximum.

The trouble is that oil oxidizes, and so over time it degrades, plus condensation can form on the inside of the gearbox and gradually contaminate the oil. Realistically, it is usually worth changing the auto gearbox oil and filter every 80,000 miles, but there is a word of caution: if you buy a car that has done well over 100,000 miles and not had a gearbox oil change then it may have jelly-like deposits inside. These will not interfere with the gearbox unless they are disturbed. New auto gearbox fluid has detergents in and may dislodge the lumps, causing the gearbox to stick in one gear or behave oddly. If this happens then you may have to strip the auto gearbox down, remove the valve block and clean it (a big job that requires great care). If you continue driving the car in this condition then one of two things will happen: either eventually the blobs will be flushed through and your gearbox will start working properly again, or they will lodge somewhere bad, cause oil starvation and completely destroy your gearbox.

Dipstick readings are only accurate when the engine is running and you have run the selector through all positions due to fluid held in the torque converter and valve body. The latest Discoverys had the dipstick deleted and instead a level plug, similar to the manual box, fitted to the front of the sump.

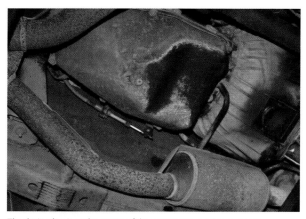

The drain plug is at the centre of the automatic gearbox sump. The sump has a magnet inside to trap metallic particles and if you change the auto gearbox oil filter, you have to clean off the magnet too. Access to the filter is by removing the sump, which is not as scary as it sounds.

I bought one 200-style Discovery with 98,000 miles. It had not had a change, but the fluid was in good condition so I left it. Eventually I sold it on eleven years later with 182,000 miles, still working fine. So it can last well sometimes, but if there is any contamination (oil looks brown or smells strongly) then it probably needs changing straight away.

To change the oil simply undo the drain plug at the bottom of the auto gearbox sump. You refill it by pouring ATF down the dipstick tube on most models, so be patient. Note that on some later models the dipstick tube was deleted and there is just a screw-in plug at the front of the gearbox sump. This makes filling quicker and is similar to filling the transfer box in that you need a bottle with a long spout to get the oil in.

Automatic gearbox filter change While the oil is out it is usually worth changing the oil filter too. This is a metal gauze plate in a slim steel cartridge in the sump.

1. Start by undoing the sump bolts and lowering the sump. The valve block will continue to drip oil all the time you are working on this so make sure you have a broad oil-catch tank and wear arm-length gloves.
2. Clean the residue out of the sump. Note that there is a magnet on the sump, which should collect fine particles and should be cleaned off and refitted. If there are chunks of metal on the magnet then one of the clutches is breaking up and the gearbox should be stripped down and fixed.
3. Unbolt the old filter and discard.
4. Bolt in the new filter with a new O-ring.
5. Refit the sump with a new gasket. The old one will have hardened and getting it to reseal will be almost impossible.
6. Refill with ATF. Note: a fair amount of oil is held in the torque converter and valve block, so you only get a reliable reading on the dipstick when the engine is running, you also have to run the gear selector through all positions to let the oil fill all the passages in the valve block.

You can see the selector lever on top of the transfer box. As it has a flat ledge, mud and grit accumulate here and can jam the mechanism.

The transfer box oil level plug is obscured by the handbrake cable, which makes it a bit awkward to access.

So the procedure is fill it until the oil is at the high level on the dipstick, start the engine and move the selector through all positions. Then with the engine idling recheck the oil level and fill as required. Add a little at a time to avoid overfilling.

TRANSFER BOX

The transfer box lever can seize up and often it can be brought back to life with a bit of wiggling, but stubborn items may need to be lubricated from underneath the car, or in severe cases the linkage must be stripped down and rebuilt.

It is vital to check the transfer-box oil every year or so, more often than the gearbox as the transfer box has a greater tendency to leak. Do this by undoing the oil level plug at the back of the box next to the handbrake drum. Ideally a little oil should just dribble out. If nothing comes out then add oil using a small oil bottle with a long spout; I use an old ½-litre ATF bottle filled with EP80 or 90. Put the spout in the level hole and slowly add oil until it just starts to dribble out, and then put the plug back in.

AXLES

Axle oil Just like the transfer box, the axles tend to leak, but they are also more likely to be submerged in flood water and so are even more prone to contamination. Checking the oil level is similar to the transfer box: undo the level plug and the oil should be up to the edge of the hole. If it is not then fill using a small oil bottle with a long spout.

If a lot of fluid comes out, or if the fluid is grey and contaminated, then it needs changing. To do this simply undo the drain plug underneath, drain the oil, clean off the drain plug and refit it. Then fill with fluid as above. Finally investigate how it became contaminated – is the gasket or seal leaking?

Front swivel housing oil The front swivels on Discovery 1 cars originally had EP80/90 gear oil in. Because the swivel seal was not the greatest, water could get in when wading

By contrast, the axle oil-level plug is quite accessible. The plug is near the middle of the differential pan and is a little delicate on later models, so use the right socket to remove it. The drain plug is near the bottom of the axle.

The oil in early Discovery 1 swivels tended to leak past the swivel seal at the slightest opportunity, so it was replaced by thicker 'One Shot' grease.

The steering box adjuster is on the top and comprises a hex-drive bolt and a lock nut. It must be adjusted with the steering central. Tighten it until there is no slack then loosen it a little, otherwise the box will wear more quickly.

and contaminate the oil, and so on the service schedule it says replace the oil every so often and there is a drain plug at the bottom of the housing.

This was not the greatest idea so eventually Land Rover changed to using a special grease in the housing instead of oil. This was known as 'One Shot' grease because it came in a single application packet and should last the lifetime of the car. The part number is FTC3435. Later Discovery 1 models had the drain plug deleted altogether.

If you're not sure whether your Discovery has had One Shot, here is what you do: undo the lower drain plug (if the swivel doesn't have one then it has the grease); if oil comes out then let it drain and fit a tube of One Shot. If you remove the plug and nothing comes out then put a clean rod up into the housing; if it comes out clean or oily then it had oil and this has all leaked out, so fill with One Shot; if the rod comes out greasy then it already has grease so just refit the plug.

Propshafts Grease the propshafts. In fact, do it right now! These are very often forgotten about and end up running dry, which leads to very rapid wear and potential failure. If a universal joint (UJ) fails then the prop shaft can come free at one end and cause the car to be pushed off the road or break into the body.

Often, worn joints result in a rumble, vibration or droning noise that is particularly bad at one road speed, often between 50 and 70mph, depending on the length of the

defective shaft. If it is making a noise then the UJ bearings need replacing.

There is a grease point in each UJ and also in each shaft for the sliding joint, so each propshaft has three greasing points. Make sure they are all done.

Steering box adjustment The steering box wears with age and this leads to a vagueness in the steering and wandering at speed. Luckily the box has a good range of adjustment, which should keep the steering reasonably sharp.

Jack up the front axle and support on two stands so the wheels are not on the ground and the axle is level. Set the wheels to the straight-ahead position. Remove the drag link from the steering box drop link. Wiggle the drop link; there should be no play in it. If there is then loosen the lock nut on the adjuster at the top of the box and gradually tighten the adjuster with a hex (Allen) bit until the play is just about removed. Do not over tighten it or it will wear the gears inside the box and make the steering tight. Once done, tighten the lock nut and recheck. Sometimes tightening the nut can knock it out of adjustment again, so hold the hex bit steady while doing this. Then refit the drag link and the job is done.

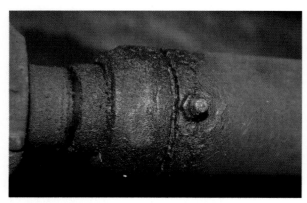

To allow for axle movement the propshafts are telescopic, and for that to work properly it needs grease in good condition.

The drop link here is covered in oil from a leaking steering-box seal, so check for play and make sure the big nuts on the output shaft are tight and locked. This early car also has a grease nipple on the ball joint.

Because the toe adjusters get pounded by road grime, the screw threads tend to corrode tight. Before adjusting, clean off the rust and allow to soak in penetrating oil. This Discovery 2 item took considerable work to free off.

Always use the two-spanner method, and never twist the rod against the ball joint. Turn the steering out to make access easier.

If you try to do it by just wiggling the steering wheel then you have to factor in the play in the hydraulic control valve too, and this can give misleading results.

Steering toe angle adjustment Normally this should not need adjustment unless the track rod ends or swivel bearings have been changed, but if you suddenly find you have too much toe-out then check that the link rod behind the axle is not bent.

The lock nuts will probably be corroded on, so before starting adjustment clean off corrosion from the exposed threads with a wire brush and soak them in penetrating oil thoroughly.

Always use two spanners to loosen the lock nuts, never twist the rod against the rod end or the ball socket will be damaged.

See the Non-standard Techniques chapter for a simple way of checking toe angle using string.

These Discovery 1 front radius arm bushes have become rounded at the edges and no longer press firmly against the mounting plate, resulting in some slack in the suspension and a vagueness to the steering.

SUSPENSION

Check the condition of the bushes in all the links and the dampers. Any play or looseness will make the handling feel vague and less predictable. Bushes should be replaced if there is any sign of cracking.

Check the dampers for oil leaks. If a leak is apparent then replace both dampers on that axle. Wash mud and dirt off the damper shaft if possible. Check the springs for cracks, often found at the lower coil. Treat any flaking paint to prevent corrosion weakening the spring.

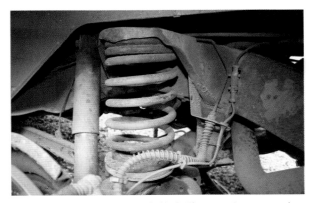

Check the dampers for any signs of oil leaks. They are quite easy to replace and not hugely. Worn dampers allow the wheel to hop and reduce braking and cornering safety.

Discovery 2 air suspension system The pump and valves are in a box on the side of the chassis. It is worth taking the lid off and ensuring there is no build-up of mud and dirt under there. I periodically put a small squirt of WD40 on the connectors to help keep corrosion at bay.

The air feed into the pump comes from an air filter located behind the rear left lamp cluster, and this may need replacing more frequently if working in dusty environments.

Keeping the air springs clean, particularly on the part that rolls over the lower location cone, will extend their life. Raising the car to full off-road height gives better access, and gently washing with a hose should get all the lumps off. Do not use a pressure washer as it can force water into the rubber and damage it.

The Discovery 2 air suspension valve block is in the firing line for road grime and water. Keep the block area clean so rot is unable to set in.

The air suspension bag rolls over a central cone and any grit here will grind away at the rubber, so keeping grit away from the bag extends its life.

If, when braking, the car twitches, pulls to one side or vibrates, then the brakes need checking. Replace brakes as complete axle sets; never just do one side.

TYRES

Check the condition of your tyres regularly. Small cuts that do not go through to the cords should pose no problem, but if the cords are exposed or damaged then a replacement tyre is needed.

Tyre technology has moved on in recent years, which makes some of the tyre pressure recommendations in the official books obsolete. Tyre pressure has a profound effect on handling, grip and safety, both on- and off-road, so check tyre pressures regularly and adjust them to suit the job the car is being used for. Just like any other tool, they have to be set up correctly, and just as the settings on a MIG welder are set up to suit the job being tackled, tyre pressures should be adjusted to get the best from them. Generally road work needs a higher pressure than off-road work. Some tyres work very well at pressures above 40psi, but others have a maximum of only 30psi, while some off-road situations may need as little as 15psi. The safest course of action is to consult the tyre manufacturer, explain what you are doing and they will be able to make sound suggestions that could transform the car's handling.

Generally the front tyres on a Discovery work best at a lower pressure than the rears.

BRAKES

Brake fluid The brake fluid must be replaced every couple of years for best performance, as once it gets old it becomes more prone to fade when the brakes are used heavily.

The principle is fairly simple: put new fluid in the master reservoir and pump it through the system using the brake pedal.

ABOVE: It is shocking how often tyres are neglected and taken for granted. If you fit just two new tyres, put them on the rear axle as this affects stability more than the front.

RIGHT: See how all the extra load from passengers or luggage goes on the back axle; even the driver sits half way between front and rear axles.

In service the fluid should need very little topping up, just allowing for minor piston movement as the pads wear. If you are constantly adding fluid then stop and repair the leak.

1. Start at the wheel closest to the brake master reservoir, the front driver's side, jack up and remove the wheel.
2. Clean up the area around the brake nipple, put a good-quality ring spanner on the nipple and fit a well fitting hose to the nipple. Ideally this would be a tube with a one-way valve at the bottom that you get in simple brake-bleeding kits.
3. The best method uses two people, one works the pedal whilst the other works the spanner on the brake nipple. The way I do it is that the one on the nipple calls 'down', the one on the brake presses the pedal firmly down and calls 'down' to confirm, then the one on the nipple opens the nipple to let fluid out and closes it again as the flow reduces. This minimizes the chance of air getting back in at the calliper end. Once that is done the person at the calliper calls 'up' and the one at the brake releases the brake pedal and calls 'up' to confirm. By one person calling and the other confirming you avoid accidentally opening the brake nipple when the brake is released and letting in air.

   Start the process by pumping the brake pedal a few times to compress any trapped gas that may already be in the system, then use a series of strokes to push fluid through until clean fresh fluid comes out of the calliper nipple. Keep the fluid level topped up at the reservoir, checking it every five strokes of the pedal.
4. Move to the front passenger side and repeat the process.
5. Move to the back driver's side and repeat.
6. Finally do the rear passenger side.
7. Check the brakes are not spongy. If they are then start again.

Always renew pads and discs as a complete axle set, otherwise your brakes will pull the car to one side.

For standard brakes one brake disc will last as long as two sets of pads. If in any doubt as to the condition of either part then replace both discs and pads at the same time. They are not very expensive and they are vital for safety.

BLEEDING THE ABS SYSTEM

If you follow the bleeding procedure and never let the level in the reservoir get low then no air will be drawn into the ABS valve block and no further action will be needed. But if air does get into the ABS unit, with its complex labyrinth of passages, it can be very difficult to remove airlocks. The only way is to operate the solenoids in the valve block while applying brake pressure. There is a special service procedure in the dealer diagnostic equipment to do this, but increasingly modern DIY diagnostic systems also have this procedure.

The complex paths in the ABS unit make bleeding all the air out tricky, so be very careful to not let air in. Make sure the reservoir does not run dry when bleeding.

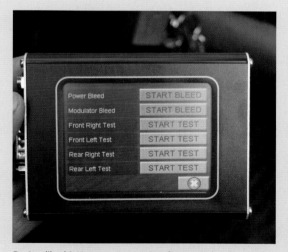

Devices like this Nanocom are getting cheaper and make complex tasks like bleeding the ABS valve block really easy.

Sometimes the air can be driven through the system by forcing an ABS stop on loose ground, if you are lucky enough to have access to a safe private gravel track or a nice flat field! Repeated ABS stops can then be followed by repeating the basic bleeding procedure to let the air out of the bleed nipples.

See the tiny gap at the joint between the pad material and the steel back plate? That is a perished pad about to fail in a very dangerous way.

Brake pads On Discovery 1 cars:

1. The pads are replaced by removing the two pad retaining pins from the back of the callipers, which are held in with small split pins. Always fit new split pins, the old ones will be weakened after being bent and unbent.
2. While the pads are out check the calliper piston seal for damage and the piston for corrosion. Any spots of rust will cut into the seals when you push the pistons back in and so must be addressed. New pistons are reasonably priced, but if there is just a small pinpoint of corrosion it might be enough to clean that up with a bit of 1200-grade grit paper. Personally I would rather just fit new ones. Also clean the compacted road debris and pad dust from the calliper so that it will not bind on the new pads.
3. Put the pads into the calliper, making sure they can move without binding on the caliper body.
4. Refit the retaining pins and fit new split pins.

> *Compress the calliper pistons (twin pistons on the front calipers, single on the rears) by using a large G-clamp and using an old brake pad to spread the force and keep the pistons in nice and square. Do this gradually and keep checking the fluid level in the reservoir. If it gets too high then draw some off using a big clean syringe, such as the sort gardeners use for dosing plant food.*

Early callipers had no protection for the pistons as they come out, resulting in corrosion. If this is present when the pistons are pushed back in, when fitting new pads, then it will cut up the piston seals and start leaking or binding. The pistons should be cleaned up or replaced.

Driving the brake calliper pistons back in should be done carefully, ensuring the piston is pushed squarely so that it does not tilt and bind. These plastic DIY clamps are ideal.

Discovery 2 callipers with sliding yoke systems:

1. Undo the lower guide-pin bolt and hinge the calliper upwards on the upper pin.
2. The pads can then be retrieved from the calliper carrier.
3. Clean up the calliper and remove any compacted pad dust and road dirt.
4. Rotate the disc and scrape any loose scale and dirt off it, and remove any grease or oil with brake cleaner.
5. Compress the piston carefully and squarely so that it does not jam.
6. Fit the new pads to the carrier.
7. Hinge the calliper back into position.
8. Re-tighten the guide-pin bolt.

Discovery 1 brake discs Here the brake discs are bolted to the inner edge of the hub drive flange, and so to change the discs you have to remove the wheel hub.

1. Jack up and remove the wheel.
2. Remove the calliper and tie it up to prevent strain on the brake hose.
3. Clean all the dirt away from the front and back of the hub.
4. Prize off the hub centre cap.
5. Tap the lock tab back.

The Discovery 1 calliper comes off relatively easy. The disc is another matter as it is bolted to the back of the hub, which has to come off first.

The rear face of the hub must be clean and the mating surface to the brake disc must be absolutely flat and dirt free. A fraction of a millimetre out here and in a few thousand miles the brakes will have warped.

6. Undo the outer hub nut, remove the lock washer and remove the inner hub nut.
7. Pull the hub slightly out and then push it in to release the outer hub bearing, recover the bearing, making sure it stays clean.
8. Pull the hub from the car.
9. Ideally hold the hub in a large vice, or put it on a sturdy work bench with a large bar bracing the wheel studs (ensuring the stud thread is not damaged), and turn it so the disc is facing upwards.

During this part of the procedure take precautions to ensure no dirt gets into the hub bearing and inner seal. I find a large coffee jar lid covered the seal quite nicely.

10. Undo the bolts holding the disc to the hub.
11. Tap the disc to help release it from the hub and remove it.

The mating face of the brake disc must be completely flat and clean – if there is any dirt there then the disc will gradually warp and about 2,000 miles later you will have vibrating brakes.

I use the edge of a chisel to scrape all the scale and debris off first, then finish it with a new Stanley knife blade.

Cleaning the mating surface is the most important part of a disc change. Here I'm scraping the surface of my Discovery 2 hub with the side of a chisel to get it flat.

12. Clean the hub face completely so there is absolutely no dirt, corrosion, old grease or debris on the disc mounting surface. This is vitally important.
13. Clean the new disc with brake cleaner.
14. Push the disc onto the hub, ensuring no debris gets trapped on the mating surface as the centre hole goes over the hub.
15. Apply thread-lock to the disc bolts and tighten them to the correct torque.
16. Refit the hub and reset the hub nuts (*see* section on hub bearing replacement).
17. Refit the calliper, put thread-lock on the two calliper bolts and tighten them to the correct torque.

Discovery 2 brake discs By comparison Discovery 2 discs are much easier to fit as they simply bolt onto the front of the hub.

1. Jack up and remove the wheel.
2. Remove the calliper (two bolts holding the carrier to the hub) and tie it up to prevent strain on the brake hose.
3. Undo the screw that retains the brake disc. This can be corroded and if somebody has been there before then it might be damaged. If so you will need to fit a new one. The tool needs to be a good fit into the screw head. Most are hex (Allen) drives, so make sure all debris is removed from the screw head first. If the screw is difficult to remove then use an impact driver, do not use a long lever as you will most likely round off the screw head.
4. Remove the disc.
5. Clean up the mating face thoroughly. This is very important as there must be no dirt, corrosion, old grease or debris on the disc mounting surface.
6. Degrease the brake disc with brake cleaner and orient the disc so that the locating screw holes line up.
7. Fit the disc.
8. Put a drop of thread-lock on the retaining screw and tighten it to the correct torque.
9. Refit the calliper, put thread-lock on the two calliper bolts and tighten them to the correct torque.

Brake discs come coated with a film of protective oil, which must be removed. Automotive brake cleaner is a suitable solvent that evaporates and leaves no residue, and so is ideal.

When new discs and pads have been fitted they will need to be bedded in to get best performance. Press the brake pedal several times with the engine running before moving off to push the pistons out to grip the disc properly. When driving the vehicle for the first time after fitting new brakes, drive with extreme caution as braking performance may be unpredictable the first few times.

Check the brake parts' manufacturer's instructions. Most say start the test drive at low speed and check brake operation, build speed gradually and use increasingly hard braking to bed the pads in. This must only be done where safe to do so, and never with traffic behind you.

All Discoverys have a bolt-in window frame that has to be correctly adjusted to press firmly enough against the door seal to prevent wind noise, but not so hard that you are unable to close the door.

CHASSIS

Areas, such as the cross member where the rear A-frame mounts on Discovery 1 cars, tend to trap moisture and mud. So when cleaning off after off-roading ensure that all the debris is blown clear from these areas with an air line or similar, including the top of the main chassis rails where the small gap between chassis and body can trap clods of dirt.

Areas on the chassis that have the most stress tend to rust first, so inspect the body mounts, rear cross member and spring seats, which often start rusting along the welds.

The chassis can be protected with chassis sealant, but the metal underneath must be free of rust and dirt before applying, otherwise the rot will be trapped under the sealant and corrode through. Often on off-road courses parts of the chassis will be scratched and the underseal damaged, so as part of the servicing regime regularly apply a little light oil to the welds and scratches, then every year redo the underseal where needed. If the car is going to be used off-road then chassis maintenance has to be considered a regular task.

BODYWORK AND TRIM

Window lift Window lift mechanisms are prone to failure if not serviced every few years. This may occur for a number of reasons. On Discovery 1 cars as the mechanisms wear and become a little looser, the plastic guide blocks inside the sliders in the door can be pushed just slightly too far and fall out of the guide rails. Remove the door card and pop the blocks back into place, and then adjust the mechanism to prevent it happening again.

Another cause is the steel channel that holds the bottom edge of the glass in the mechanism, which can rot out completely (glass drops down) or lets go (glass stays up when the mechanism goes down). To prevent this make sure any rust is treated before it takes hold. A little spray grease (the sort that is not harmful to rubber) can be sprayed into the area in case there is rot starting where you can't see it.

Keep the mechanism lubricated with a small amount of grease, but remove lumps of old hard grease first.

Plenty of hiding places for rust about the various crossmembers. This is a Discovery 2.

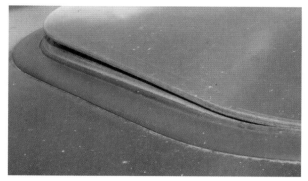

An important summer job is cleaning and lubricating the sunroof seals.
If they go hard then water leaks into the roof space above the headlining
and pours onto the occupants when the car moves.

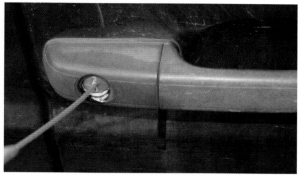

Side door locks also need lubricating. Most cars have remote central
locking and the door lock rarely gets used unless in an emergency, by
which time it has often seized solid.

Spray grease is good for the latch mechanism.

Keep the rear door latch working with spray oil on the back of the handle.

Sunroof The rubber seals on sunroofs age faster than
other rubber parts due to greater direct sunlight. As they
harden or crack they start leaking into the headlining, so
to keep them supple wipe them with silicone grease once
a year.

Door locks Door locks must be lubricated and operated
regularly, at least once a year. As the cars have remote locking, the key lock in the door may not get used for years,
which often results in it seizing. I put a small squirt of WD40
or similar directly into the key hole and then put the key in
and turn it to get everything moving.

Rear door lock The rear door handle on Discoverys can
corrode and seize. To prevent this, keep it lubricated with
spray oil such as WD40, removing the badge to get good
access.

Rear door hinges The rear door hinges have a hard life.
With the spare wheel on, the back door is a heavy lump and
only supported at one side. I give the hinges a coating of
light oil or WD40 and lift the door up as I open and close it
a few times to allow the oil to get right into the hinge. Clean
the excess oil off with a cloth.

The rear door retaining rod is also often forgotten. Without lubrication the
pivot at the boot floor will corrode and could pull out completely.

Back door hinges take a lot of force and should not be ignored. Spray
some oil on and move the door to work it into the hinge.

The retaining rod detent mechanism should also get some lubrication to
prevent it becoming stiff and wearing rapidly.

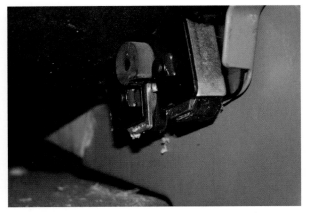

Light oil is best for seat latches, as you do not want big blobs of grease marking the interior. Make sure any fluff or rubbish is removed from the latch before lubricating.

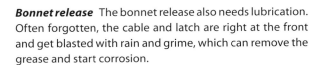

Wipers grind dirt against the windscreen, creating micro scratches. These make it more difficult for the wipers to clear water off and also increase the effect of glare when driving toward lights or the sun. They can be polished out, but it is hard work.

Seat latches The second- and third-row seats have latches to hold them in the seated position, and become stiff unless lubricated at least once a year. A quick squirt of light oil such as WD40 followed by operating the mechanism a few times should keep things moving properly.

Wipers and screen Windscreen wipers have a hard life. Scraping the blade across a screen covered in mud or grime wears the edge very quickly, so always use the washer jets on the first wipe. In the winter if the blades have frozen to the screen wait until the heater has defrosted them before using them and never pull them off a frozen screen or the blade edge will be damaged.

Mud contains fine grit particles and using the wipers to clear a muddy screen not only damages the wipers but rubs this grit across the window, and just like sandpaper it scratches the glass. So again use the washer jets extensively or, if there is a lot of mud, stop and remove it manually before continuing.

Eventually the screen will become scratched, which makes it harder for the wipers to remove rain water and can cause blurring of lights at night. These micro scratches can be removed by polishing with domestic glass polish and lots of hard rubbing.

To stop the wipers and jets freezing on very cold journeys increase the screen wash concentration significantly. I use neat concentrate in the worst part of winter.

Bonnet release The bonnet release also needs lubrication. Often forgotten, the cable and latch are right at the front and get blasted with rain and grime, which can remove the grease and start corrosion.

ELECTRICAL

Changing the battery Before changing the battery make sure the car is unlocked and not immobilized. Also note the radio code if applicable.

1. Always disconnect the negative terminal first. This is for safety, because if your spanner accidentally hits the body and you are working on the earth terminal, nothing happens, but if you start with the positive lead and touch the body then it will short out and potentially damage the battery, the spanner and your hand, as it glows red hot!
2. Then undo the positive terminal.
3. Undo the battery clamp. Quite often the threads are corroded, so if the clamp bolt or nut does not undo easily then bathe it in penetrating oil for a while first. If the clamp is broken then fix it or get a new one. Do not drive with the battery loose as it could jump up when you go over a pothole and either stress the terminals or possibly short on the bonnet. Additionally, if the car is in a crash, an untethered battery turns into a missile.

The bonnet latch should be regularly lubricated to prevent corrosion. If this end gets stiff then the bonnet release cable will stretch and eventually snap.

Always undo the negative terminal first. There are so many things the spanner could touch that are earthed, and if you undo the positive terminal first, you could seriously injure yourself.

The new battery should meet the requirement for Cold Cranking Amps (CCA) and capacity in Amp Hours (Ah) – both of these figures are important. The CCA dictates how fast it can turn the engine over, and the Ah dictates how long it can keep that up for. All engines need to turn over at a given speed for a given time to fire up cleanly.

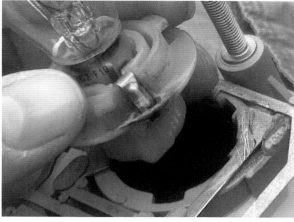

This rear light failed an MOT, but the bulb was fine. It turns out the holder had burned out because the connection on the bulb holder was slack.

Periodically operate all infrequently used switches to keep switch and relay contacts clean.

4. When lifting the battery out be careful – it's heavy.
5. With the battery out, remove the battery tray and check the bodywork underneath. This is a prime spot for corrosion, so deal with any rot or peeling paint before putting the battery in.
6. Clean the terminal clamps on the leads; any corrosion or dirt in there will reduce starting capability.
7. Make sure the new battery fits the space. Some modern batteries are physically smaller for the same electrical performance, which is fine as long as they can still be fitted securely.
8. Clean the battery terminals to remove any oil, grease or dirt.
9. Refit the battery tray.
10. Fit the battery.
11. Refit the clamp.
12. Refit the terminal leads, fitting the positive first for safety. Have the key fob ready just in case the alarm goes off when you connect the earth lead.
13. Finally, smear a little petroleum jelly on the terminals to stop corrosion setting in.

Bulbs Bulbs degrade as molecules from the filament gradually migrate off and become deposited on the glass, turning the bulb grey or silver. Eventually the filament will be degraded enough that it will burn out.

Check the bulbs and replace any that are starting to go silver or grey to minimize the chance of one failing when you are driving.

Periodically remove the bulbs and check that the holders are clean. Tarnishing or corrosion here will reduce performance and cause hot spots, which can cause them to fail.

Bulb glass should be completely clear. Grey or silver deposits will have come from the filament wearing out. Halogen bulbs have to be completely clean. Any grease from a finger print can cause the glass to become porous when hot and burn the filament out.

Headlight bulbs can be replaced with higher efficiency modern alternatives. Other bulbs can be replaced with LED upgrades, but avoid cheap units as they are likely to fail. Good-quality LED bulbs will outlast the car.

Switches On all models the hazard-light switch can stop working because it never gets used and the contacts tarnish. So before the car's annual test just operate the switch several times until it starts to work properly. The same goes for all rarely used switches – use them or lose them.

Connectors There are a lot of electrical connectors in the engine bay, which are prone to corrosion, so check them. If they are in good condition coat them in spray grease to protect them long-term. If they are already corroded clean up the terminals or fit new connectors to avoid systems failing when the car is miles from help.

Programming new keys to the immobilizer alarm system
Discovery 1:

1. Start with the ignition off, all doors unlocked and the bonnet closed. Then, within 8 seconds, complete steps 2–5.
2. Turn the ignition on then off again.
3. Lock and then unlock the doors.
4. Release the bonnet.
5. Turn the ignition on and off again.

There is a myriad of electrical connectors in the engine bay and under the car that are exposed to fumes and weather, which attack the connector. A light coating of spray grease helps protect them.

If that worked then the horn will beep and the LED will light. Now you have only two minutes to program up to two key fobs. Press and hold the fob button until the dash LED flashes, and then repeat this for the second fob if you have one. The dash LED will go out when two fobs have been successfully programmed.

Discovery 2:

To program a new key you need to use a suitable diagnostic tool, or take the car to a dealer. If you have a suitable system, such as Nanocom or Rovacom, then start with the vehicle unlocked and the immobilizer off. Plug in the diagnostic tool and follow the on-screen instructions. You will have to manually enter the key-fob code number, which should be on a label on the circuit board inside the new key fob. If

you buy a second-hand fob and it does not have a written key code then it is useless and should be sent back. The fob is made by Valeo and is the same unit used on the Rover 75 and many other cars, so there is a wide variety of sources for a good second-hand unit.

Discovery 2 dash illumination light One odd thing is that the procedure to replace the dashboard back lights is not covered in the official Land Rover workshop manual or the handbook, so when mine blew I had to find out for myself.

1. Remove the steering-column shroud, noting the orientation of the ignition switch surround so you get it lined up when it comes to reassembly.

307582
24/07/02

Keys are frequently lost and so getting a spare is often desirable. Programming the Discovery 2 item requires the key code written on the label to be manually programmed into the BCM with a suitable diagnostic tool.

The dash illumination bulbs are on the back of the instrument cluster, and quite a lot of trim has to removed to get access to them. If you have to replace one bulb it is worth renewing them all at the same time.

2. Remove the dash surround by undoing the two screws at the bottom using a stubby screwdriver.
3. The upper cowl is retained by two spring clips at the back of the top. To release them pull the cowl firmly towards you.
4. Now the four screws can be undone that hold the cluster in and it can then be leaned outward to allow access to the three twist-lock bulb holders.
5. There are three back-light bulbs in small twist-lock holders in the back of the dash circuit board. The bulbs are normal clear press-fit dash bulbs, they have a green translucent sleeve that is simply peeled and rolled off and fitted to the new bulb.

When reassembling remember to get the ignition barrel surround the right way round.

Discovery 1 300 style and Discovery 2 clock illumination bulb This is another one strangely missing from some manuals. It is a little awkward to get the clock out:

1. First prise off the switch cover next to it (lock switch on Discovery 2, hazards and a Land Rover logo on Discovery 1).
2. Slide a slim rule, or similar thin-gauge but wide blade, into the gap between the clock housing and the dash frame. There are two plastic lugs that hold the unit in.
3. Slide the unit out – there is no need to disconnect the wiring so the clock will not have to be reset.
4. The bulb holder is a normal twist-lock unit in the middle.
5. When the new bulb is in, test that it works before refitting.
6. Refitting is simply by sliding the unit back in until it clicks into place.

The dash illumination bulbs are conventional clear items but have a green rubbery sleeve on. I found it easiest to roll it off and on to the new bulb.

There is a pair of tabs on the underside of the clock module and a thin blade is needed to open it up.

Big jobs are often no more difficult than the small jobs, but they take longer and may need special tools.

servicing – big jobs

These jobs will require better tools and facilities than the ones in the previous chapter. If you do not have the skills or confidence then you might be better off getting these done at a specialist garage. Alternatively it might help to get a few friends over to help out. As you will be taking chunks of the car apart it can be really useful to have someone about who can help lift heavy parts, pass you tools or run errands to the local motor factors to buy the bits you forgot.

Most of this chapter is written based on personal experience, but some of it is based on the experience of friends who also own Discoverys. There were a great many variations in design through the Discovery's production life and it is essential that you check to see if your car is different to that described here.

This chapter is not an alternative to the official workshop manual, just a bit extra. Make sure you are familiar with the official procedure before starting a big job.

As well as making sure you have all the parts needed before starting the job, also have a few spare parts in case fixtures and fittings fail. A selection of nuts and bolts, O-rings and hose clips is a very good thing to have available.

You may see in most workshop manuals that almost every job starts with 'first disconnect the battery'. This is good advice as there are several places on the car where a slip of the spanner could result in a short circuit, particularly near the starter motor and alternator.

Always disconnect the negative terminal first and reconnect it last.

ENGINE

Cam belt and front oil seals change, 200Tdi

1. Disconnect the battery.
2. Drain the coolant.
3. If it has air conditioning then remove the drive belt, undo the wiring plug, undo the bolts holding the pump to the engine and push it to one side, taking care not to strain the hoses.
4. Remove the top hose from the radiator.

Genuine timing pegs versus some alternative versions. Timing tools must be a snug fit so that the pulley cannot move by more than a fraction of a degree.

5. Remove the intercooler to induction manifold duct.
6. Remove the viscous fan and coupling.
7. Remove the fan cowl.
8. Remove the drive belts.
9. Undo the four bolts that hold the crank pulley to the crank damper.
10. Lock the crank by either putting the car in gear if it has a manual gearbox, or by using the crank locking pin (explained a bit later) if automatic.
11. Remove the crankshaft pulley retaining bolt using a socket and a very long bar. It was done up to 340Nm (250lb ft).
12. Recover the big washer.
13. Remove the pulley, if necessary using an extractor
14. Disconnect the hoses from the coolant pump.
15. Hold the coolant-pump pulley steady by wrapping an old belt round it and undo the three bolts holding it on.
16. Remove the coolant-pump pulley and then extract the coolant-pump bolts.
17. Remove the coolant pump and gasket.
18. Remove the intake air duct from the air filter to the turbo.
19. Remove the alternator.
20. Take the bolts out of the power steering pump and move it to one side, taking care not to strain the hoses.
21. Now you can unbolt and remove the bracket that holds the power steering and alternator on.
22. Remove the nine bolts securing the front cover plate, noting which ones go where as they are different lengths. The top two bolts also retain the thermostat hose clips.
23. Remove the cover plate complete with gasket.

> **When removing lots of bolts from the front cover, get a bit of cardboard, draw the outline of the plate on it and make holes in so you can push the bolts into it to store them in the right order. Then you know which one goes where.**

24. Remove the small gasket from the centre bolt boss.
25. Remove the worn seal from the cover and clean the recess.
26. Put a socket on the crank-pulley bolt and with a long lever turn the engine to top dead centre (TDC) on No. 1 cylinder.
27. Next you need to put a locking pin in the flywheel. There is of course a Land Rover special tool for this, but as an alternative I use the smooth part of a drill bit that is just the right size to fit snugly.

There are some variations on the theme here:

The manual gearbox versions have a blanking plug in the flywheel housing, which must be removed for access; the electronic diesel control (EDC) version has a different size hole to the non-EDC version.

The automatic gearbox versions have a blanking plate on the engine backplate at the back of the engine sump. Remove the two blanking plate bolts and insert the drill bit shank, or special tool, into the larger bolt hole, making sure it is fully engaged with the slot in the flywheel.

28. At the front of the engine check that the timing marks on the cam gear are correctly aligned, and that the crankshaft key aligns with the cast arrow on the housing.
29. If all is well then insert another drill bit/tool through the timing hole in the injection pump gear and into the recess in the pump flange.
30. At this stage if you are also going to change the cam oil seal then the cam gear retaining bolt should be slackened before the timing belt is removed.
31. Slacken the belt tensioner bolt and the belt will become loose. You do not need to remove it, just loosen it.
32. Remove the idler pulley completely.
33. Now you can remove the timing belt.

The bell housing drain hole provides access to the timing slot in the flywheel. The timing tool screws into the plug thread and should only be hand tight.

In use a cam belt develops a wear pattern that depends on which way it was running, so if the original belt is going to be reused then it must be fitted so that it goes in the original direction. Mark it using soft chalk.

Belts can be sensitive things and must be stored on their edge on a clean surface, avoiding oil and water. They do not like tight bends either, so do not bend belts at a radius of less than 50mm.

200Tdi idlers worked so well that they were adopted as an upgrade for 300Tdi engines. The bearings can be pressed out and replaced, but this usually costs more than just buying a new set of idlers.

At this stage it is probably a good idea to change the crankshaft front oil seal.

1. The crank cam belt gear should come off by hand. If it doesn't then use a puller, but be careful not to damage the crank pulley bolt-hole threads. The crank gear should come away with its O-ring.
2. Then prise out the oil seal from the front cover.
3. Use new engine oil to lubricate the new crankshaft oil seal and push it in with the lip side towards the engine.
4. The crank O-ring needs lubricating with petroleum jelly, and then slide it onto the shaft. Be careful not to damage the seal on the woodruff keys.
5. Now the crank gear can be refitted and gently tapped fully home.

It is also probably a good idea to do the cam front oil seal too:

1. Start by removing the bolt from the cam gear and then you can remove the gear.
2. Extract the old oil seal from the front cover using a small hook.
3. Use a few drops of clean engine oil to lubricate the new camshaft oil seal.
4. Now, with the lip side facing the engine, push in the seal squarely.
5. Then refit the gear.

Timing belt fitting and tensioning The cam belt has to be tensioned carefully. It has a hard life and if you get it wrong here then it just will not last. The official procedure involves tensioning the belt twice so that it is equally tensioned between each gear. Interestingly, new and original belts are tensioned to different figures.

1. First check that all the timing marks are still correctly aligned, and that the drill bits/tools are still properly seated in the injection-pump gear, cam gear and the flywheel.
2. Offer the belt up, keeping it tight on the drive side.
3. Fit the idler pulley and torque up the bolt.
4. Slacken the injection pump gear bolts to allow the gear to move slightly.
5. Adjust the belt so that it sits neatly in the gears.

6. Make sure the belt tensioner securing bolt is finger tight and use a ½in square drive extension bar in the tensioner plate to pull the tensioner up against the belt.
7. Now, the official procedure says that belt tensioning should only be carried out using a dial-type torque meter having a range not exceeding 60Nm (44lb ft). Certainly a click-type torque wrench will not work too well against a springy rubber belt. The tension required is 14–16Nm (10–12lb ft) for a new belt or 11–13Nm (8–10lb ft) for an original belt. Interestingly this torque is equivalent to a mass of about 3kg (or 2.4kg for old belts) hanging off the socket breaker bar at a distance of half a metre from the bolt centre. I am not saying that is an alternative method, but it may be of interest if you have to do an emergency belt change in the middle of a desert expedition.
8. When tension is correct tighten the tensioner clamp bolt.
9. Then tighten the injection-pump gear bolts and remove the drill/tool from the injection pump gear.
10. Remove the drill/tool from the timing slot in the flywheel or ring gear, but do not put the cover back on just yet.
11. Rotate the crankshaft one-and-three-quarter turns clockwise; then continue rotation until you can get the drill/tool back in the flywheel or ring gear.
12. Refit the drill/tool in the injection-pump gear and through into the pump flange.
13. Slacken the injection-pump gear bolts.
14. Slacken the tensioner and re-tension the belt.
15. Tighten the injection-pump gear bolts and remove the drill/tool from the injection pump gear.
16. Now remove the drill/tool from the flywheel and refit the plug or plate.
17. Fit the front cover plate using new gaskets and seals. Tighten the nine bolts to 25Nm (18lb ft).
18. Refit the bracket that held the power steering and alternator on.
19. Refit the power steering pump.
20. Refit the alternator.
21. Refit the intake air duct from the air filter to the turbo.

22. Refit the coolant pump and fit a new gasket.
23. Refit the coolant pump pulley. Hold the coolant pump pulley steady by wrapping an old belt round it and do up the three bolts holding it on.
24. Reconnect the hoses from the coolant pump.
25. Refit the crankshaft damper, lightly greasing the spigot. Tighten to 340Nm (250lb ft).
26. Now do up the four bolts that hold the crank pulley to the crank damper.
27. Fit the drive belts, fan cowl, viscous coupling and fan, intercooler to induction manifold hose and finally the top hose from the radiator.
28. Fill with coolant.

300Tdi cam belt and front oil seals change

1. Disconnect the battery.
2. Drain the coolant.
3. Remove the top hose from the radiator.
4. Remove the intercooler to induction manifold hose.
5. Remove the viscous fan and coupling.
6. Remove the fan cowl.
7. Remove the drive belt.

Use a long bar to undo the crankshaft pulley bolt. Put a sheet of cardboard in front of the radiator to protect it while working on the front of the engine.

Make a sketch of the front cover on some cardboard and poke the bolts through to make sure you get the right length bolts in the right holes.

8. Lock the crank by either putting the car in gear if it has a manual gearbox and having an assistant stand hard on the brakes, or by using the crank locking pin (explained a bit later) if automatic.
9. Remove the crankshaft pulley retaining bolt using a socket and a long bar.
10. Remove the pulley, if necessary using an extractor.
11. Remove the fourteen bolts securing the front cover plate, noting which ones go where as they are different lengths. The top two bolts also retain thermostat hose clips.
12. Remove the cover plate complete with gasket.
13. Remove the small gasket from the centre bolt boss.
14. Remove the worn seal from the cover and clean the recess.
15. Put the crank pulley bolt back in and with a socket and a long lever turn the engine to TDC on No. 1 cylinder.
16. Next you need to put a locking pin in the flywheel. There is of course a Land Rover special tool for this, but I use the smooth part of a drill bit that is just the right size to fit snugly.

There are some variations on the theme here:

The manual gearbox versions have a blanking plug in the flywheel housing, which must be removed for access. The EDC version has a different size hole to the non-EDC version.

The automatic gearbox versions have a blanking plate on the engine backplate at the back of the engine sump. Remove two blanking plate bolts and insert the drill bit shank, or special tool, into the larger bolt hole. Make sure the drill/tool is fully engaged with the slot in the flywheel.

17. At the front of the engine check that the timing marks on the cam gear align correctly, and that the crankshaft key aligns with the cast arrow on the housing.
18. If all is well then insert another drill bit/tool through the injection pump gear and into the recess in the pump flange.
19. At this stage if you are also going to change the cam oil seal then the cam gear retaining bolt should be slackened before the timing belt is removed.

This belt had walked forward and worn a groove in the front cover. It was half normal width! The plastic tensioner shoulders are not up to the job of holding it in place, which is why the system was replaced with a new crank pulley and tensioner set.

The timing peg locks the pump drive flange to a hole in the front timing casing. With this locked you can loosen the pump pulley bolts to make lining up the belt easier.

Of course, any shaft of the right diameter will do, even a drill bit.

The idler is on the tension side and so is the first part to come off after relaxing the tensioner, and it is the last part to go back on before tightening the tensioner.

20. Slacken the belt tensioner bolt and the belt will become loose. You do not need to remove it, just loosen it.
21. Remove the idler pulley completely.
22. Now you can remove the timing belt.

At this stage it is probably a good idea to change the crankshaft front oil seal.

1. The crank cam belt gear should come off by hand. If it does not then use a puller, but be careful not to damage the crank pulley bolt-hole threads. The crank gear should come away with its O-ring.
2. Then prise out the oil seal from the front cover.
3. Use new engine oil to lubricate the new crankshaft oil seal and push it in with the lip side towards the engine.

4. The crank O-ring needs lubricating with petroleum jelly, then slide it onto the shaft, being careful not to damage it on the woodruff keys.
5. Now the crank gear can be refitted and gently tapped fully home.

It is also probably a good idea to do the cam front oil seal too:

1. Start by removing the bolt from the cam gear and then you can remove the gear.
2. Extract the old oil seal from the front cover using a small hook.
3. Use a few drops of clean engine oil to lubricate the new camshaft oil seal.
4. Now, with the lip side facing the engine, push in the seal squarely.
5. Then refit the gear.

Timing belt fitting and tensioning The cam belt has to be tensioned carefully. It has a hard life and if you get it wrong here then it just will not last. The original official procedure involves tensioning the belt twice so that it is equally tensioned between each gear. Interestingly, new and original belts are tensioned to different figures. However, a new procedure was issued when the belt kits were improved to avoid premature wear problems, as explained below.

1. First check that all the timing marks are still correctly aligned and that the drill bits/tools are still properly seated in the injection-pump gear, cam gear and the flywheel.
2. Offer the belt up, keeping it tight on the drive side, which is the right-hand side as you are looking at it.
3. Fit the idler pulley and torque up the bolt. Note that the studs can fail, so it is best to replace the idler stud and nut. Also check that the stud thread hole in the block has a 2mm chamfer to avoid it pulling out a high spot

– if it does not have a chamfer then make one with a countersink tool.
4. If the belt will not go on you can slacken the injection-pump gear bolts to allow the gear to move slightly, but only if the timing peg is a good tight fit so the pump timing is unable to move.
5. Adjust the belt so that it sits neatly in the gears.
6. Make sure the belt tensioner securing bolt is finger-tight then back it off one full turn. Now use a ½in square-drive extension bar in the tensioner plate to pull the tensioner up against the belt.
7. Now, the official procedure says that belt tensioning should only be carried out using a dial-type torque meter having a range not exceeding 60Nm (44lb ft). Certainly a click-type torque wrench will not work too well against a springy rubber belt. The tension required is 14–16Nm (10–12lb ft) for a new belt or 11–13Nm (8–10lb ft) for an original belt. Interestingly this torque is equivalent to a mass of about 3kg (or 2.4kg for old

Getting the tension right is crucial, and is easiest with one person holding a steady tension and another tightening the bolt.

belts) hanging off the socket breaker bar at a distance of half a metre from the bolt centre. I am not saying that is an alternative method, but it may be of interest if you have to do an emergency belt change in the middle of a desert expedition.

8. When the tension is correct tighten the tensioner clamp bolt.
9. Then tighten the injection-pump gear bolts and remove the drill/tool from the injection pump gear.
10. Remove the drill/tool from the timing slot in the flywheel or ring gear, but do not put the cover back on just yet.
11. Rotate the crankshaft one-and-three-quarter turns clockwise; then continue rotation until you can get the drill/tool back into the flywheel or ring gear.
12. Refit the drill/tool in the injection-pump gear and through into the pump flange.
13. Slacken the injection-pump gear bolts.
14. Slacken the tensioner.
15. Re-tension the belt.
16. Then tighten the injection-pump gear bolts and remove the drill/tool from the injection pump gear.
17. Now remove the drill/tool from the flywheel and refit the plug or plate.
18. Fit the front cover plate using new gaskets and seals. Tighten the fourteen bolts to 25Nm (18lb ft).
19. Refit the crankshaft pulley, lightly greasing the pulley spigot. Tighten to 80Nm (59lb ft).
20. Fit the fan cowl, viscous coupling and fan, intercooler to induction manifold hose and finally the top hose from the radiator.
21. Fill with coolant.
22. Refit the battery.

Cleaning out the intercooler – all diesels

This should be done once a year for cars that are used regularly.

To access the intercooler on Discovery 1 cars:

1. Undo the two ducts from the top of the intercooler. It is worth taking them off completely and cleaning the oil out of them too, and replace the clips if they are less than perfect.
2. Remove the upper fan cowl.
3. Remove the radiator top cover. On 300Tdi vehicles you will need to release the power steering fluid reservoir too.
4. The intercooler should now simply pull up and out. Check that the two locating grommets from the bottom do not fall out and get lost.
5. Rinse the intercooler with a degreasing fluid and make sure it is completely dry before reassembling.

To access the intercooler on Discovery 2 cars:

1. This is a bit more involved than on earlier Discoverys. You have to take the front grille and headlight trims off, along with the air deflectors behind the grille.

A 300Tdi intercooler on a test rig. You can see how the angle of the hoses means oil tends to accumulate at the bottom of the intercooler.

2. The radiator will have to be leaned back later, so take the fan and the radiator top cowl off. It can just about be done without removing the fan if you are very careful, but it is much easier to take the fan off.
3. Take the ducts off each side and remove them from the car. Clean these out too, check for damage and replace the clips if they look weak.
4. It is also worth cleaning the gunge from the exhaust gas recirculation (EGR) valve area whilst the intake is off.
5. There are two brackets that hold the air conditioning condenser onto the assembly. Remove the brackets completely.
6. Undo the two bolts that hold the top of the intercooler to the radiator. Now you should be able to lean the radiator back enough to get good access to the intercooler.
7. Remove the intercooler, bearing in mind that it may have a substantial amount of oil in it, so be careful not to accidentally tip it on the floor or over the engine.
8. Once out, hold it over a bucket while the majority of residue runs out, then lay it down and use carburettor cleaner, or similar solvents, to clean out the sticky mess inside.
9. Thoroughly dry it out before refitting. Any cleaning agent left inside may cause the engine to misfire or rev up uncontrollably. It is best to blow it through with an air line if one is available, or let it drain overnight.

On Discovery 2 cars the intercooler sits across the front of the radiator pack and requires a bit more disassembly to get at.

10. Inspect the intercooler fins and gently straighten any bent ones, being careful not to snap them off. Touch up any corrosion with spray paint.
11. Reassemble and replace any worn or damaged clips.

V8 thermostats

I have included the thermostat in the servicing section because it seems to have a limited service life and after about ten years seems prone to sticking shut (causing overheating) or open (causing under-heating, excessive fuel consumption and oil contamination).

Discovery 1 thermostats are a simple element accessed by undoing the two bolts on the thermostat housing. When refitting you will need a new gasket. Use the later neoprene-covered variety and clean the mating surfaces up so they are flat and smooth with no corrosion.

The Discovery 2 thermostat is a more complex plastic assembly that has to be replaced complete. This is just a matter of undoing the hoses, but check the condition of the hose clips and replace as needed.

The cooling system is complex and can be poorly described in manuals, so take a picture to help when reassembling. Be careful taking the hoses off, as some of them are no longer available new.

Cam belt, Mpi

1. First remove the drive belt.
2. Now, unless you have the special tool to hold the crank pulley steady whilst undoing the crank pulley bolt, put the gearbox in a high gear and get an assistant to stand on the brake pedal whilst you loosen the crank pulley bolt. Do not undo it, just loosen it enough so that it can be easily undone later.
3. Remove the five bolts securing the timing belt top cover and remove it.
4. Remove the five bolts securing the timing belt centre cover and remove it.
5. Now rotate the crankshaft, by using a socket on the crank pulley bolt, to align the timing marks on the camshaft gears to 90 degrees BTDC.

Never use the camshaft gears, gear retaining bolts or timing belt to rotate crankshaft.

6. Use a suitable drill bit or special tool in the back of the engine block to lock the flywheel.
7. Lock the camshaft gears by fitting a special tool between the two gears. There are general-purpose tools available at most auto tool shops, or you could hire one.
8. Loosen the camshaft belt tensioner pulley bolt and move the tensioner to release the timing belt tension.
9. Temporarily re-tighten the tensioner pulley bolt to keep it out of the way.
10. Remove the four bolts securing the crankshaft pulley to the crankshaft timing gear.
11. Remove the crankshaft pulley bolt and the pulley.
12. Remove the timing belt lower cover.
13. Remove the old timing belt.
14. Clean the crankshaft pulley, timing belt gears and pulleys.
15. Fit the timing belt to the gears, starting at the crankshaft gear and working in an anti-clockwise direction.

16. Ensure the belt run between the crankshaft and exhaust camshaft gear is kept taut during the fitting procedure as this is the tension side.
17. Refit the timing belt lower cover and tighten the three bolts to the correct torque.
18. Fit the crankshaft pulley to the crankshaft timing gear. Fit the four bolts and tighten to the correct torque.
19. Fit the crank pulley bolt and tighten moderately. Do not use enough force to damage the flywheel locking pin and the hole it is sitting in.
20. Remove the cam gear locking tool.

Tension the belt and reassemble
1. Loosen the timing belt tensioner pulley bolt so the tensioner sits against the belt.
2. Apply 40Nm (30lb ft) anti-clockwise torque to the inlet cam pulley bolt and release to settle it.
3. Tighten the tensioner pulley bolt to the correct torque.
4. Remove the drill bit/tool from the flywheel.
5. Fit the timing belt centre cover and tighten the five bolts to the correct torque.
6. Fit the timing belt upper cover and tighten the five bolts to the correct torque.
7. With the car in gear, get your assistant to stand on the brakes, and tighten the crank pulley bolt up to the correct torque.
8. Finally refit the drive belt.

CLUTCH REPLACEMENTS

Do not try your luck with the clutch. Replace the disc before the friction pads wear down to the rivets, or you will be replacing the flywheel too.

The TD5 is the only variant to be fitted with a dual-mass flywheel. If the clutch disc is replaced when it is due then the dual-mass flywheel will not need replacing at the same time. If the clutch is allowed to wear until it starts to slip then it may cause the dual-mass flywheel rubber to overheat, resulting in clattering sounds and potential misfire. That is an expensive repair. Changing the clutch disc is a cheap repair so do it as per the service schedule or at the first sign of trouble, whichever is sooner. I personally would not convert the TD5 to a solid flywheel (i.e. non dual-mass) as this may result in crankshaft failures.

The first job is to remove the whole gearbox assembly:

1. Start by undoing the propshafts.
2. Release the gearstick shroud and transfer-box shroud (or release the transfer-box cable on Discovery 2 cars) and release the linkages.
3. Undo the clutch slave cylinder and support it so the hose is not strained.
4. Undo the reversing light and speedo wiring.
5. Undo the handbrake cable.
6. Support the box securely on a suitable transmission jack.
7. Undo the bell-housing bolts.
8. Move the gearbox assembly back and then down. Be careful – it is very heavy!

Now undo the clutch assembly:

1. Restrain the flywheel by fitting a suitable tool between the engine casing and the ring gear, being careful not to damage the ring-gear teeth.
2. Working in a diagonal sequence, progressively loosen the six nuts securing the clutch cover to the flywheel.
3. Remove the clutch cover and clutch plate.
4. Renew all worn or damaged components.

Refit:

1. Clean the clutch cover and flywheel mating faces and spigot bush in the end of crankshaft. Brake cleaner is ideal for this.
2. Put a small amount of anti-seize paste on the splines, such as Rocol MV3 or MTS1000.
3. Position the clutch plate to the flywheel. The discs will be marked 'gearbox side' facing towards gearbox, or 'flywheel side' against flywheel
4. Position a suitable spigot-shaped tool through the drive plate into the spigot bearing in the crankshaft to get it all centred.
5. Fit the clutch cover and locate it on the dowels.
6. Fit the clutch cover nuts and progressively tighten in a diagonal sequence. The torque depends on the variant, 25Nm (18lb ft) for TD5, 40Nm (30lb ft) for V8 Discovery 2, 28Nm (21lb ft) for other engines.
7. Finally refit the gearbox assembly.

Slightly blue marks on the clutch cover show where the disc was slipping and overheating.

The rear oil seal will leak into the handbrake drum. Oil stains round the back of the transfer box like this are common.

TRANSFER BOX REAR OIL SEAL

To change the seal you will need a new fibre washer, a new M20 Nyloc nut and of course the seal.

1. First chock the car securely. Do not put the handbrake on, but put the gearbox in gear or park.
2. Remove the rear propshaft, compressing it so that it clears the rear flange.
3. Undo the drum retaining screw. Always use the right screwdriver bit or the screw head will be ruined. If it is tight, or already a mess, then it is best to use an impact screwdriver straightaway.
4. At this point the brake drum should be loose and simply slide out rearwards. However, several times in the past I have found that it will not move back more than a few millimetres, the reason being that either there is grit in there, which is binding between the shoe and the drum, or that it is worn to such an extent that the shoes have dug a groove into the drum. The solution is to wind the adjuster bolt out until the drum moves freely, making a note of how many turns you have applied so you can set it up as you found it later.
5. With the drum off you can clean all the oil off it and also clean up the handbrake shoes.
6. Remove the large nut that holds the drive flange on. This will be done up quite tight and so the flange has to be locked. If your Discovery has a differential lock and is very securely chocked then you stand a fair chance of getting it off with a long breaker bar on your socket, but beware that as the slack is taken up the car will move slightly. If you do not have a differential lock then you will end up driving the front driveshaft with the same force that you apply to the nut, which could potentially drive the car off the chocks, so this method should not be used. An assistant standing very hard on the brakes may help, but if the nut is very tight then even this will not stop the car moving. In either case it is far safer to use a special tool to lock the drive flange. Proper tools can be rented for the day or if you are a competent fabricator you can make one out of two lengths of steel bolted together to form a Y-shape with holes at the ends that go onto the drive-flange studs.

7. Behind the nut is a plain washer and a felt seal, which is an admission that oil will always leak through the drive splines to a small extent. Remove them both.
8. You can now try extracting the drive flange. If you are really lucky it will pull off easily, but for most of us it will need a three-jaw puller and some effort. Once it comes out there will be a small amount of oil following it, so have a drip tray ready.
9. Hook the old oil seal out, being careful not to scratch the seal mating surface.
10. Clean up the area and lubricate with fresh gearbox oil.
11. Slip on the new seal. Make sure to get it on straight, possibly using a large socket to push it on.
12. Slip the drive flange back on, followed by the new felt washer, plain washer and new Nyloc nut.
13. Torque up the nut, observing the same precautions as when you undid it.
14. Refit the drum. If the retaining screw was damaged then fit a new one.
15. Before putting the propshaft back on put the transfer box in neutral with the differential lock off and spin the drum to make sure it rotates freely. Tighten the brake adjuster bolt so that with the handbrake lever fully off the brake locks, and then back it of 1.5 turns.
16. Once this is all working properly the propshaft can go back on and the job is done.

Differential input seals traditionally leak like this although the differential could go on for many more miles if the oil level is topped up, but it is far better and cheaper in the long run to change the seal.

AXLES

Differential oil seal

These seem to last about ten years with normal road use. The only problem is that they are a press fit. Getting new ones in is easy; getting the old ones out is less so.

1. Chock the vehicle securely.
2. Remove the propshaft.
3. Get an assistant to stand on the brakes very hard while you undo the drive-flange nut.
4. The flange should pull out reasonably easy, but if it does not then use a block of wood and a hammer to drift it up.
5. Now you need to pull the seal out – it has a metal outer part, which is a press fit. Ideally you would have a specially made hook and slide hammer so you could work it out. I have managed to get them out using small pry bars, although it takes a lot of time, while being careful not to damage the input shaft or knock any debris into the differential.
6. Once it is out, clean up the recess and drift the new one in, making sure to keep it parallel to the shaft so it does not get jammed half way.

7. Then put a smear of differential oil on the seal lip and refit the drive flange.
8. Put a drop of thread seal on the flange nut.
9. Again get an assistant to stand on the brakes very hard while you torque up the drive-flange nut.
10. Refit the propshaft.

Wheel bearings

Discovery 1 wheel bearings are fairly cheap. The downside is that there is a bit of work involved in fitting them. By comparison, Discovery 2 wheel bearings are very easy to change as they come in a pre-assembled hub that just bolts on, but the downside here is that they are quite expensive.

Discovery 1 wheel bearing replacement

1. Chock the car securely and loosen the wheel bolts on the wheel in question. Jack up the axle and remove the wheel.
2. Remove the brake calliper bolts and tie the calliper up so as not to strain the brake hose.
3. On the front axle the driveshaft is held into the drive flange by a circlip and its end-float is set by a washer behind the clip. The thickness of the washer is important, so be careful when you remove the circlip and washer. On the rear axle the shaft is attached to the flange and comes out as one unit.
4. Unbolt the drive flange and you will see the big nuts that hold the hub on. They are locked in place by a big washer that is bent up against the nut's sides. Using a suitable drift, such as an old screwdriver that you will never use for undoing screws ever again, knock the sides of the washer back so the nut can be undone.
5. With the nut removed you can see a groove or flat machined in the stub axle, which stops the washer rotating. Remove the washer and throw it away – you will need a new one later. Some people hammer them flat and reuse them. You might get away with this sometimes, but the washer metal will be fatigued and is more likely to fail in service, so it is really not a good idea.

The inside of the hub needs to be clean so that the bearing races do not jam as you drift them in. The same goes for the stub axle. Make sure the shoulder that the inner race butts up to is clean, as any lumps will knock the bearing out of true.

6. Now the inner nut can be removed. You will need a fairly deep socket for this.

7. With the last nut off there should be nothing preventing the hub from coming off. I usually pull it out a bit and then push it back to release the smaller outer wheel bearing, otherwise it may drop on the floor.

8. With the hub removed you can fish out the inner bearing and the seal too.

9. Clean out the inside of the hub. There is a lot of space in there and all the old grease needs to be removed, otherwise once it gets hot and melts it will contaminate the new grease.

10. The outer race of each bearing is a light interference fit in the hub and so has to be drifted or pressed out. If you have a press and the right size tool then that is great, but most of us do not and will have to work the race out by gradually tapping it using a steel rod (an old screwdriver or socket set extension bar will do) with gentle taps all round the race periphery to ensure it comes out straight and does not jam in.

11. When they are both out, clean up the housing so there is absolutely no dirt or grease under their seats.

12. Drift the new outer races in. It is vital to get them in straight or they will get stuck. I use a flat piece of wood across the face of the race and gentle hammer blows in the middle initially. Once the race is flush with the hub, I drift it in a few more millimetres using the old race as a drift, being careful not to knock it in so far that it gets stuck. From then on I use a small steel rod as a drift and tap the race home, alternating between the left and right as I go. When the race is home the hammer blows make a slightly different sound.

13. When both races are seated the hub needs a good clean again. Even a small bit of grit will eventually destroy the new bearing.

14. Now pack the new bearings with grease and work it into the cage. Put a dollop in the hub too.

15. Put the inner bearing in first and then tap the new seal into place using a soft-faced mallet, or a piece of wood across its face. Smear some grease on the seal lip.

16. Now wipe the stub axle clean and carefully offer up the hub, making sure that you do not damage the seal.

17. With the hub approximately in place you can fit the outer bearing along with its thrust washer and the first nut, finger tight to start with.

18. Now you need to set the pre-load by tightening the nut until the hub will not rotate quite as easily. It is important to rotate the hub several times to allow the grease to be forced out of the gaps. The official tightening procedure was revised to make it easier. Initially the end-float was specified (0.01mm), which had to be tested by pulling the hub in and out while watching a dial test indicator. Later the procedure was revised to tightening the nut to 61Nm (45lb ft), rotating the hub a few times, then fully slackening the nut off and re-tightening to just 4Nm (3lb ft).

19. Fit a new lock washer.

20. Fit the outer lock nut and tighten to 61Nm (45lb ft).

21. Bend the edges of the lock washer in so that it holds the inner and outer lock nuts.

22. Fit a new gasket to the drive flange, refit and torque up the bolts.

23. Refit the brake calliper and wheel.

Hub bearings, Discovery 2 On the Discovery 2 the hub bearings come as a complete new hub assembly. The good thing about this is that there is no grease and bearing pre-load set-up involved – you just bolt it on. The bad thing about it is the cost, but do not be tempted to buy a much cheaper non-genuine item; the bearings take huge forces and the assembly incorporates the ABS sensor and reluctor wheel. Cheap copies can result in early bearing failure and a variety of interesting ABS faults.

Discovery 2 hubs come as a pre-assembled unit with the ABS sensor built in. Simply bolt it in from the back.

One challenging thing about this operation is the relatively high torque that the hub nut is done up to. You will need a substantial torque wrench to do it up later and it may be worth renting or borrowing one for the day.

1. First turn the steering slightly to the left, this way you will be pressing down on the breaker bar and if it comes off it will not hit you in the face or smack into the front wing.
2. Ensure the car is chocked securely.
3. Loosen the wheel nuts, raise the wheel using the bottle jack under the axle and remove the wheel.
4. Undo the ABS sensor connector on the inner wing and feed the wire back through the panel.
5. The hub nut is secured by bending a section of its collar into a slot on the shaft. To release it you have to bend that bit out again using strong long-nose pliers or a suitable drift.
6. Now you need a very good-fitting socket and a long bar to get the nut to release. The socket should be well designed with six sides (and not a bi-hex because that puts the turning force on the nut too close to the corners). If your 32mm socket seems a bit loose on the nut then it might round it off; sometimes a well used 1¼in AF socket can be a better fit as it should be just a quarter of a millimetre smaller than the 32mm. To hold the hub stationary you could put the gearbox in gear/park and engage the differential lock (if available) and select low range. Alternatively have an assistant stand very firmly on the brake pedal.
7. Remove the brake calliper and brake disc, and tie the calliper up in the wheel arch so that the brake hose is not stressed.
8. Undo the four bolts at the back of the hub that hold it onto the steering knuckle. One of these four bolts has a clip that holds the ABS sensor wire in place – make a note of how it is routed.
9. It will not fall off yet. It fits into a recess in the knuckle, so it will need a bit of tapping to free it off. Also it is still held on by the drive shaft. The official method is to remove the hub with the driveshaft still attached, then when refitting you need to fit a new oil seal to the shaft. An alternative is to leave the driveshaft in place and use a three-jaw puller to ease the shaft out of the hub while it is being progressively tapped free. It is vital to not stress the CV joint while doing this, so a little at a time is best and loosely fit two of the bolts in the back of the hub.
10. Carefully withdraw the hub while feeding the ABS sensor wire through the steering knuckle. The new hub will

> *Discovery 2 ABS sensors in some replacement service packs came ready fitted with a very long length of wiring loom so they could be fitted directly to the ABS unit. This allowed the wire to be threaded through the hub without removing the hub. The downside is that often the way the wire is spliced into the original loom at the ABS unit leaves a lot to be desired.*

come with the ABS trigger ring and sensor pre-fitted, do not disturb them as the tolerance is quite fine.

11. Before fitting the new hub you must make sure the mating surface is completely clean, and that the driveshaft splines are clear of any old retaining compound or dirt. A very light smear of suitable anti-seize compound on the hub mating surface will help if you ever need to take it off again in the future.
12. The drive splines are prevented from chattering in the hub by using retaining compound such as Loctite 640. Put a bead of about 3mm width around the end of the splines, then when it is fitted the compound will be drawn in along the length of the splines.
13. Reassemble the whole lot, remembering the ABS wire clip on the top hub-retaining bolt.

BRAKES

Handbrake

The handbrake uses shoes and a drum on the rear transfer box output. It is fairly easy to change and if you are slim enough it can be done without jacking the car up.

1. First make sure the front wheels are chocked securely. The next step involves disconnecting the brakes, so it is vital the car cannot move.
2. Fully release the handbrake.
3. Undo the four propshaft bolts at the brake drum. If you need more access to some of the nuts then rotate the propshaft by jacking up one rear wheel and turning it very slowly (remember the prop goes round nearly four times faster than the wheels). If there is enough plunge in the propshaft, you may be able to release it from the studs and tie it up to one side. If not, then undo the rear prop bolts and remove the shaft completely.
4. Undo the drum retaining screw. This may have been damaged by previous owners because many people try to undo it with the wrong size screwdriver bit. Make sure you use the right one – it is often best to use an impact driver to get it started.
5. At this point the brake drum should be loose and simply slide out rearwards. However, several times in the past I have found that it will not move back more than a few millimetres, the reason being that either there is grit in there, which is binding between the shoe and drum, or that it is worn to the extent that the shoes have dug a groove into the drum. The solution is to wind the adjuster bolt out until the drum moves freely.
6. Now you can see the shoes. Undo the little round spring caps that hold the shoes to the back plate – you have to push them in and twist 90 degrees. Be very careful here. If you slip, they will ping out never to be found again, and could injure your eyes.
7. Before going any further make a note of how the springs attach to the shoes. Over the years there have been many variations, so it is best to note down or photograph the ones on your car.
8. Now you can release the lower spring that holds the two shoes together. I use a small hook with a big handle

as the spring is tight. Avoid using cheap pliers as they will probably just slide off and you will hurt yourself.

9. Remove the upper retaining spring in the same manner.

10. Now one shoe should come out.

11. Undo the C-clip and spring that holds the abutment lever to the back plate.

12. To release the other one you have to unhook the handbrake cable.

13. When refitting, some kits come with a new adjuster bolt with thread-lock already on. If so then throw away the old one, but if the kit does not have one then you must apply thread-lock compound to the old bolt to stop it rattling out of adjustment.

14. First fit one shoe and attach the handbrake cable.

15. Lubricate the cable lever pivot pin with copper grease or similar.

16. Put the other shoe in and fit the springs.

17. Fit the retaining springs and caps.

18. Ensure the adjuster is wound out and refit the drum. Then refit the retaining screw with a dab of thread-lock.

19. Before putting the propshaft back on, put the transfer box in neutral with the differential lock off and spin the drum to make sure it rotates freely.

20. Refit the propshaft and torque up all the nuts.

21. With one rear wheel jacked up, tighten the brake adjuster bolt so that with the handbrake lever fully off the brake just locks, and then back it off 1.5 turns.

The handbrake is a transmission brake drum and after wading or heavy off-road work it can get mud inside, which eats away the shoes. The transfer box tends to leak oil into it too. It has a hard life, so inspection and service is well worthwhile.

non-standard techniques

RUSTY NUTS

One of the problems with older cars is that when it is time to remove parts, the chances are that the nuts and bolt heads will have rusted and so once the rust has been wire brushed off you may find that the spanner or socket does not fit too well. One cunning solution is to swap between metric and Imperial tools, for instance if a 13mm nut has lost about a quarter of a millimetre on its width due to corrosion then you could use a ½in spanner as this is 12.7mm. Another point worth noting is that tools wear. A new socket set will be slightly softer than a well-used one and the sockets will open out very slightly during their early life. Once they have been used a few times they work-harden and the size will tend to stabilize. So a very well-used ½in socket might very well be closer to 13mm anyway.

To remove this bolt all that rusty thread has to be forced past the nut threads, so clean it off to avoid trouble.

Spot the difference – just 0.1125mm in it.

Here are a few relevant size measurements:

7/16in = 11.1125mm
½in = 12.7mm (battery terminals and some engine/gearbox bolts)
9/16in = 14.29mm (early prop bolts)
¾in = 19.05mm (some engine sensors)
1¼in = 31.75 (hub nuts)

More rusty nuts Many of the fixings that go through the floor pan have lengths of thread exposed to road grime and salt corrosion, including rear seat bolts and the ones that hold the body onto the chassis. The exposed thread corrodes and may fail when you try to undo it, so first wire brush all the loose corrosion and mud off and soak the thread in penetrating oil for a day before undoing. This should maximize the chances of undoing it without damaging any of the surrounding parts.

Once the bolt is out then throw it away and replace it with a stainless item of the same or higher strength rating. This makes things much easier if you are going to keep the car long-term.

WATER WATER EVERYWHERE

The Discovery is a superbly practical machine, and if maintained properly, there is very little that will stop it, including deep water. Splashing through puddles is unlikely to cause many issues, but driving through winter floods or crossing deep rivers can cause a few problems for the unwary.

The main area to look at is the axles. If the car has been driven a few miles, the differential gears will have warmed up a little, and so will the oil. Also the hub bearings will have warmed and the grease expanded a little. All this is as it should be, but if you then encounter water deep enough to cover the axles then the sudden drop in temperature causes the air and oil to contract, and this can cause water to be sucked into the differential or bearings. If that does occur then you will not notice straightaway, but the wear rate will dramatically increase and wheel-bearing failure or excessive differential play can result a few months later.

Good maintenance is essential. The axles have breather tubes, which can get damaged, so check them before an off-road trip and before winter sets in. Also the differential and hub bearing seals must be in good condition. As

Although the Discovery 2 does not have the same swivel seal issues, it does have a boot over the CV joint, and a split will let water in. Regular inspection can help avoid problems later.

Before entering deep water and rivers, ensure breathers are okay.

they have rubber parts in it is worth replacing them every ten years or so, but also replace them if there is any sign of oil leaking out. Remember that driving through thick deep mud can grind away at seals, so if that is what you do with your Discovery then check the seals more often. If water has got in to the axle then the differential oil and/or bearing grease will have to be completely removed and replaced with new. Discovery 1 hub bearings can be removed and cleaned out before repacking with grease, but Discovery 2 bearings come as a non-serviceable assembly although thankfully this is a little more robust against water ingress.

Wading also affects the brakes. Brake pads can absorb some water if left submersed for very long periods, and become weaker. So before parking up use the brakes hard a few times to dry them out. This will also slow the corrosion rate on the discs.

The handbrake is a drum and can retain quite a lot of water. If it is left on while saturated then over time it will corrode on. Also the drum will rust in the gaps between the two shoes, resulting in vibration at speed. So again, after wading go for a run so the water is flung out of the drum.

The gearbox, transfer box and engine all have breathers of one sort or another. Just like the axle, when cold water surrounds them the gasses inside contract and any weak gaskets or seals will let water in. So check them all and if there are any signs of oil leaks (yes, I know all old Land Rovers leak oil) then the gasket must be replaced. Pay particular attention to the engine sump gasket, crank seals, transfer box lower cover plate, output shaft seals and on automatic gearboxes the gearbox sump gasket.

After wading check the oil for contamination – water turns oil milky or grey. Check the engine oil, gearbox, transfer box and axles.

The next area to look at is the electrical system. Early cars had some connectors that were a little less robust than we might have liked. Connectors can be kept in good order with a light covering of contact grease. After wading, a small squirt of water dispersant oil such as WD40 can reduce the chances of corrosion setting in. The connectors in greatest jeopardy are the lights, those on the chassis and the ones in the engine bay.

Petrol engines can suffer ignition problems if water gets in. The V8 has breather holes in the base of the distributor – water thrown up by the viscous fan can be drawn in through these holes as you drive into deep water. If this happens then pop the distributor cap off and apply a small amount of water dispersant to the base and wipe the cap out with a dry cloth.

Water dispersant oil can extend life of connectors in exposed locations, particularly if you intend to do any wading.

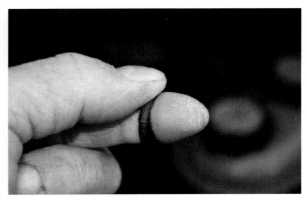

Emergency grommet machine – a finger and a loop of self-amalgamating tape.

Using self-amalgamating rubber tape to make a temporary repair on an intake duct. The tape has to be stretched and wound back onto itself to make a homogeneous seal.

As well as changing the seat bolts, I changed the seat-belt bolts for motor sport seat-belt mounting eyes. They are stronger and make useful cargo securing points too.

Finally, the body and chassis have many water traps built in, particularly the sills and rear body cross member. As well as attending to any paint defects or rust spots, I squirt some WD40 into voids while they are still dry, plus high-stress areas such as where the spring hangers are welded to the chassis.

SEALING DUCTS

Air leaks between the air meter and engine will cause problems. As these parts age the best solution is to replace them. But if you are unable to get hold of one and need to use the car, then cracks can be temporarily sealed using self-amalgamating rubber tape, which has to be stretched and then wrapped around the duct, making a large overlap. Hold it in place for a few seconds and the rubber will flow into itself, making one continuous band.

TEMPORARY O-RING

You can also use self-amalgamating tape to make emergency O-rings. Wrap a piece round your fingers to make it the right size and roll it off, thus making a ring. Although it will not fit perfectly it can be a great 'get you home' temporary repair. Similarly it can be used to make grommets where cables or hoses pass through the bulkhead etc.

Discovery 1 and 2 rear seats can be removed easily, which provides much greater load space. There are four small

bolts holding each part of the rear seat to the car floor. They secure a clamp bracket, which houses a plastic bush to allow the front support tube of the seat to hinge forwards. Move the carpet out the way to get at the front bolts, and then fold the seats forward to access the bolts at the rear of those brackets.

Unfortunately as these bolts protrude through the underside of the body they are exposed to road grime and corrosion. So if you are thinking of taking the seats out on a regular basis, it is worth replacing these bolts with stainless cap-head bolts and keeping them well lubricated.

With the seats out a standard industrial pallet can be forklifted in – as long as it goes in long ways it just fits between the wheel arches.

STRING THEORY

Setting up suspension geometry is best done using professional garage equipment, but there is a much cheaper option that is almost as effective and it is so good that a lot of racing teams use it when they are at an event. All you need is four axle stands and a ball of string.

Accuracy and precision It is very easy to spend ages taking detailed readings, but beware: it is easy to have accidentally moved the string, thus highlighting the difference between accuracy and precision. For example, if you measure a block of metal that is in fact 50mm wide with a cheap

Setting up the string box takes a little practice. The first time you do it you will probably have to make several adjustments before it measures parallel, but with practice it becomes very easy.

digital vernier that reads 47.9836mm then it is very precise but not very accurate. By contrast if you use an old tape measure then it may read 5cm, which is not very precise but completely accurate. With the string method we are looking for accuracy, and consistent results.

Procedure Park the car on flat and even ground. This is very important; you can't do it on grass. Attach a piece of string to a suitable stand at each end, one that will not move when you pull the string tight, such as a sturdy axle stand or a breeze block. The string must be at the same height, give or take a couple of millimetres, as the wheel hub centres and extend beyond each end of the car by a foot or so. The string should be as close to the car as possible without touching it. Ideally we would get this parallel to the centre line of the car, but as that can be difficult to define just make it parallel to the sills to start with. It can be adjusted in a moment. Next put the other string on the other side in the same manner.

Now measure the distance between the strings at the front and the rear of the car to check they are parallel and adjust the string stands evenly until the same measurement is achieved at both ends.

When taking a measurement hold the ruler just underneath the string and take a reading from the edge of the string closest the car. With practice, and fine string, it is quite possible to get precision to 0.5mm, more than enough for our purposes. You will need an assistant with a steady hand for this part.

You should now have two parallel lines at hub height, so to measure toe angle you can measure at a right angle from the string to the front and rear edges of the wheel rim.

Now, as we will not be measuring between the wheels, but instead from the string to the wheel, we are effectively looking at half the car. So what we need to do is combine the readings from both sides.

For example, on the car pictured here, the measurements from the string to the front left wheel are 47mm at the front of the wheel rim and 46mm at the rear edge. So the front edge is 1mm further inboard than the rear. Now onto the right front wheel and I have 51mm at the front edge and 49mm at the back. So it is 2mm inboard at the front. That means that I have a total 3mm toe in. And the car is slightly closer to the string on the left and I also have not got the steering set quite as straight as I thought, but the latter does not affect the results.

Measurements at the rear are 47mm on the left and 50mm on the right. In both cases it is the same at the front and rear edges. So the rear wheels are completely parallel.

All this makes the assumption that the wheels are not bent or dented, so it is useful to check the run-out first.

Jack up and properly support the axle until the tyre is just off the ground. Then place a suitable datum, a breeze block perhaps, next to the wheel and clamp a ruler onto it so that its edge is just touching the wheel rim. Next, spin the wheel and see if the gap opens up or the ruler gets pushed back. Anything more than a fraction of a millimetre is less than ideal although its amazing how much wobbly wheel factor some people live with. If the wheel is bent then it is still possible to check the geometry, but the wheel has to be set so that the front and rear edges where we take measurements from have the same offset. But it is obviously best to get it fixed first.

Next we can check to see if the front and rear axles are centred properly. The first step is to check the wheelbase on both sides, which for both types is 100in.

Having set the strings up to be parallel, measure to the hub centres, and also to suitable datum points on the body/chassis such as the seam on the sill. If the car has been badly repaired after a shunt then one axle could be offset causing the car to crab. Should the results show the car is out of alignment, it might be a case of rebuilding the suspension or possibly the chassis may need straightening. However, before embarking on any drastic action based on the string method it is worth having it double-checked at a professional alignment facility first.

Checking your car's steering and suspension geometry can be quite simple, once you get the hang of it, and although the accuracy is not as fine as with laser alignment kit it does give a very useful idea of which way your wheels are pointing, can help highlight suspension faults and is a technique used by some of the top motor-racing teams to this day.

Practise this method until you become proficient and you will have a simple and easy-to-set-up system ready for use almost anywhere.

Measure from the inside edge of the string to the wheel rim front and rear edges to find the toe angle. The wheel must not be bent! Move the car forward so the wheel turns half a revolution and then check again.

The Discovery was designed so that major repair is possible, and almost anything can be fixed or replaced to keep these cars going for a very long time.

repair

Most repair operations are well described in the relevant manuals, but occasionally there are problems that were not thought of when the original texts were written. Additionally, years of driving experience by millions of owners have thrown up some unusual quirks and also some handy tricks for diagnosing and fixing them. So this chapter is intended to be an enhancement to a standard workshop manual, to spread some of the knowledge about the things 'they' don't tell you, gained the hard way.

ENGINE

V8 valley gasket

The valley gasket can be deformed by high crankcase pressures, so if it is bulging or the ends have been bent up then check that the breather hoses and flame trap are in good order. If the engine is difficult to start and has a smokey exhaust then there may be worn piston rings, bore or valve guides. That said, the valley gasket does seem to give up

after a number of years, leading to possible coolant loss, air leaks, poor running and the ever-present spectre of oil leaks.

To change it you have to remove the intake manifold, which is slightly more complicated on Series 2 cars but still quite straightforward for the home mechanic.

It is the little things that they don't tell you, like how to gently prise up a plastic trim screw while turning it because it will not come out.

SRS AIRBAGS

Airbags are astonishingly good at saving lives, but a big explosion in front of your face is always going to have a downside. In most types of crash they will not activate, only where the crash is severe enough that if they did not deploy the occupants would definitely be significantly worse off. In some of the operations in this chapter you may want to temporarily remove them, but extreme caution is required.

Airbags are explosive devices and although they have several fail-safe devices fitted you must treat them with respect. If you have to remove an airbag then make sure the system is deactivated by disconnecting the battery and waiting at least ten minutes before working on the system.

The explosive is triggered by a 12V signal, but they will fire at much lower voltages too, so never test one with a multimeter or it may well go off!

There are several reasons why you really do not want an airbag to accidentally go off. If your head is too close you could suffer severe head injuries and a snapped neck, not to mention being deafened and blinded. Then there is the residue containing material such as sodium azide, which is explosive and flammable and can burn your skin.

All the airbag wiring is yellow, and the connectors are protected such that when you unplug an airbag the wires short out so it cannot be accidentally fired due to static electricity. So only unplug and never cut airbag wires. Make sure the battery has been disconnected for ten minutes before working on any part of the airbag system.

Removed airbags should be stored with the trim pad surface pointing up. If you store it the other way up and it accidentally goes off then it will launch itself across the workshop and is quite capable of breaking bones.

The connector on the airbag has a device to prevent it going off due to static electricity when it is disconnected, but nothing is completely reliable and when the connector is two decades old I would not rely on it. So it is recommended that the removed airbag is stored in a steel box (or a car boot if a steel box is not available).

---

1. Disconnect the battery earth lead.
2. Drain the coolant.
3. Remove the top hose (from the thermostat on Discovery 2 models, to the thermostat on Discovery 1).
4. Release the throttle cables.
5. Remove the intake duct from the throttle area.
6. Undo the crankcase breather hose and clean it out.
7. Depressurize the fuel system. The pressure drops slowly after the engine has stopped but it can still be several bar the following day, so extreme caution is needed to avoid fuel squirting all over you and the car.
8. Wear safety glasses.
9. Put a rag under the fuel union connection and put two spanners on the fitting ready to undo it, but before you apply force put another rag over the union to catch any fuel that may spray out.

The valley gasket closes off the top of the block as well as forming the intake manifold gasket – a clever idea but poorly executed. Even mild crankcase pressure from a blocked breather will act on that large surface area and distort it, resulting in a leak.

10. Loosen the nut just enough for fuel to weep out slowly, then gradually undo it further until no more fuel comes out.
11. Remove the fuel-soaked rags and dispose of them safely. There are alternative methods so please investigate them and make your own decision on the safest way to proceed.
12. On Discovery 2 cars undo the plenum top bolts and move the casting forwards so you can remove the coil pack from the back.
13. Fully remove the plenum top.
14. Release the electrical connectors from the fuel injectors.
15. Undo the bolts securing the manifold to the cylinder heads. Note that some of them are different lengths, so make a note of where they go.
16. The intake manifold should now be free although they are usually stuck and need some gentle persuasion to free off. If it is very reluctant to move then you have left a bolt in. Some coolant will spill out of the manifold, so be careful to ensure none of it gets spilled down an intake port, or the engine will be damaged.
17. While the intake manifold is off inspect the injector nozzles for any tar-like oily deposits, and clean them with carburettor cleaner if necessary.
18. Mop up any remaining coolant from the valley gasket.
19. Undo the bolts that hold down the two end clamps and remove the clamps.
20. Now the valley gasket should come free with a bit of a tug. The ends will have been stuck down with gasket sealant.
21. Retrieve the two rubber seals from the front and rear of the block and throw them away – these are where most of the oil leaks come from so do not reuse them.
22. Clean up the area and remove all traces of old gasket sealant.

23. Early cars had a plain steel valley gasket while later models had a neoprene-covered gasket, which is a much better seal and is a direct replacement for the early type. To refit, first apply a small amount of gasket sealant to the ends of the block and fit new rubber seals.
24. Offer up the new valley gasket, making sure the intake ports on the heads are not obscured.
25. Loose fit the end clamps and bolts, with a drop of thread sealant on the bolts.
26. Re-check the valley gasket alignment and then torque the clamps down.
27. Refit the intake manifold, apply a dab of thread-lock to the bolts and loosely assemble them. The manifold needs to be torqued down evenly to avoid distorting the valley gasket, so turn the bolts in a scatter pattern, similar to the way you do head bolts, until they are all at the correct torque.
28. Fit the injector loom (inspect the connectors and repair any faults).
29. Put the plenum top on. For Discovery 2 cars get it approximately in place first, allowing enough room to refit the coil pack.
30. Refit the hoses, intake duct, fuel lines, throttle cables etc.
31. Refill the coolant and purge air from the top hose. Now is a great time to replace the coolant if it is due.
32. Reconnect the battery earth lead.
33. Before starting the engine, bear in mind that there will be a small amount of air in the fuel line. Prime the system by turning the ignition on but not starting, the pump will run for a few seconds. Do this two or three times to get fuel pressure up.
34. Check for fuel leaks and tighten the union if necessary.
35. Start the engine and immediately check for leaks. Stop the engine if any are found and repair before restarting.

Only four small bolts hold the rocker covers on, so the clamping load that holds the gasket in place can be poor. The later moulded plastic gasket is much better than the early cork items.

V8 rocker cover gasket

If you have a V8 then you have an oil leak. The rocker cover gasket is a particularly challenging design. On Series 1 cars it was cork, but later it changed to a moulded plastic part, which fitted a little bit better but still had a tendency to fall out and leak. One of the main causes for the gasket falling out is that there are only four bolts holding the cover on and they tend to undo by themselves, so when you replace the gasket it is worth using thread lock on the bolts.

On both Series 1 and 2 Discoverys the intake plenum top will need to be removed first. The small-diameter coolant hoses to the throttle tend to perish and may break, so it may be worth having some spare tube ready just in case.

V8 head gaskets

The original 3.5-litre V8 was very robust and is unlikely to need a head gasket change unless it has overheated. By contrast the 3.9-litre and later engines seemed to have difficulty holding their cylinder liners up. When this happens the head gasket is no longer held securely and is gradually eaten away until it starts leaking. If the leak is to the coolant gallery, it will blow coolant out of the header tank. If it leaks to the oil way then it burns oil. So if the head gasket needs to be replaced, you must first fix the cause of the failure, otherwise it will simply fail again a few hundred miles later.

1. Start by removing the intake manifold and associated parts as described in the valley gasket section above.
2. Now remove the rocker covers by undoing the four bolts on each. Throw away the cover gaskets and get new ones for refitting.
3. Undo the rocker shafts by progressively loosening the bolts so the shaft is not distorted. While it is off it is worth cleaning it out as the oil ways are notorious for clogging. Also check for wear between the rockers and shaft, and if very worn then fit new shafts.
4. Now you can recover the pushrods. I use a piece of cardboard with the rods pushed through small holes in order to store them in the correct order.
5. Now clean any sludge out of the top of the cylinder heads and make sure the head bolts are clearly visible. Undo them progressively in the scatter pattern described in the official manual to avoid distorting the heads.

The outer row of V8 head bolts cause more problems than they solve. With modern composite head gaskets it is questionable whether they are needed at all.

Always apply cam lube before fitting. This sticky oil will prevent the followers grinding through the thin hardened surface when you first start up the engine. Once the oil pressure is up this is washed away and the engine oil takes over the job.

6. The heads should simply lift away, maybe needing a mild tap from a soft-faced hammer just to break the seal. If they prove very difficult to move, then you have missed a bolt.

7. Once removed, get the heads checked for flatness. Slight distortion can be fixed by skimming but only by a fraction of a millimetre otherwise the compression ratio will be affected too much and the intake ports will not line up with the intake properly.

8. Also check the block face for flatness, and check the liners have not sunk. Run a finger nail across the join between liner and block, there should be no noticeable step. If the liners have sunk then it's a big job. The block will have to be removed and new liners fitted, or a good second-hand unit used instead.

9. When reassembling, use the later type of composite head gasket, which offers much better reliability.

V8 camshaft

This is one of the first things to wear down if the oil is neglected. A slightly worn camshaft will still allow the car to pull away, but it will run out of puff when you put your foot down. It will not start rattling until it is severely worn because the hydraulic followers will adjust automatically.

Changing the camshaft involves the same steps as above for the valley gasket change, plus taking the front pulley and front cover off. It is just about possible to change the camshaft with the engine in the car as long as you take the radiator out.

When changing the camshaft always change the followers at the same time and check the push rods are all straight by rolling them on a very flat surface such as a mirror.

It is also worth considering changing the camshaft type to get a bit more performance and economy. In my opinion it is best to go for lower duration to improve low-down torque at the expense of high-rpm power, which also improves fuel economy and makes the car nicer to drive on and off road. But opinions vary.

When you first fire up the engine after a camshaft change, hold it at about 2,000rpm for a minute or two. It may sound odd, but at this speed the forces on the cam lobe are at their lowest. If you just let it idle after starting, the cam will start to wear within a few thousand miles.

Also check that the cam gear and chain are in good order. Hold the chain sideways and if it droops down then it needs replacing.

V8 lambda sensors

The lambda oxygen sensors are the only way the engine management knows if it has the fuelling right. If they fail then you could end up running rich (washed bores, poor fuel economy, smoke, contaminated oil etc.) or lean (pinking, overheating, poor performance, misfires, catalyst damage etc.). Luckily they are fairly reliable, and the most common cause of a lambda failure is not the sensor itself but a leak in the exhaust manifold gasket, which causes the engine to run too rich, so always check that first before condemning the sensor.

There are two type of sensor: early cars used Titania-type sensors whilst later models used Zirconia. The differences

The V8 oxygen sensors play a vital role but age just like everything else. Air leaks ruin their performance, so fix leaks before fixing the sensor.

between these and sensors on other types of car was mainly just the connector and lead lengths, so if you are careful and know what to look for then you can get much cheaper sensors and splice them onto the original connector. But be careful, never try to solder oxygen sensor wires, as this will eventually cause the sensor to misread, and it's really difficult. Oxygen sensor leads can only be joined using a crimp connector that hermetically seals. These are available from good electrical shops. First you make a normal crimp connection and then you use a heat gun, which causes the heat shrink outer to contract around the joint and a resin to melt and expand into the joint to seal it completely.

This is a 300Tdi pushrod after the cam belt snapped. The rod bent and the engine was saved.

The Tdi engines have adjustable rockers to control valve gap. If the gap is too small then the valves could burn out; too big and the shock loadings will wear the cam and rockers. Either way performance will be lost, so adjust them correctly.

You can buy a universal sensor kit from Bosch, which contains these special crimps and is cheaper than a genuine replacement part. Second-hand parts cannot be relied upon.

What to do if your Tdi cam belt snaps

If your Tdi (200 or 300) has lost its cam belt while running then some damage is likely, but hopefully only to the pushrods.

If the engine cranks over quickly but without any knocking, squeaking or grinding noises then you may have got away with it. But if it does make a bad noise then it is time to either rebuild the engine or simply buy another second-hand engine.

If you have been lucky then start by removing the rocker cover and rocker shaft. Extract the pushrods and one or two will be very bent. At this stage I would throw all the pushrods away and buy a new set. If funds are tight, you can check to see if a rod is slightly bent by rolling it over a very flat surface such as a pane of glass – even a very slight bend will probably render the rod scrap. Although some specialists may offer to straighten the rods by rolling them, this is unlikely to work long-term and the rods are relatively cheap anyway.

When fitting the new cam belt spend some time checking for remnants of old belt wrapped around behind pulleys. If the strands are tightly wound then the pulley will have to be removed to get them all out. Do not leave any in there or they might work loose and nudge the new belt off.

When the engine is back together spin it over with the ignition off (12V onto the starter) to check there is nothing mechanical clashing before firing it up for the first time. *See* Servicing chapter for details on changing the cam belt.

Tdi head gasket fix

Changing the head gasket is relatively straightforward because it is a pushrod engine, so there is no need to disturb the cam or timing. The procedure is as shown in the official manuals but note the following:

The dark area between the cylinders shows where the head gasket was leaking. The brown triangular area is where the coolant gallery was. This engine emitted white vapour at idle as the coolant was drawn into the chamber on the intake stroke through the leak.

You can see the injector and glow-plug tips protruding from the head surface. Never put the head on the bench such that they get damaged. If you need the head face down, support it with wooden blocks at the ends.

When you remove the intake and exhaust manifold assembly some studs may snap, so it is worth buying new studs and a gasket before you start.

When undoing and removing the injector pipes, be careful not to bend them or allow even the tiniest piece of dirt to get into the pipes or injectors. They work on tiny tolerances and can easily get blocked.

To be safe you could remove the injectors and glow plugs, but if you are careful you can leave them in. They poke out proud of the head, so take precautions before putting the head on the bench.

The injectors can be freed off by prising them up gently with a 12mm spanner on the shaft pivoting on the clamp stud. Do not push too hard here or you will damage the stud. Do this while rotating the injector with a spanner on the flats at the top.

Throw the rocker cover gasket away, as you will be fitting a new one because the old one will have distorted and will never go back properly.

Store the pushrods in a piece of cardboard or use a similar method of ensuring they go back in the right holes.

There are several different lengths of head bolts, so again use the cardboard storage method, or better still fit new bolts.

The head should now be free, but is likely to be slightly stuck, so give it a gentle tap with a soft-faced hammer or a block of wood. Never hit the head with a metal hammer, as it could deform or crack.

It is best to use an assistant or crane to remove the head. It is a bit of a stretch over the engine bay and it is vital that you do not damage the head or block. Have some soft wood on the bench ready so you can put the head down without damaging it.

The cardboard method of getting things in the right place is vital for pushrods and head bolts.

If the engine has overheated then the head may have warped slightly. Often the areas between chambers can soften and become concave allowing the gasket to leak. To fix this, take the head to an engineering company and have it skimmed.

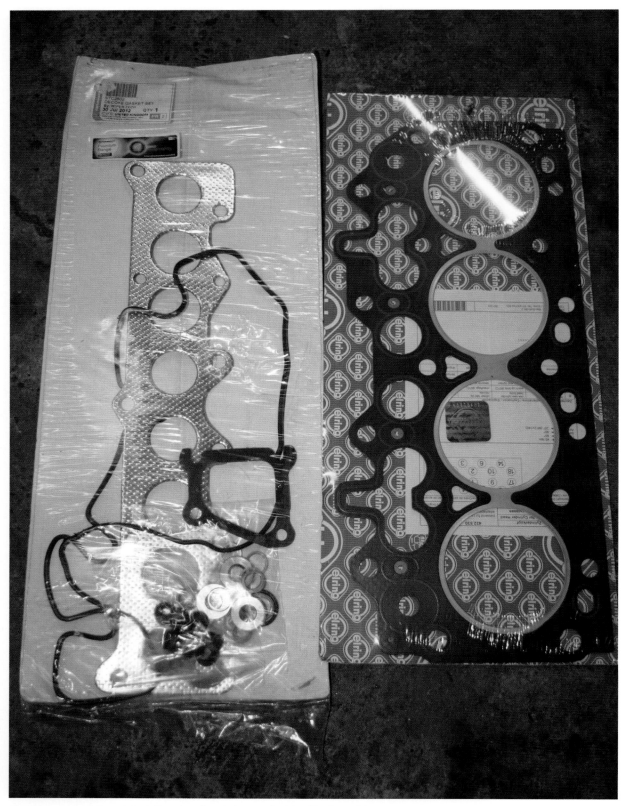

Always buy good quality gasket sets. Never buy cheap bolts or studs – it is asking for trouble.

When the head comes off some coolant and oil will fall into the cylinders. Clean it all out and spray grease or oil round the ring area. If you rock the engine back and forth to make the pistons go up and down slightly, the dirt will be trapped in the oil and can be removed, preventing ring wear.

300Tdi vacuum pump losing its suck

The problem is that the soft aluminium rivets that hold the top of the pump on stretch and eventually lose their grip on the sealing ring. As well as noticing that the brake pedal has gone hard you will also notice engine oil leaking out of the join between the vacuum pump body and the top.

One solution is to drill out the six rivets and fit six M5×20 bolts and nuts, although you may also need to fit a new seal or put some sealant around the edge if the pump top has warped. Of course the other alternative is to fit a new pump, but obviously this will cost a lot more, and second-hand pumps run the risk that they may be just about to fail in the same way.

The Tdi vacuum pump tends to lose its grip in the diaphragm as the rivets weaken, resulting in high blow-by and poor brake assistance.

The solution is to drill out the rivets, fit a new gasket and put a ring of bolts in. Note that one of them is very snug against the body of the pump.

Oil dripping from the TD5 ECU connector is bad news, usually resulting in a 'misfire'. The solution is to fit a replacement injector wiring loom.

TD5 injector loom fix

This is located inside the cam cover (which is why it's oily) and has a plug that protrudes through the end of the cylinder head casting and is sealed by O-rings. So to get at it you need to take the cam cover off, then the injector connectors can be unplugged and the new loom clipped on with new O-rings. Clean out the oil from the connector to the main loom first and blow it dry. Once that is replaced you also need to clean off as much oil as possible out of the main loom, plus clean the oil out of the red plug at the ECU end. Carburettor cleaner is a good solvent here, but make sure the connectors are dry before reattaching, and if using an air line then wear eye protection.

TD5 fuel purge trick

To purge the low-pressure fuel line from the in-tank pump to the engine you can try the following procedure:

1. Turn the ignition on.
2. Press the throttle to the floor six times.
3. The Check Engine (MIL) light will come on and the pump will cycle for a few minutes.

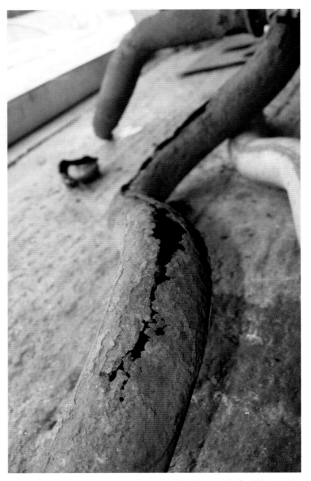

I thought my Discovery was getting noisy. The blue band of weld along the exhaust tubing had rotted out for about a metre.

4. When it has completed Purge Mode the Check Engine light will go out.

It may not work on all cars due to varying software used in production.

When removing the catalyst from the manifold, it is vital to prevent any particles of gasket or dirt entering, as even tiny pieces will rattle round and gradually erode the catalyst surface. When the catalyst is off, clean up its flange and then hold it upside down to shake any particles out. Also clean up the exhaust manifold flange and blow all the dust away before the catalyst goes back.

When refitting catalysts to the manifold, new gaskets should be used. Used gaskets are already crushed up and will not seal the joint fully. Gasket sealant paste should be avoided due to the risk of some of it falling into the catalyst or contaminating the oxygen sensor.

The upstream gaskets, which are the ones between the catalyst and manifold, and the ones between the manifold and cylinder head, must be absolutely gas tight. Even a small leak draws air in, which results in the oxygen sensor reading lean, and this causes the engine to run excessively rich.

I removed the manifold to replace the gasket. The leak was causing the lambda signal to drift and run the engine rich. The gasket is designed for two pipes and so does not seal on this style of down-pipe.

To get the exhaust out jack up the chassis and let the rear axle drop. Ensure it is secure before starting work.

EXHAUST

It is quite common for the welds in mild-steel systems to rot out, but wading and playing in mud speeds this up considerably. Small holes can be patched with exhaust seal tape, but this tends to work loose and is susceptible to damage off-road. A better solution is to weld a patch of steel sheet over the fault where possible.

Eventually the faulty exhaust must be replaced, at which point the sleeve-type joints will refuse to budge. When this happens the faulty part can be cut near the joint and then the remainder that is stuck in the joint persuaded out with a hammer and chisel.

The CV joints are capable of going through extreme angles, but any water contamination from a leaking seal will lead to corrosion and the thin surface hardening will fail rapidly.

However, on cars with catalysts restraint must be applied. Catalysts are very susceptible to damage from hammering, so if retaining the catalyst section then avoid heavy shocks that might fracture the ceramic catalyst brick.

The rear section of the exhaust goes over the rear axle and is almost impossible to remove unless the car is raised allowing the axle to drop sufficiently.

On older cars there is a chance that the exhaust will have to be taken apart again at a later date for further work, so a little copper grease on sleeve joints and sealing rings will make life easier later.

AXLE

CV joints

If the car makes a knocking noise when turning tight corners then it is possible a CV joint on the front axle has broken. If unchecked the parts will break up and could seize dangerously, locking the wheel. Luckily, it is fairly simple to fix:

1. Remove the brake calliper.
2. Remove the hub and stub axle and the CV joint is right there.
3. Slide it carefully off the half-shaft in case there are any loose bits.
4. If it has broken up then all the debris has to be removed from the axle to avoid it causing further damage.

Replacing propshaft bearings and seals is reasonably simple. Propshaft failure can be very dangerous, so only use quality parts.

Leaking ACE rams are not uncommon. It will be either the shaft seal or the hydraulic unions, and both are repairable.

Propshaft bearings

The bearings in the propshaft universal joints (UJs) are reasonably simple to replace.

1. Make sure the car is chocked securely, as removing the rear propshaft means no handbrake.
2. Remove the propshaft and clean all the dirt from the UJ area. It is very important that no grit gets into the new bearings. Also mark clearly where the grease nipple goes.
3. Remove the C-clips, but be careful that they do not ping off the C-clip pliers and disappear.
4. Remove the bearing cup and all the tiny rollers will fall out too. The cup is a press fit, but if you do not have a press then you can do this in a bench vice using two sockets, one small enough to press against a bearing cup and the opposite one big enough that the bearing cup can pass into it. Squeeze it until one cup is just proud of the UJ, then remove it from the vice and use the vice to hold the protruding bearing cup. Wiggle the bearing cup free.
5. Now use an even smaller socket to push the spider the other way and repeat the process to remove the opposing bearing cup.
6. Repeat this for the other pair of bearings. Now you should be able to separate the two halves of the UJ and release the spider. Most UJ repair kits come with a new spider, but if not then inspect the spider for damage. If they have dents or flat spots then they will cause the new bearing to wear very quickly.
7. Clean up the area and remove all the old grease.
8. Apply grease to the bearing rollers and cup. They need to be about a third full of lithium-based grease.
9. Pump grease through the grease nipple on a new spider to make sure any debris left inside from manufacturing is driven out, then clean off the excess grease.
10. When refitting, make sure the grease nipple is in the same orientation as the old one to preserve propshaft balance. And also remember the nipple points away from the flange, otherwise you will not get a grease gun on it later.
11. The UJ is reassembled by pressing the new bearing cups in – again, the two socket method in a vice seems

to work. Be very careful not to squeeze too hard; the bearing cups need to be in just far enough to get the C-clips back in and no more.
12. When the joint is all back together apply the grease gun and work the joint to ensure the grease is spread to all areas before refitting it to the car.

Active Cornering Enhancement (ACE)

Luckily most of the ACE system seems fairly robust, but the solenoids and sensor on the valve block can give problems. Depending on the exact fault the system may fail with the anti-roll bar locked (giving some roll but not too much) or unlocked (giving higher rates of roll). It is reasonably straightforward to fit replacement solenoids or a pressure sensor, but to find out which one is at fault you have to use a diagnostic system.

Changing any of these units could let dirt into the hydraulic oil, which in turn could damage seals and cause further faults, so it is very important to clean the valve block area before you start work. Do not forget to clean the bodywork above the block too, as it is easy for hands to knock dirt from this area into the parts you are working on. I spray a little WD40 on the area to be worked on so any remaining dust is held.

If you are replacing the solenoids or sensor on the ACE valve block, loosen them before undoing the three bolts that hold the block to the chassis. Be careful not to strain the metal pipes.

The solenoids can be replaced by first slackening them off with a spanner, then removing the valve block bolts and allowing the block to droop enough to give room to unscrew the valves upwards. A small dribble of ACE oil in the socket before fitting the replacement valve means less chance of trapping air and having to bleed the system.

The pressure sensor is on the side of the block and so can be simply removed in situ. The downside is that a small amount of oil may be lost and air will get in, requiring the system to be bled.

Bleeding the system requires the solenoids to fire and requires a special diagnostic routine available in the official Land Rover dealer system or one of the better aftermarket systems such as Nanocom. Have a look in the Parts and Tools chapter later in this book.

SUSPENSION

Air suspension bag replacement

This is really easy. There is a mounting lug at the bottom and two spring clips at the top. After undoing the air line the bag can be removed in just a few minutes, but beware of high pressure air lines, which can injure the unwary. The system runs at about 16 bar, and even when the air spring appears flat it may still have over 1 bar in. So wear eye protection and all other appropriate safety equipment.

1. The car must be raised with the chassis on stands and the wheels off the ground.
2. The system needs to be depressurized before any work on the air lines can commence. The official procedure is to use the dealer tool Testbook to run a special program commanding the system to vent all the air. There are some aftermarket systems that can also do this. However, if your starting point is a car on its bump stops then the pressure is fairly low already, and by carefully partially undoing the air line at the air spring it will release the remaining pressure. Only once all the pressure is released should the air line be fully removed.

With the two clips pulled out and the bag deflated it should drop down easily. Then you can undo the air-line fitting.

3. Before removing the air line at the bag ensure the area is clean, as any small particles of dirt will compromise the seal later on.
4. On the cars I have worked on the spring clips that hold the top of the air spring to the chassis are heavily corroded and not worth reusing, and any reputable supplier should sell a new spring with a new pair of clips anyway, so you can be fairly harsh in removing them. They can be difficult to remove, but when they go they can ping off quite violently, so keep the eye protection on.
5. The lower part of the bag is a twist lock, so turn it 90 degrees and it should just pull out.
6. Before fitting the replacement bag make sure the mounting faces are clean. Any rust should be treated before the new bag goes on.
7. Fit the lower end first then locate the top and slide the two new spring clips on.
8. Ensure the air-line connection is clean and gently tighten it to the specified torque. Be careful here as the plastic threads in the air-spring bag can be damaged easily if the fitting is not in straight.

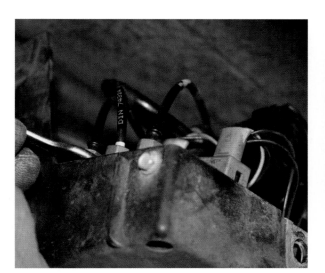

To let the pressure out of an air spring carefully loosen the pipe fitting at the valve block and let the air release gradually.

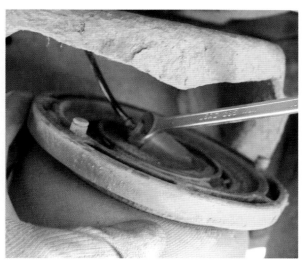

Only once the air spring was lowered could I get access to undo the pipe fitting.

The perishing of the air-spring rubber is apparent here and is worst at the edge where the spring rolls over the centre cone.

The new spring used a push-fit system instead of a screw-in fitting, which requires a cleanly cut pipe end.

Note: Both air springs wear and age at similar rates, so it is definitely worth replacing both at the same time. Once it is all back together it should automatically pump up to the right height next time you start the engine (with the doors closed).

Watts link

The back axle on the Discovery 2 is located by a Watts link that controls its side-to-side motion. This is absolutely critical to stability and if it is worn then the steering will feel vague and uncertain. As you go into corners and start to turn the steering wheel there will be a short delay before the car starts to turn, closely followed by a little more turning than expected.

CHECKING FOR AIR LEAKS

The best way is the old way. A bucket of soapy water and a brush. Cover the connections and air bag in soapy water and bubbles will form on any air leak.

Another sign that it is on its way out is when you get a hard knocking noise from the back when driving over ruts in the road, a bit like the noise you get when the back door is not quite shut properly.

The bushes in the link endure quite high forces, so about ten years of road use is usually when the weakest one starts to go. If you regularly tow or drive off-road then they will go a bit sooner. Because of the high force on them it is wise to only use genuine Land Rover parts, they are not very expensive and so the cost saving of using a pattern part is just not worth it. I have heard of even well regarded pattern part brand items lasting only a few months.

To fix it you first have to remove the whole link assembly. This is relatively easy, but it is vital to park the car on level ground and support the chassis before you start as the link is the only thing that stops the back axle going sideways and you do not want to be under it if it does that.

1. Jack the car up and support it on the chassis, not the axle. Letting the axle droop gives better access to the link bolts. The centre bolt on the axle is very long indeed so will need to be below the fuel tank guard to give you enough space to draw it out.

The new bag fitted with new clips. There is no point reusing the old rusty ones. I also cleaned up the chassis and axle where the bag locates.

The Watts link is ingenious, and makes the centre point of the axle stay exactly central as it rises and drops, unlike the Panhard rod on the front axle. The downside is that it has five bushes instead of two and is more prone to wear.

2. Before removing it I would check which bushes are worn (usually it is only one or two) by using a pry bar to wriggle the link about and listen for the clonk. Make sure the car is very securely supported first. There are three bolts that hold the link on: one on each side and one in the middle. The ones holding the link arms onto the chassis will be largely corroded, so it is worth cleaning up the protruding thread and giving them a good soak in penetrating oil before starting to undo them. The one on the left is obscured by the exhaust, so it can be a slow job with a couple of spanners.

3. The centre bolt that holds the link to the axle also holds on the mass-damper retaining wire, so you need to undo the nut that is in front of the axle first, slide the wire retaining washer off and then take the main nut off,

which is set at a fairly high torque so may put up a fight. Then begins the slow process of trying to wriggle the incredibly long bolt out. Make sure any rust or mud is removed from the forward threaded end before it jams in the hole.

4. With the three bolts removed the assembly should come out.

5. Now the two side links can be removed from the central link by undoing the two rusty bolts. This could be done while it is still on the car, but I found it more comfortable to do this at the work bench.

6. The bushes are press fitted, and getting the old ones out may take well over 5 tonnes equivalent force, so a hydraulic press is ideal. An alternative is to use a large bench vice and two sockets, but it has to be a vice big

This is the really long bolt from the middle, and the axle must be lowered (or the chassis raised) to allow enough room to extract it.

The two-socket method can be used on most of the bushes and bearings in the suspension. All the parts have to be exactly in line or else it will jam.

enough to take the width of the bush plus the two sockets. The idea is that a socket bigger than the bush is on one side and a socket the same size as the bush outer is placed on the other. The little socket pushes the old bush into the big socket. Then to get the new bush started I removed the big socket and used the little socket to push the new bush halfway in and then put the big socket back to finish the job. The little socket must only push against the bush outer cylinder. If it pushes against the inner part, it will ruin the bush.

This method is very fiddly, so if you can it is better to use a press or take the link to a workshop that can fit the bush for you.

7. The outer ends of the side links get road grime thrown at them from the wheels and so the paint does not stand much chance and corrosion sets in. As it is a solid bar the corrosion is usually superficial and so taking it back to bare metal and repainting it should extend its life significantly. If the rust is severe and has weakened the weld or fork end then a new link or substantial repair will be needed.

8. Once completed the refurbished link can be refitted. I put a little anti-seize grease on the bolts before refitting in case I ever have to take them out again. I put the central bolt in first, which takes most of the weight and makes it a little easier to fit the other links. What you may find at this stage is that one side link goes on easily but the other no longer lines up with the mounting hole on the chassis. This is because the car has moved sideways a little. The axle needs to be lined up centrally again: as the chassis is already well supported it should be possible to move the axle over by lifting it on a trolley jack and pushing the jack handle to one side or the other. At this stage do not fully tighten the bolts, just enough so there is no slack.

9. Next the car needs to come off the stands and settle at its normal ride height (air spring cars may need the engine to run briefly). Now with everything at the right angle the bolts can be tightened fully.

BRAKES

Often the pistons in the callipers corrode where they are exposed to the elements between the calliper seal and the

Brake calliper dust seals prevent piston corrosion. This one split a long time ago and if I had just pushed the piston back the corrosion would have ripped the inner oil seal.

> *On non-ABS cars, if one wheel locks up when braking hard then look at the brake on the opposite wheel as it is putting less braking force into the wheel than the side that locked up.*
>
> *ABS cars will compensate for the poor performance of one calliper and prevent the other wheel locking, which hides the problem. For this reason the callipers should be inspected yearly to check for seal and piston damage.*

WARNING

The air suspension system remains active for several minutes after the ignition is switched off. This means that the car could move down and potentially crush anyone working under it. Do not even think of working with your hand between the axle and the chassis unless the system is disabled.

The easiest way of disabling the system is to undo the battery. When working near the rear suspension make sure that both the chassis and the axle are supported.

pad. Cars that have been run for long periods with worn pads will have suffered the most. Light piston corrosion can be removed with fine sandpaper, but they are chrome plated and if this is damaged or flaking then the piston and calliper seals will need replacing.

The callipers have two distinct seals on each piston. An inner seal is square in section and keeps the oil in the caliper. The square section distorts when the brakes are applied and returns the piston to its normal position when the brakes are released. If oil is leaking out then this seal has failed. The outer seal is a thinner design and its function is to keep road grime out of the calliper bore. These can become gummed up and sticky, which causes the pads to constantly rub on the disc and may result in a squealing noise when the brakes are not on.

If you are only changing the pads then this is as far as you need to go on a Discovery 2. To change the disc the carrier has to come off too.

You can get stainless-steel replacement pistons, which will not corrode and will last decades. However, they are expensive and standard pistons usually last a decade anyway.

To replace the pistons or seals you first have to drive the pistons out, and this is best started while the calliper is still on the car.

1. Remove the brake pads.
2. Press the brake pedal repeatedly to push the piston(s) out. On the Discovery 2 there is one piston in each calliper, but on Discovery 1 callipers there are four at the front and two at the back. Here you will have to check that they have all come out as frequently one is a lot more sticky than the others.
3. When the piston is contacting the disc, undo the brake hose, seal the master reservoir with cling film and also seal the brake hose end. I do not use hose clamps as they can damage the hose.
4. Undo the calliper and clean the area around the piston(s).
5. Hold the calliper in a sturdy vice and work the piston(s) free. Slip-jaw pliers can be useful here, but use thick card to prevent the jaws damaging the piston surface.
6. Replace all the inner and outer seals.
7. Clean the piston. If it is pitted then replace it.
8. Lubricate the seals and piston with fresh clean brake fluid and fully insert the piston into the calliper to minimize the amount of air trapped.
9. Ensure the brake disc is clean.
10. Refit the calliper and pads.
11. Remove the cling film from the reservoir and top up the fluid.
12. Open the bleed nipple and pump some fluid through.
13. Tighten the nipple and pump the brakes to seat the pads.
14. Bleed the brakes.

It is not only braking-system faults that can cause a wheel to lock up when braking. Worn dampers allow a wheel to bounce and reduce traction dramatically. Also tyres have to be in good order for the braking system to apply force to the road, incorrect tyre pressures or hardened and perished tyres reduce traction dramatically.

ABS SHUTTLE VALVE FIX

There are two shuttle valves that push down onto a pair of switches to tell the ABS ECU when they have worked. When the ECU does not get the signal it was expecting it logs a fault and lights the ABS, TC and HDC warning lights. Sometimes this signal can be intermittent, and sometimes worse in damp conditions, so the fault can seem to come and go.

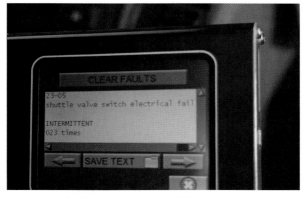

When the ABS fault light came on I checked the code with a Nanocom diagnostic tool, which showed the traditional shuttle valve fault. Without a diagnostic tool there is a danger of replacing parts unnecessarily to hunt down the fault.

Here I have got the ABS valve block upside down on the bench to test the shuttle valves by pressing them manually, but this could be done in the car without removing the ABS block if you are careful.

With the switch pack unbolted you can test it by checking the resistance between the ground and signal pins on the ABS valve block connector. Normally the resistance should be about 3k ohms until one or more switches are pushed down; if either switch is pressed you should see about 2k ohms and if both are pressed then it should read about 1k ohm.

A replacement ABS shuttle valve switch pack unit is available from Land Rover at a reasonable cost. Fitting it involves removing the three mounting rubbers from the ABS valve block, easing it up just enough to get a hex (Allen) key onto the three bolts underneath and pulling the old switch pack down. However, often the fault is a crack or dry joint in the valve block itself and so this fix will not always work.

As the shuttle valves were okay the problem had to be the internal connection in the valve block. To bypass this I first cut away some plastic and re-routed the two wires to come directly out of the switch pack.

This is the wire that goes back to the ABS ECU. I cut it near the valve block connector and spliced it into one of the switch-pack wires. As the switches are in series it does not matter which one is used.

I used a spade connector so I could unplug it if I had to remove the valve block for any reason in the future. I then wrapped the connector in self-amalgamating rubber tape to seal it.

The other wire from the switch pack needs to go to a good earth point. I used one of the existing bolts on the bulkhead but removed the paint from the metalwork. Once the connection was tight I gave the area a protective coating.

The wires from the shuttle valve switch pack can be brought out underneath the valve block to bypass the troublesome internal connection. One wire is spliced onto the yellow/green wire to the ABS ECU, and the other goes to a good earth point.

CHASSIS

If a number of chassis repairs are needed then it may prove easier and safer to fit a replacement chassis. With a few friends round to help it is possible to swap a chassis in a couple of weekends, but be prepared for several bolts to snap in the process.

The chassis twists and bends during off-road manoeuvres. It has to put up with huge forces and so any repairs must be of the highest quality. Any welds must be done professionally, so if your skills are anything other than perfect, get the professionals in.

It is interesting to note that the front sections of the chassis are usually well protected from corrosion by the many oil leaks that seem to come as standard. Often from the transfer box forward there is a thick coating of black oil, the transmission, engine, front differential and power steering system all contributing to this phenomenon.

Ironically well-maintained, leak-free cars suffer from the worst chassis rot, but on all cars the rear section suffers terribly from rust if it is not well maintained.

The rear cross member gets road grime thrown at it and mud gets trapped on the upper surface. New rear cross members are available, which can be welded in.

Typical chassis rot on the upper surface and along the seam. It can be patched but there is probably more rust hidden and it may be easier to replace the chassis.

> *Making little jigs is good practice on any area of chassis repair involving mounting points.*
>
> *This could be a bar tack-welded across the part being replaced, with pieces descending to bolt into the mounting points. These are fitted before cutting out the original part, ensuring the mounting points will be in exactly the same place after welding.*

The outriggers that support the body also have flat upper surfaces that trap wet mud. Again new repair sections are available, but before cutting out the old outrigger both the chassis and body must be well supported to stop them moving relative to each other during the process. To ensure the new item is located accurately, the body mounting can be temporarily reassembled before welding the outrigger to the chassis.

Any welding on the main chassis will burn off the protective paint on the inside and promote rust, so after any such

The rear crossmember corrodes fastest. Here a previous owner has tried to slow the rot with a little paint, and you can see the original paint is flaking off all over. This one will take a lot of work to take it back to bare metal and give it a proper paint job.

To get the Discovery 1 centre crossmember in, two jacks can make the job a lot easier, as shown on this Range Rover Classic.

Do not worry about shearing the retaining studs when removing the damper tower. They come on a ring and are still readily available, so just buy a new one before you start work.

repair the chassis should be sprayed internally with paint via a flexible nozzle or with a wax-based sealant.

Many chassis have been wax treated in their past, but one problem with this is that welding the chassis can set fire to the wax inside the chassis rails. So always have a big CO_2 fire extinguisher ready in case it gets out of hand.

Removal of the central bolt-in cross member can be made easier by securely putting a high-lift jack between the chassis rails and easing them apart very slightly. Never work under this jack as it can fall and cause serious injury.

Front damper towers rust at the top and bottom. Luckily these are simple bolt-on items, but often the mounting bolts, which are welded onto their own mounting ring, corrode too and need replacing at the same time.

Rear damper mounts are bolted in, but rust can form between the mount and chassis, weakening this critical area. Again the chassis must be repaired properly to remain strong enough for the job, but as it is a flat plate the job is not too hard.

Spring mounts have a hard life. Grime trapped where the spring meets the mount is constantly ground in, and the stress where the mount is welded to the chassis results in corrosion. This usually means that if the mount needs replacing then that area of the chassis needs repairing too. It has to be cut back to good sound metal, and then a strengthening plate welded on before the new spring mount is attached.

BODYWORK

> *Before welding bodywork ensure that all trim and wiring is removed from the area where heat and weld spatter may fall. Ensure all repairs are done to the highest standard so that the body remains strong. Just think about what happens in the event of a crash – it could be a matter of life and death.*

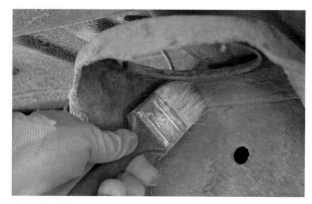

Clear away debris and inspect the spring mount carefully. There is a lot of stress where it is welded to the chassis and that accelerates rust right where it matters most.

When welding the roof remember the main wiring loom is tucked in the cant rail. Removing it is tedious as it drops down every pillar.

The bracing between the sill and the floor traps mud and corrodes if left untreated, and the underseal peels away from the joints first.

The sill trims can trap and hide rot, so it is worth unclipping them every couple of years to check and treat any issues.

Sills

The sills support the A, B and C/D pillars, holding the body together, and in a side impact they are vital for your survival. So it is rather unfortunate that they are one of the top rust traps. There are two approaches to repair. The usual method is to cut out the old sill and weld in a new piece. Ready-made repair sections are available and make the job a lot easier. The other method is to replace it with something stronger such as a heavy-gauge box-section 'jackable' sill, which if tied into the body mounting points means you can then jack the car up on the sills – a very useful technique in some off-road situations.

Front inner wings

On all models these are flat steel sheets and corrode where mud and moisture accumulates on the flat top and at the bulkhead joint. Repair panels are available although they are simple enough to fabricate from flat sheet. If the joint at the bulkhead is corroded then a sheet may be needed to repair the bulkhead before commencing on the inner wing.

Discovery 1 rear inner wings and seat belt anchors

A repair section is available, which replaces the outer part of the arch. The old arch is cut at the junction of the rear wing and at the sill, then along the arch seam. Welding near the rear wing is problematic due to the proximity of the

You can see how close to the rear arch the seat belt anchor is, so take no chances with this area. This is a good example with no evidence of corrosion or repair.

Discovery 1 inner wings and arches can be made easily from flat sheet steel, similar to this RRC, but Discovery 2 items are contoured pressings.

Peel back the carpet and most of us will find this. There is a line of corrosion above the crossmember support and all round the edge of the panel.

Also keep an eye on the rear-door-stay mounting point, which can also rot through. This one has completely disappeared and the rear panel has been crudely patched and painted.

aluminium panel – if there is insufficient bare metal available in front of the wing, then the wing must be released and held away from the join area.

These repair sections do not include the seat-belt-mounting area. This has to be a sound and solid piece of metal, so great care is needed when repairing it. Cut the surrounding metal back to full-thickness sound metal and fit a sheet of the same strength as the original to the underside of the area, so that in an accident it would have to pull through the floor to fail. Attach a replacement strengthening piece under the mounting point to spread the load as per original design.

Boot floor

Moisture collects under the matting in the boot floor, corroding it mainly around the joints. New steel floors can be welded in, and again some repair to the surrounding steel work may be needed.

The floor is joined to the chassis via two small adjustable mountings that incorporate the inner two rear seat-belt mounts. The mounting bolts that go through the belt mounts may be heavily corroded underneath where they are exposed to road grime so will need to be cleaned up and lubricated before attempting to undo them.

Extreme caution is needed while working in this area with grinding or cutting tools as the fuel tank is directly below.

Replacing door skins

The door skins are aluminium alloy and are crimped and glued onto a steel frame. Small holes and dents can be readily filled, but if the bottom half of the door is completely rotten then it is far easier to fit a new skin.

For best results remove the door first. It can be done in situ, but the edge near the hinges always seems to go a bit wrong.

1. Remove the outer weather strip, door card and the outer door handle.
2. To remove the old skin, trim the edges off with a grinder. Try not to cut into the door frame – you will know when you hit the steel frame with the grinder because steel generates sparks; aluminium does not.
3. Clean up the frame, removing all the old sealant and glue. What you will probably find is that some sections of the frame have rusted through and must be repaired before going any further. Ensure all the paintwork on the frame is in good order. Any exposed steel will start corrosion off as soon as the aluminium skin touches it.
4. Apply a bead of sealant all round the frame edge where the door skin gets crimped on, both sides and about 4mm thick.
5. Apply sound-deadening strips to the new door skin, otherwise it will boom like a drum.
6. Put some soft matting on the bench or flat floor. Put the new skin on the mat and lower the door, with the help of an assistant, to the skin so you can get to the flange. Alternatively, have the frame sat on a pedestal allowing access all round and lower the skin onto it.
7. Crimp the edge on all round. Do not use pliers directly or you will mark the outer surface, the aluminium is thin enough that most of it can be done by hand. Tricky bits can be done with tools, but make sure you have some soft spreaders in place, such as small bits of soft wood or plastic.
8. Now paint the skin and let it dry.
9. Finally put all the furniture back on the door and refit it to the car.

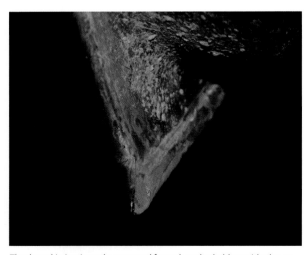

The door skin is crimped over a steel frame but also held on with glue, so be careful not to bend the frame when removing the old skin.

The front wing is bolted on, but there is also sealant, which seems to glue it on. The bolts are on the top, front and rear edges.

Wing bolts hide in the front door gap. Remove the front door to make life easier.

Front wing

The front wings are simply bolted on, but there is sealant on the A pillar joint to prevent galvanic corrosion. So when you remove the old wing it will need a good pull to get it off here, then clean all the old sealant off, fix any paint issues and allow to dry, then put a bead of sealant down before bolting the new wing on.

Top of the A pillar

If the rust has broken through here then it will need welding. This is the primary load area if the car rolls over, and if it is weak then it could just fold in and offer the occupants no protection.

Start by removing all the trim and headlining. Discovery 2 cars have an A-pillar finisher on the outside, secured by plastic plugs that can be released by pushing the centre in. You should also really remove the windscreen. Then grind out all the rot and make sure you have a good area of clean metal to weld onto.

Replacement A pillars are available but may be difficult or expensive to get hold of in some countries. If only the top of the pillar has gone then it can be fixed by fabricating a small steel collar from the same grade and thickness steel as the A pillar.

If the roof has rotted where the pillar attaches then grind the area back and weld in a strengthening plate to the underside of the roof so the pillar has something to attach to.

If it seems likely the joint will have to be completely cut through, then jig the pillar into position first so it is unable to move. This can be done by tack-welding a steel brace between the A and B pillars, but remove the B-pillar trim and seat belt first.

Door mirror glass, Discovery 2

The door mirror glass can become detached if the unit is struck. The glass clips onto the adjuster unit, but the clip part of the adjuster can become weak and snap off, leaving the glass dangling on the heater wires. The best solution is to buy a new clip (STC4625), which is a press fit. Getting the old clip off the adjuster unit is made easier if you carefully snap it so it releases its grip. If you need a temporary fix then another method is to use two self-tapping screws with spring washers screwed into the clip to form a new locating point. It is fiddly but the mirror can be guided onto the washers and the large clip on the outer edge engaged.

The top of the A pillar is a prime rust spot. This is my Discovery 2 with the windscreen removed. All the trim and filler just seems to trap moisture and make it worse.

This plastic frame is available as a spare, part number STC4625. Fit it to the mirror by squeezing it up a bit, then simply push the mirror and frame onto the circular adjuster.

These bolts hold the window lift mechanism to the door. If you are removing it then wind the window down first so you have room to manoeuvre the glass out.

Window lift

Symptoms include the window jamming and twisting in the frame, suddenly dropping into the door or failing to come up.

This may occur for a number of different reasons. On Discovery 1 cars as the mechanism wears and becomes a little looser the plastic guide blocks inside the sliders in the door can be pushed just slightly too far and fall out of the guide rails. The initial solution is to remove the door card and pop the blocks back into place, then adjust the mechanism to prevent it happening again. If it is too far gone for adjustment then a new mechanism is needed, but beware buying second-hand because although there are many bargains there are also similarly worn items for sale.

The C channel that holds the door glass in the lift mechanism has a tendency to rust and lose grip of the glass. Often the window will still go up and down but may make a crunching sound and may drop in a jerky or sudden way.

It is possible to fit a new C channel to the glass, but it is very difficult to get the right clamping load to make a durable repair, so it is often easier to fit a good second-hand window with the grip already attached. Just make sure you inspect it before handing over the cash.

Fitting the glass requires the removal of the door card and the window frame. When refitting the frame after the

The thin window frame is easily pushed in or out. To set it, loosen the securing bolt just enough to allow the frame to move when pushed. It should compress the door seal enough to stop wind noise.

Here the plastic guide from the lift mechanism has failed and fallen off, allowing the pin to drop out of the rail and let the glass drop in the door.

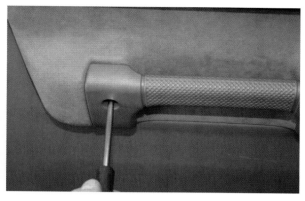

ABOVE: This is what the lift mechanism should look like, with a nicely greased plastic guide seated in the rail.

TOP RIGHT: To get the door card off first unscrew the handle. On Discovery 1 cars the handle will then come off; on Discovery 2 cars it remains bonded to the card.

RIGHT: There is a retaining screw hidden in the door-release-lever cowl. Pull the leaver out to gain access.

glass has been inserted the frame must be adjusted to fit snugly against the door seal to avoid gaps and increased road noise. This can be a bit tricky, but a fairly simple method is to bolt the frame in loosely then close the door to get a rough starting point, then open the door and adjust the frame inward very slightly. Tighten the bolts and recheck.

Loose rear-window washer jet

This is usually caused by one of the plastic locating lugs breaking. Fitting a new one is just a matter of pressing it in, but before removing the old unit secure the water tube – if it falls back into the car then the rear interior trim has to be removed to get it out. Gently pull the old unit away then tape the tube to the car before removing the tube from the washer jet. The part number is PRC6496. Fit it by twisting 90 degrees.

Windscreen

On Discovery 1 cars the windscreen is held in by a traditional rubber strip. To remove it:

1. Start by pulling the trim strip out of the seal to release its grip.
2. Ease the old screen out, but chances are that due to its age it will have partially bonded to the rubber. So carefully feed a long length of fine wire through the seal and use it like a cheese cutter to separate the screen from the seal.

If the seal has not been replaced in the last ten years then it is likely to have become hard and prone to cracks. In this case it would be better to replace the seal with a new item.

The rear-window washer jet seems to get knocked quite easily and break one of its mounting lugs. Replacements are cheap and simply push in.

The Discovery 1 windscreen seal is rubber and perishes just like all rubber parts. Cracks not only reduce the security of the screen but also let water into the bodywork and accelerate corrosion.

The 300-style cars had more trim around the seals. These distort when removed and never quite go back properly. So if you have to remove them, buy replacements first.

If the seal is still supple enough then ease the screen out. I use the old-fashioned foot method:

1. First run a few strips of sticky tape over the screen just in case it breaks, and put a large cloth on the dash to catch any broken glass should the worst happen. Drape a large blanket over the screen to stop it falling flat on the bonnet and breaking.
2. Sit in the driver's seat and have an assistant sit in the passenger seat. Wear goggles just in case! Then put your feet up against the screen and push from the top corner first and work round the screen until it pops out.
3. Clean up the old seal or fit a new one.
4. Lay a feed wire or strong cord in the seal.

5. Fit the screen and use the wire or cord to pull the seal lip over the edge of the screen.
6. Fit the trim strip.

On Discovery 2 cars it is a lot more difficult, as the screen is bonded in and contributes to the car's structural strength.

1. To get at it you have to remove the upper trim strip, side trims, front gutter corner pieces, rain guard and wipers.
2. Cut the glue with thin high-tensile wire.
3. Clean up the metalwork thoroughly, then touch up any rust and let the paint dry completely.
4. Clean the new screen thoroughly.

The sides of the bulkhead trap leaves and moisture and so tend to rot. Early treatment will prevent costly repairs later.

My Discovery 2 with the windscreen out. I removed the bonnet so I could remove the lower panel.

The Discovery 2 windscreen is bonded on to increase body strength. To locate it while the glue sets there are orange blocks at each side. This screen has thick wires for the heated front screen option.

5. Apply the correct glue to the car and make sure it has the correct thickness all the way round. Ask the screen supplier for details.
6. Drop the lower edge of the screen onto the orange plastic spacers first, and then ease the top edge into place.
7. Fit the trim, but be very careful not to push the screen off the little spacers, otherwise it will break the bond and never seal properly, leading to high wind noise and leaks.
8. Wait for the sealant to cure before driving.

Rear seat hinge failure, Discovery 1

One of the more common failures is the rear seat-back hinges on Discovery 1s coming undone. The hinge is made with a domed-head hex-drive bolt and a small collar, which allows one part of the hinge to rotate freely about the other. After many years of service the bolts work loose and fall out, but it is quite simple to replace them and return the seat to service. If the fixings have vanished then you will need a domed head bolt and a steel sleeve so that the bolt head does not press hard against the seat-back bracket and it can move freely.

Sagging headlining

The fabric is glued to a fibrous backing and over time the glue gives way, leading to a tent-like effect.

Usually the fibres in the backing are also loose and so attempting to stick it back on is tricky. A temporary fix is to use spray glue applied with a straw poked through small holes cut in the fabric. Inevitably this fails as the fibres that the glue holds on to fall out. The only real repair is to remove the headlining, peel back the whole fabric, clean off the loose fibres and apply a liquid glue that will soak into the backing. Once this is almost dry, but still tacky enough to hold the fabric, with the help of an assistant lay the fabric over the backing and press it into position. Put some old pillows and blankets on with books or suitable weights on them to compress the assembly evenly.

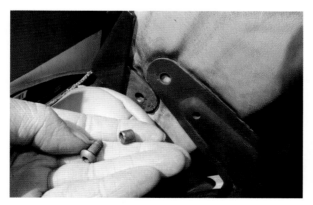

The rear seat hinge bolts tend to undo themselves and fall out. When fitting a new one ensure the spacer sleeve is present, or the hinge will lock solid, and use thread-lock on the bolt.

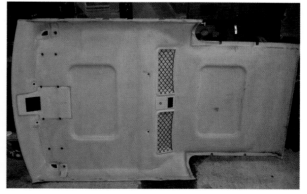

The headlining is a single piece, which is as wide as the car. Getting it out requires the seats on one side to be laid flat so the headlining can be withdrawn at an angle through the back door.

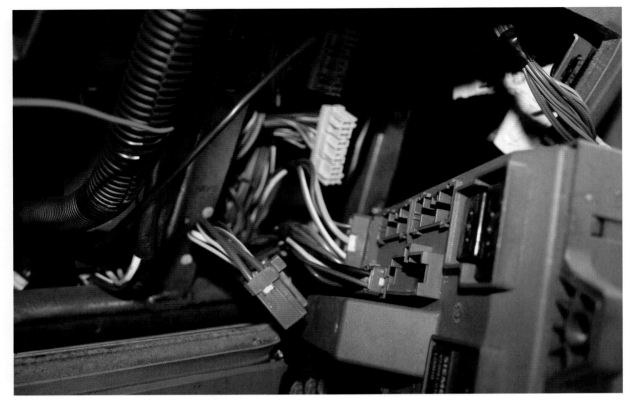

Connections are the number one cause of electrical faults. Fuse boxes under the dash are prone to corrosion if the screen seal lets in water.

Do not put the fabric on wet glue or it could soak through, making unsightly marks and potentially gluing your old pillows to your headlining – not a great effect.

As you can imagine, it is usually easier to get hold of a replacement headlining.

ELECTRICS

TRACING FAULTS

If the fault is intermittent, try to identify what else is happening when the fault occurs. For example, is it when something else is switched on/off, when you go over a bump or when turning left? This indicates where to start looking for the fault.

Intermittent faults are frequently associated with a connector that is loose or corroded. In fact it turns out that joints and connectors are the single most common cause of electrical faults. The pins in a connector should be bright shiny metal. If they are tarnished and very dark, or if they have a white powdery surface, then they must be cleaned up or replaced. Most connectors are plated in some way, so scraping them will risk damaging the coating, so it is best to be gentle and use spray-on 'contact cleaner' and a stiff, fine-haired brush. Often simply unplugging and reconnecting will clean the connector enough for it to work for a short time, and while it is not a permanent fix it can be helpful in letting you know where the problem lies.

There are two main problems with old electrics: first is that all the connectors age; second is that most cars have suffered at the hands of a keen but unskilled amateur and have a bird's nest of added wires.

Some people 'get by' without fully understanding the system, just trying things out almost at random until the problem seems to go away. This is a potentially disastrous method. First, you do not know what the fault's root cause was, so you don't know if it has been fixed or just temporarily masked, ready to pounce on you later with even more venom. Second, you would not know if you have stressed some other circuit, storing up more problems for later on. So you have to understand how the circuit works first before you can work out how to fix it.

Connections

Never make a 12V feed by splicing in a link to another wire nearby that has 12V on it. This will increase the load on the second circuit, causing fuses to blow.

Never bridge a fuse, because if they keep blowing then it may be due to an intermittent short where the loom has chafed going through the bulkhead. The fuse prevents burnt-out wires.

Splicing wires together can be one of the top reasons for electrical faults on an old car. First of all, just twisting wires together and wrapping them in sticky tape is a recipe for disaster. Cars vibrate and go through extremes of heat and cold, and engine bays get to enjoy an atmosphere of fuel and oil vapours too. Not only will twisted wires loosen but sticky tape will go soft, gooey and unwrap.

When fitting a connector like this the first step is to make a solid mechanical connection. One pair of tags crimp the conductor part of the cable, making the electrical connection, while the other pair of tags crimp the insulation to hold the cable in place.

Using the right type of tool for the specific type of terminal is very important if the connection is to be formed properly.

A good connection needs to start with a solid mechanical join, such as a good quality crimp. The mechanical joint should be strong enough that the wire cannot be tugged out. The crimp must have two stages, an inner crimp onto the bare wires to make the electrical connection, and an outer crimp onto the cable's insulation, which takes any mechanical strain away from the conductor. Getting the right crimping force is very important: too much and the wire strands will be pinched out and break, too little and they will work loose. For this reason professionals use a ratchet crimp tool that automatically applies the right force. The alternative is to use the cheap crimp pliers and practise on scrap wire until you can get it right consistently.

Soldering is another option, but as well as being a little more tricky it can result in a concentration of stress at the edges of the soldered joint, leading to fractures in later life. That is why F1 cars do not use soldered joints. If you do use solder then the finished joint must be wrapped with amalgamating tape or heat-shrink tube in order to take the vibration and stresses.

Once the mechanical joint is made it must be insulated, to prevent anything shorting out, to prevent moisture corroding the joint and to give the wires some strain relief. As mentioned above, a good solution is to slip a tube of heat-shrink plastic over the joint, which when heated with a hot-air gun shrinks and seals the connection. You can even buy crimps that have integral heat-shrink insulation plus a resin that melts through the whole joint, making a very durable connection. Another very effective method is to use self-amalgamating rubber tape. It looks like insulating tape but is not sticky. Instead it is stretched and wrapped round the joint and over a minute or so it flows into itself forming a single homogeneous, waterproof seal. It is brilliant stuff and has loads of other uses round the car, from making grommets to fixing small air leaks – every tool box should have a roll.

Sticky-backed PVC electrical insulation tape will not survive in a car for any length of time; the glue just gives up in the harsh conditions. However, PVC does have its uses. Ordinary non-sticky PVC tape, sometimes known as loom wrap, can be wound round a wiring loom to hold all the wires together neatly and offer protection against chafing. Start by threading the end of the tape into the loom then winding over it, then wind in a spiral up the loom, overlapping by about half the tape width as you go. To stop it unravelling, the final winding must be tied off by threading through the loom and tying in a knot. To finish it neatly the ends can be dressed in self-amalgamating tape or heat shrink.

Main fuse box repair on Discovery 2

1. Start by ensuring the car is in an unlocked state and not immobilized. Then disconnect the battery.
2. Open the lower dash panel by undoing the two twist locks. The fuse box is nearest the side of the car.
3. Undo the connectors on the front side. All the connectors have one tab on the side, which you press in to release, but they will still take a bit of wiggling to get out.
4. Undo the securing nut at the top of the fuse box.
5. Gently ease the fuse box forward. It is located at the bottom by a plastic peg and lifts out, but there is not much space to manoeuvre in there.
6. Remove the plugs on the back of the unit. I found it easiest to remove them from the side nearest the steering column first, then ease the fuse box out a little more and turn it so I could get at the other connectors

Here I have finished the terminal with self-amalgamating rubber tape to form a weatherproof seal. If moisture can get to the end of the wire it will tarnish the conductor and gradually work up the wire from the inside.

ABOVE: *On the Discovery 2 the fuse box under the dash is an 'Intelligent Driver Module' (IDM), which communicates with the Body Control Module (BCM) via a data link. If you replace it, leave the ignition on for five minutes to re-synchronize the IDM and BCM.*

LEFT: *If the screen has been leaking then the contacts inside the IDM will have corroded. This unit controls all the body electrics such as windows, locks and lights. Cleaning up the contacts can revive a failing unit.*

more easily. The connectors are keyed so you cannot get them in the wrong hole, but it is worth noting their positions so that you do not end up trying to fit the wrong one unsuccessfully later.

7. Now the fuse box should come out.
8. On a workbench, release the plastic tabs all round the casing simultaneously. This is near impossible, but I found I could do one corner by inserting flat-blade screwdrivers all along one side and under one tab at the end. I repeated this on the other side and it came free.
9. Lift off the rear cover. If there is any corrosion, gently remove it and resolder any defective joints. Then reseal the circuit board with electrical lacquer.

10. Put it all back together, remembering to connect the plugs closest to the side of the car first.

Key fob antenna unit, Discovery 2

1a. On cars with a rear sunroof pull the sunroof trim out of the headlining, also pop the sunroof switch out so you can undo the screw that holds the switch panel up. This screw is not mentioned in some workshop manuals.
1b. On other cars, remove the rear trim including third-row headrests if fitted, rear pillar trims and the rear interior light.
2. Then pull down the headlining just enough so you can

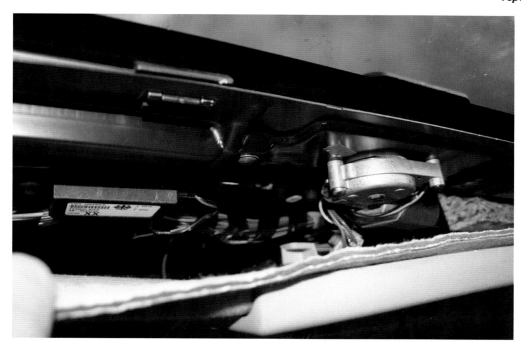

On a Discovery 2 the radio receiver for the remote key fob is in the roof, just in front of the rear sunroof. You have to pull the headlining down a bit to get at it.

What they don't tell you in the manual is that there is a screw behind the rear sunroof switch that needs to be removed to get access to the key fob receiver.

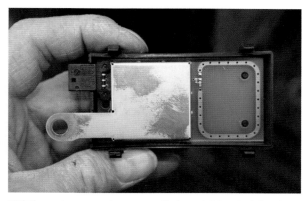

With the receiver removed you can see the large stainless steel plate that forms the vital earth point. Corrosion between this and the roof stops it working. The loop on the circuit board is the actual aerial.

reach the radio unit that is bolted to the roof just in front of the rear sunroof area.

3. Disconnect the multi-plug.

4. Undo the two small bolts holding it to the roof.

5a. The unit usually goes wrong because of water from a leaky sunroof corroding the circuit. If you have caught it early enough then you can open the case and gently remove any corrosion with an anti-static stiff brush, such as a glass-fibre one available from electrical component shops. Once dry and clean, resolder any failed connections. Then the board must be sealed again.

5b. If the board is too far gone then fit a replacement second-hand unit. There is no programming involved so just plug it in, but first check the circuit board for corrosion to make sure it was not taken from a car with a similar problem.

6. Another common fault is the earth connection tarnishing. There is a small eyelet with a black wire that provides the earth from the vehicle. The earth connection on the unit is a stainless steel tab on one of the bolt holes. Both of these can tarnish, becoming black

over time and reducing earth quality, which ruins radio-code reception from the key fob. Cleaning the earth tabs can be done with some cardboard that has a squirt of WD40 on it and a lot of rubbing.

Snapped key (replacing the key blade)

Discovery 1 keys can be copied and cut by any reputable high street key shop as they are separate from the alarm system electronics.

Discovery 2 keys can also be cut at high street shops, but the blanks are less common and you may have to buy one from a specialist or a well-known internet auction site first. The blade has a small black plastic moulding at the end that clicks into the fob. To get the old one out you have to twist it to one side.

On the internet there are several companies that will supply a pre-cut key, for any model, for you if you supply them with a photograph of your old key blade. They will read the actual key code from your picture and cut a key to that code rather than making a simple mechanical copy,

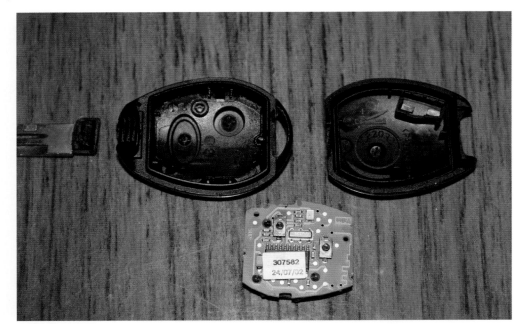

Replacement keys need to be programmed to the BCM using the code written on the circuit board. The original keys were made by Valeo and were the same circuit as on some Rovers such as the 75.

which is far more reliable and avoids the problem of copied keys not working quite as well as the original.

Discovery 2 auxiliary driving light control module

This optional device usually fails after about ten years. The relay overheats inside the sealed unit and is almost impossible to extract.

One alternative is to rig up a new relay circuit. To do this you also need to change the type of switch in the dash because the existing one is only a momentary action switch, meaning it only closes its contacts while you are pushing it. On the original control unit this momentary action sets an electronic latch. Pressing the button again resets the latch and when you turn off the ignition it also resets the latch, the idea being that you could not forget to turn them off when you park up.

I used a spare cruise-control switch and swapped the switch covers over so it had the right graphic on for the driving lights. But it is not quite that simple, as the other dash switches have different internal wiring. For instance the cruise-control switch has a common earth for the illumination and the telltale light on pin 5, but on the original spot lamp switch it is on pin 4. Heated rear window switches have a common 12V feed on pin 4 for both lamps and the switch, so the solution depends on which type of switch you use. If you struggle to find a switch second-hand, the same type of switch is still used today (at time of writing) in the Puma Defender as its heated seat switch with the same connections as the Discovery 2 cruise-control switch.

As I was using a cruise-control switch I carefully released the connector and swapped pins 4 and 5 over, by using a small jeweller's screwdriver to push the locking tab in.

The optional auxiliary light unit is filled with resin to form a solid block, so when the relay fails it is useless. Alternative units can be made from relays.

The original auxiliary light switch is momentary action, so if converting to a relay control then an alternative switch body is needed. The switch cap is a clip-on item and can be swapped over.

Working in the engine bay, first release the control module by undoing the two bolts that hold it to the fuse box. You can see the extra fuse attached to the control unit, so remove this for safety while you work on the circuit. Cut the wires to the control unit as close to the connector as possible to give you the most wire to work with, and discard the control unit.

The small red wire that goes up to the switch (pin 1) needs to have a positive feed from the Blue/Orange wire, which is the high beam circuit. So splice those two together and seal the joint.

The small blue wire that comes back from the switch needs to go to one side of the relay coil, so attach a crimp and fit it to the relay pin 86.

The other side of the relay coil needs to be connected to earth, as do the driving lights. I connected the two black earth wires from the lights to the black earth wire that goes to the body and put them all into a crimp onto the relay pin 85.

The two power feeds to the driving lamps need to be spliced together in a crimp and fitted to pin 87 of the relay.

Finally the power feed into pin 30 of the relay is the big red wire from the fuse.

Now pop the fuse back in and it should all work, with the lights on main beam and the ignition on, the driving lights should now also come on.

This is not quite the same functionality as the original as the driving lights would come on when you flash main beam with the ignition off too, and the telltale light in the switch only works when you are on main beam.

A simplification is to do away with the switch and use the main-beam wire to power the relay coil instead, that way the driving lights always come on with main beam.

Discovery 1 (200 style) heater fan switch burns out

The fan speed switch suffers from weak contacts, which overheat and burn out. Sadly the switch is part of the heating unit and does not really lend itself to replacement so I fitted a non-standard switch instead.

First I removed the front panel. Then I could see and remove the wires from the burnt-out switch. There is a power feed and three output wires with resistors of different values to give different fan speeds.

The new switch has to be able to cope with the full current that the fan motor can draw, a small neat switch will just burn out.

The 200-style cars had a tendency to burn out the interior fan switch. The wires for this can be brought out and an alternative changeover switch fitted. As it takes the full fan current the switch has to be a high-power item.

Discovery 1 fusible link replacement

The 200-style Discoverys had a number of fusible links built into the positive feed wires from the battery, and these often corroded and failed. Although it is possible to replace them by crimping in new fuse wires of the correct rating, it is arguably easier to replace them with a fuse box.

The box can be attached to the inner wing just behind the battery. Suitable fuses are made by companies such as LittleFuse or MegaFuse. Check your wiring diagram for more details on your model. Do not try to save time and space by joining two or more circuits to one fuse. You need a separate fuse for each fusible link wire you are replacing.

Alternator

The alternator is rebuildable. Kits are available to replace the bearings and brushes, and you can even get new windings. The back of the unit houses the regulator electronics, but take care when undoing the connection nuts as they can snap or make the studs rotate and snap the connection wire.

The main body is held together with three long bolts, which may need a bit of soaking in penetrating oil to free off.

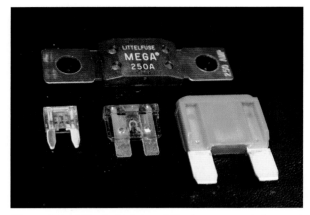

When replacing failing fusible links on 200-style cars, use equivalent-rated fuses. Littlefuse make a range of bolt-on high-value fuses from 50 to 500A. The large spade fuse on the right is available up to 100A. Traditional car fuses like the blue one only go up to 40A.

There are several different variations on the basic unit, so be very careful to order the right parts for your unit. Read the full part number on the casing first.

Of course it is often cheaper and easier to simply buy a good second-hand unit instead, but avoid ones covered in mud as this accelerates bearing and brush wear.

Alternators are available in a variety of specifications. Before ordering parts remove the faulty one and read the full part number.

The Discovery has the potential to be almost anything you want. Its shape suits larger tyres and modest lifts, a snorkel allows the engine to run under water. But modifications do not have to be simply practical; aesthetics also count. Note how the clear indicators make the front look cleaner.

9

improvements

The Discovery is already a very good car, but sometimes a few subtle modifications can make it work that little bit better.

WHEELS AND TYRES

Tyres

The most important component on any car is the tyres. They are the only parts that link the car to the ground and fitting the right tyre can make all the difference.

Most Discovery owners will spend most of their time driving on roads, with the occasional trip onto mild off-road terrain. For this application there are very good performance tyres such as the Pirelli Scorpion S/T or Yoko Geolandar AT, which handle well on the road but are still absolutely fine for green laning and useful on snow and ice-covered winter roads.

Chunky off-road tyres can be very vague on road and lead to snaking under braking. These are best avoided if your main use is on road or towing a heavy trailer. Also the chunkier the tread the worse the fuel consumption.

There are different tyres for summer and winter use, and in many countries swapping to winter tyres when the cold weather starts is compulsory. Winter tyres have a softer compound and have lots of small deep blocks with extra

---

WARNING

I hope it is obvious that any modifications should only be undertaken by competent mechanics, and even though many of us have had years of experience tinkering with cars, this does not equate to proper qualifications.

When it comes to tyres the choice is endless. Tyres are the most important component on the car. They have the most profound effect on handling and safety, so choose the right one for how you use the car.

tiny grooves in them so they can even get some grip on ice. Winter tyres do not work quite so well in summer. On a hot day they do not grip as well and also they wear down faster than a summer tyre, so it is worth having a second set of wheels for the winter tyres and change over as the seasons pass.

Low-profile tyres on big wheels do not work so well on these cars. They cause the axles to be jolted about on the more uneven back roads, which makes the steering feel nervous and twitchy. The standard-profile tyres offer a far

Tyres like the Pirelli Scorpion ST have a good general-purpose tread that works equally well on snow or warm dry tarmac. The downside is that the narrow channels between tread blocks will get clogged on deep mud or heavy snow.

more relaxed drive. Off-road they are less flexible and do not offer the same traction as a higher-profile tyre.

For muddy tracks there are two scenarios. One is a few inches of mud with gravel or rock underneath, and here it may be best to use narrow tyres that will sink through the mud and get a good grip on the solid ground underneath. The other scenario is where there is no solid ground underneath, at least not within reach of the tyres anyway, and here you need a wide tyre that will 'float' on top of the mud with big lugs to dig in and give traction. Consideration must be given to the area you are driving through. If it is a green lane then you should not be doing any damage to the track, so having a tyre that cuts the ground up is a definite no.

The tyre carcass makes a big difference too; a softer one allows the tread area to flex over the lumps and bumps on the ground giving more traction, but it is also more susceptible to punctures and on long expeditions the drop in fuel economy can be a problem.

One of the problems with mud is that it sticks between the tread blocks and effectively renders the tread smooth, so tyres designed for mud have deep channels radiating out from the centre of the tread in a chevron pattern so that as the tyre moves forwards the mud is pushed out sideways. On sand a mud tyre would simply cut down too deep, so a close tread pattern similar to road tyres is much better. Gravel tyres are designed with channels about the width of the gravel pieces so they are gripped between the small flexible tread blocks, but on mud these would just clog instantly and even wet grass can send them sliding.

Standard tyres have a total diameter of about 29in. Minor body modifications were needed to fit these 33in tyres. Larger tyres than that would require significant bodywork modifications.

Some tyres have a mixture of tread types with a denser central band of blocks for road and sand, with wider spacing towards the tyre edge to cope with softer ground. Many 4×4 tyres have lugs that extend past the sidewall so that if the tyre does sink then these more aggressive chunks will get a grip.

Very deep-tread blocks and softer rubber on the most aggressive off-road tyres make the tread unstable on the road, leading to reduced braking performance and lower grip when cornering, as well as increased wear and a loud droning noise at speed. Broader tread blocks are more stable and last longer but would slide on gravel. So with all these different aspects of tyre design there is not one universally good tyre. If the car is to be used in a range of terrains then it may be worth having a spare set of wheels with different tyres on. For example, mud tyres for play days and road-biased tyres for everyday use.

Often on an older car, where annual mileages are limited, the tread will outlast the casing. Six years should be considered too old for any tyre, no matter what it looks like on the outside. Just because it still holds air does not necessarily mean it is in good condition. Those little hairline cracks can run very deep and you never know when one will develop into a complete puncture. Tyres can stay up on project cars for many decades, but a perished tyre can blow out suddenly when the car is taken up to speed, or when cornering, so it is a dangerous game of roulette, and not a game to be played on public roads.

Just because a tyre has good tread depth does not mean it is in good condition. This tyre is heavily cracked and would likely disintegrate if driven at speed.

Tyre markings Taking a 235/80R16 99S tyre as an example:

'235' – section width of the tyre carcass in millimetres, usually slightly wider than the tread, to the nearest 5mm.

'80' – the sidewalls measure 80 per cent of the section width.

'R' – radial layout of the cords.

'16' – wheel diameter in inches.

'99' – static (car parked) load index. This one is 775kg.

'S' – the actual maximum speed rating, 113mph here.

Since 2000 there will also be a date code such as '3514', which means the tyre was made in the 35th week of 2014.

The pressure rating is a maximum and not necessarily the pressure you should run at.

Traction, temperature performance and wear rates are also given a relative code, but actual performance depends on use.

The alternative notation has this in inches instead – a 750/16 has a width of 7.5 inches on a 16-inch wheel. Yet another variation might be 37x12.5R16, 37 inches total diameter by 12.5 inches wide.

Fitting bigger tyres means that they are closer to the car's bodywork and suspension parts, and the first problem that most people encounter is at the front axle when turning tight corners where the wide tyre hits the front radius arm. Big aggressive tyres with large tread lugs can even jam against the arm and lock the wheel up, so it is important to wind the lock stop adjustment bolt on the axle out so that the tyre cannot foul the radius arm. Obviously this reduces the manoeuvrability, extending the turning radius, so you have to weigh up the advantages of big tyres against the loss of manoeuvrability.

Wheels

Do not think that for hard off-road use you will necessarily need to buy new wheels. Land Rover design and test their wheels under very harsh conditions. However, sometimes it can be beneficial to swap the standard wheels. Some people have a cheaper set of wheels for use in the winter with 'Mud & Snow' or winter tyres, thus keeping their nicer wheels looking good for the summer. Some people swap their wheels to a different size in order to be able to use more commonly available tyre sizes, which are usually cheaper too.

The Discovery 2 and P38 Range Rover use a smaller bolt pitch circle diameter (PCD) pattern compared to the Series 1 Discovery and Classic Range Rover, so be careful if you just search for 'Discovery wheel'. There are adaptors available, but good ones are expensive and cheap ones are dangerous.

Land Rover offered wheels up to 18 inches for these cars, but there are a huge variety of aftermarket wheels up to a quite-remarkable 24 inches. Beware of uncertified cheap

When I fit larger tyres I run the suspension through its full travel to ensure the tyres do not catch on the bodywork under any circumstances. Here I am creating an 'axle twister' before turning the steering through its full travel.

On the left a standard Discovery 2 18in wheel and tyre, in the middle a Range Rover Sport 19in wheel and lower-profile tyre with standard overall diameter, on the right an aftermarket steel wheel and larger tyre. All fit a Discovery 2.

wheels, which could break up at high speed or in high-load situations. Any quality wheel will have the manufacturer's mark and the date when it was made either stamped or cast into the metal. If a wheel has no markings, ask yourself this: why would any proud manufacturer not put their name to their product, what are they trying to hide? The mark is usually in the hub area or on the inside of one of the spokes.

There are some voluntary tests manufacturers can put their wheels through. There is a Japanese test that all OEM wheels go through, and the mark looks a bit like 'JWL'.

The other markings it should have are the size and rim style. Taking 7J17 as an example, the 7 means that the wheel is 7 inches wide between the tyre bead seats, the J refers to the shape of the bead seat, and the 17 means the wheel is 17 inches in diameter at the bead seat. All these dimensions must match the tyre's specification, including the letter.

Obviously the wheel has to sit centrally on the hub, otherwise we would have a very bumpy ride. There are two main ways that car manufacturers do this. One is to use the hub centre to locate the middle of the wheel, which is 'hub centric', and the other is to use the nuts to do the job, which is 'bolt centric'. Discovery alloys are hub centric. There are other wheels that will physically fit but have larger hub dimensions, and these would require a collar to fit onto the hub to adapt it to the new wheel.

The wheel can be designed to put the tyre more inboard or outboard from the car; this offset has a big effect on handling. Having wheels poking out of the arches may look good, but the force pushing the tyre backwards, caused by a pothole for instance, makes the wheel turn outwards. In bad cases this can rip the steering wheel out of the driver's hand and cause the car to swerve off the road.

Changing the offset by one centimetre makes a difference to how the steering fights back, so it is crucial to get wheels with the right offset.

There is more to nut design than meets the eye. Steel wheels usually use nuts or bolts with a tapered shoulder, so that they naturally tend to centralize in the hole. Most, but not all, alloy wheels use sleeve nuts or bolts that have flat shoulders and a cylindrical part that fits inside the hole.

The two are not interchangeable and put their force into the wheel at very different angles. Using the wrong ones may crack the wheel, so make sure you get the right nuts for your new wheels.

Wheel nuts from left to right: a Range Rover Classic/Discovery 1 alloy (27mm socket), a Discovery 2 alloy (22mm socket), a Discovery 2 steel wheel (19mm socket). Locking wheel nuts shown in the centre

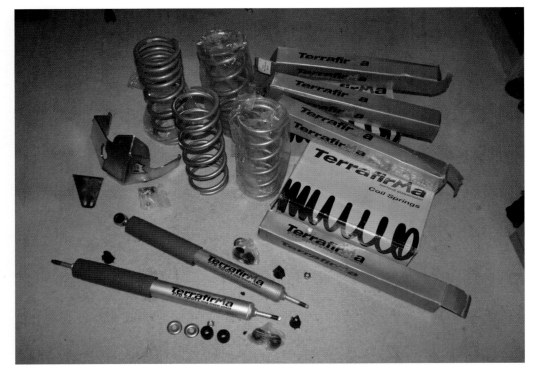

Any good suspension kit should have a matched set of springs and dampers. If you lift the ride height, you must use longer dampers and extend the brake hoses.

SUSPENSION

Talk to any ten enthusiasts about Land Rover suspension and you will get ten different opinions of what works and what is just plain rubbish. It is one of those areas where there seems to be a lot more opinion than fact.

Off-road bias

On very rough ground the standard car can end up with one or two wheels in the air, either because the suspension is unable to move far enough down or because the car has grounded out, and a wheel in the air obviously has no traction.

Here is one of my Discovery 1 cars showing that a completely standard car is still very capable – wet leaves on slippery mud on a ridged gully. So consider carefully what modifications you actually need, as it is easy to ruin a good car.

When this happens the standard differentials conspire against you by allowing the free wheel to spin, and so no drive goes to the other wheel that is still on the ground. This is where a locking or limited-slip differential comes in handy, ensuring at least some drive goes to the wheel with traction. This relieves some of the burden on the suspension when on dry ground, but on slippery surfaces you need all the tyre contact area you can get.

Big-travel suspension systems can help maintain the tyre's contact patch and significantly improve traction, but a raised car is less stable on corners. Off-road this means that side slopes become much more of a problem, but more importantly on-road emergency manoeuvres can become significantly less safe. So there is an optimum design, which depends on the intended use of the car.

As well as longer springs there are some other tricks to consider. One popular modification is to allow the springs to dislocate from their seats, so the weight of the axle and wheel makes it drop to the ground, but as the only weight pushing the tyre into the ground is half the axle and a wheel there is significantly less traction available than from the other wheel on the same axle. So again some form of slip limiting in the differential can help, or just drive gently so as to not ask too much from it. When the wheel comes back up there needs to be some sort of relocation device to make the spring sit back in the right place, usually steel cones or spikes.

Another thing that limits wheel droop is the suspension linkages and in particular the bushes, which can only bend so far before binding up and so restricting movement. One way round this is to replace the bushed links with links that have spherical-type joints in them and mount to dedicated mounting plates. Large articulation also needs modified propshafts to cope with the extreme angles.

Road bias

Of course not every Land Rover is modified for ultimate off-road capability. Many spend most of their lives on the road, often towing large trailers. The on-road handling can be improved without totally ruining the off-road ability. It won't be great off-road, but it won't be bad either.

The methods are almost the complete opposite of the ones mentioned above. The first step is the tyres, and good road tyres cost money.

After that we are looking at reducing unnecessary play in the suspension system; a good starting point is the bushes. Replacing old rubber bushes with good quality new rubber makes a big difference. After all these cars did not handle too badly when they were new, and restoring them to that condition really is a good first step. To go further you could consider polyurethane bushes, which are available in a variety of firmnesses; stiffer bushes make tauter handling but transmit a little more noise.

The next thing to tackle is roll, both to improve handling and also to make the car feel nicer to drive round twisty roads. Generally stiffer springs are not such a good move, they can make the ride a bit too harsh, and while they will

The 3,500kg towing capacity is largely due to the low-range transfer box, but even in high-range towing about 2.5 tons the car performed with ease. A robust towing bracket is essential, and for heavy loads I always put the maximum nose weight on to load up the Discovery's rear axle and improve stability.

I was given this polyurethane bush kit with a car I bought, but look closely and you'll see pock marks indicating that this is an inferior kit and may break up. Do not buy cheap kits.

Poly bushes

The phrase 'poly bush' has become synonymous with any synthetic bushing material, a bit like the word Hoover is used for any vacuum cleaner, but more accurately this only refers to polyurethane, a soft plastic.

The advantage over rubber is that it does not degrade over time so easily and that it can be made in a higher degree of firmness to suit the application. Typically a poly bush will last between three (if it is getting hammered in a harsh environment) and ten (normal road use) times longer than the rubber part.

Choosing the right grade of bush is vital. Hard ones are best suited to high-performance vehicles where minimal suspension compliance is beneficial.

Different areas of the car require different firmness depending on the magnitude of the force applied, so when you buy a kit for a car it should contain a variety of hard-nesses. All the bushes in a given kit will be dyed the same colour, and this is the manufacturer's way of denoting how sporty or comfy the overall kit is, not the individual hard-ness of each bush.

The bush material, polyurethane, is made as a liquid and then poured into moulds. It is very important to have no bubbles in it when poured, otherwise the finished bush will be softer than intended and can start to disintegrate internally too.

During manufacture, the material shrinks and the mould must be made to cope with this – the accuracy of the mould is critical, or the bush may be impossible to fit. Some bushes

reduce roll they can make the axle skitter over rough back-road surfaces. It is far better to use firmer dampers with standard springs.

In 1994 Land Rover introduced anti-roll bars to the Dis-covery, which helped the top heavy car no end on the road without making a huge impact on off-road prowess. In most circumstances they add a useful amount of stability, especially on raised vehicles, and can be retrofitted to older Discoverys.

The secret is to keep things simple and only solve the problems you actually have. Usually subtle modifications work best in the real world. After all, standard Land Rovers are pretty good.

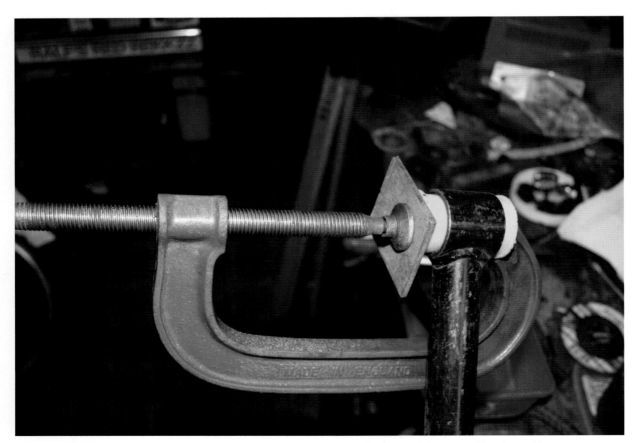

Bushes that are a press fit need to be pushed in dead straight to avoid them jamming and kinking. Push them in steadily and smoothly.

Another option when upgrading brakes is to use bigger brakes from other models. Here a Discovery 1 and Defender 110 calliper can be seen. The larger Defender brakes are now available with solid or vented discs.

need to move a fair amount, and a good bush manufacturer will know this and tailor the design to suit. By comparison the cheapest bushes on the market are often simply geometrical copies of the rubber item but made in polyurethane, and this can work very badly in some situations.

It is sometimes tempting to just replace a few bushes with polyurethane as they wear out, but this can lead to imbalance in the car's handling, so if you are doing some suspension link bushes then it makes sense to do them all.

When fitting them it is important to remove all traces of the previous bush. Any bit of rubber, rust or loose paint will reduce the life of the poly bush, and even dust and grit can cause too much wear, so get it clean.

Make sure the bush housing is not worn or bent. If it is then the new bush will be distorted and as well as not being able to function properly it may fail soon.

Some bushes need a little lubrication, such as soapy water or tyre lube, which dries out during fitment. If the bush has a steel tube insert, put this in last. If it is a cold day in the shed and the interference fit bushes are proving difficult to fit, warm them up in some hot water for a few minutes.

Only do the final tightening of the bolts when the car is sitting at its normal ride height, otherwise the bushes will be distorted and may pre-load the suspension components.

Polyurethane does not like alcohol, so solvents including methanol, ethanol and methylated spirits should be avoided.

Difficult bushes can be fitted with a G-clamp, vice or even wound in with a washer and a long bolt.

Never trim the bush to make it easier to fit, because nicks will lead to rips and early failure.

BRAKES

Solid discs are fine for most purposes off-road. After all you can't brake overly hard on mud, and vented discs just fill up with mud, which defeats their purpose. But for towing, the vented front discs fitted to later models offer better fade resistance. Moving up to harder pads, such as 'Green Stuff' from EBC, will improve braking, and many uprated discs are available, but avoid crack-prone cross-drilled ones. Some later Defender 110s used bigger four-pot callipers and different vented discs, and this offers a further bolt on, and cheap, improvement for Discovery 1 models. There are more extreme conversions using Brembo and Alcon parts costing a few thousand pounds, but these need very good traction to be fully effective so they need good suspension and tyres too.

The brake bias needs to be carefully considered too. If you have a raised car then when braking heavily it will pitch forwards more than a standard car, which takes downforce off the rear wheels and can allow them to lock up more easily. Cars with ABS get round this problem to a large extent, but are not totally immune, while cars with-out ABS need the brake bias adjusting forwards to compensate. This is not a job for the amateur, so seek advice from professionals when considering your own particular project.

Remember that if the suspension travel is increased then the brake hoses must be longer too.

There are many types of brake fluid available, but for most Land Rover applications one meeting DoT 5.1 should be the best option. I would avoid silicon DoT 5.0 fluid because it can make the brakes feel spongy, it can trap moisture in pockets which can in rare circumstances lead to brake fade, and its sponginess makes it unsuitable for the fast response of ABS systems. A good DoT 3 or 4 fluid should be okay in most cars too (check the manual for your car). The critical thing is making sure it is changed regularly, particularly if you go wading.

Brake fluid absorbs moisture. It is sold in sealed containers and as soon as the seal is broken it starts ageing and must be discarded after a time, just as if it was in the car.

Before making big changes, remember that a well-maintained Discovery is perfectly capable of wading small streams with no modification.

WADING

Splashing through lots of water is fun. It may be seen as childish by some, but they are probably just jealous because they cannot do it. Land Rovers were designed to cope with fording up to 0.5m (20in) as standard, but cars can be modified to run when almost completely submerged. Some of the river crossings in the Camel Trophy were driven with water up to the roof and the driver sitting on the window sill so their head was above the waterline.

There are a large number of snorkels available, including ones from Land Rover. When fitting a snorkel every joint must be watertight or you will risk destroying the engine. Snorkels usually restrict maximum power a little, but the intake can be pointed forwards for road use to get a little 'ram air' help.

There are a number of problems, and first is keeping the engine running by feeding it air from a roof-mounted snorkel and sealing any possible leakage points. Then it is a matter of stopping water getting into the oily bits including the engine, gearbox, axles, hubs and transfer box. And finally all the electrics have to be protected to prevent moisture getting into connectors and control boxes. After wading the car needs thoroughly dried out again, usually with a long drive; parking up a wet car results in all sorts of things seizing up and corroding.

Snorkels

The basic idea is that the inlet pipe for the air filter is extended to the top of the roof. The top of the tube needs a guard to stop debris and rain being drawn into the tube and blocking the filter. Most kits have an inlet that can be fitted facing forwards, which rams air in at speed and may make a small enhancement to performance, or backwards to protect it from overhanging foliage or flying dirt. The tube goes through the wing on its way to the air filter, and most systems use two parts, which are bonded onto each side of the wing panel after a suitable hole has been cut.

Mud flap ties

When reversing on rough terrain the mud flap can get caught between the tyre and an obstacle, which rips it off. If the flap is tied up when driving off-road then the flap is saved. This needs a reliable fitting installing into the flap; just cutting into it will lead to it simply ripping in use so the mounting hole needs to have a smooth rim and the fitting must spread the loading evenly with broad washers. Then a suitable hooking point needs to be installed onto the body.

IMPROVE YOUR LIGHTING

Things were different back in 1984 when the headlights used on 200-style Discoverys first shone out from the front of a Sherpa van. Road speeds were lower, traffic density was much less and fewer people drove in the dark anyway. But on today's roads it is becoming ever more important to get a good clear view of the road far ahead, combating the perils of faster roads and the glare of oncoming traffic.

Discovery lighting improved over the years and it is possible to update older models with later lights. Replacing the 200-style lights with the larger 300-style lights is a bolt-on fix, but the grille, light surrounds and indicators will also have to be changed. The facelifted Discovery 2 lights can be fitted to earlier Discovery 2 models, again with the full grille and trim change. It is also possible to fit Discovery 2 lights to a Discovery 1 although you will have to modify the mounting points and use the later bonnet and wings.

Luckily you do not have to go that far to improve light output. Modern bulb and lamp construction can harness the light output more efficiently, making the beam brighter and stretch to greater distances.

The best modern headlight bulbs can increase brightness by up to 90 per cent compared to halogens of twenty years ago, and extend the length of the beam on the road by over 30m, which is a very welcome improvement for very little outlay.

I grafted in lights from a BMW 3-series. With modern bulbs this gave excellent lighting for very little cost and about two days' work.

Lights from a 300 can be fitted to a 200-style car, but you need all these bits to make it work. It is a similar story for upgrading early Discovery 2 cars to post-facelift lights. Discovery 2 lights can be fitted to Discovery 1 cars but you will have to modify the bodywork.

The most recent development has been the use of LEDs. There are retro-fit headlight kits available, but they are hugely expensive at the moment. However, they do have another advantage in that because they are sealed and run cool they can be used underwater, which is handy if you like wading at night!

LED bulbs make more sense for indicators and stop/tail lights. You can get plug-in replacements, but beware of

cheap LEDs. As with many things quality costs and cheap LEDs will fail early, but quality units will last for many decades, and rather than suddenly blowing they will gradually get a little dimmer.

Adding lights

No matter how good the standard lights are, there are some situations off-road where they do not point in the direction you need. Sometimes on a dark night in the middle of nowhere, where the terrain doesn't reflect anything, it is almost like the light is being sucked out of the standard beams and the amount of road illuminated seems tiny. Here, long-range high-power spot lamps can help, mounted on the front bumper and connected with a relay that switches on with main beam. Fitting them on the roof provides extra height and range, casting slightly less shadow close up, but the downside is that they illuminate the bonnet, which can ruin your night vision.

> *Here's a bit of top trivia: halogen headlight bulbs are made in two varieties, quartz glass and hard glass. Quartz has the advantage that it can run at higher temperatures and so makes brighter bulbs. The lower thermal expansion rate means it can even cope with the occasional water splash – worth knowing if your lamps are prone to condensation from wading.*
>
> *You can tell if it is a quartz glass bulb by looking at the wires as they go into the glass. In quartz glass bulbs they will be attached via a thin strip of molybdenum metal foil in order to cope with the very different expansion rates.*
>
> *Hard glass bulbs tend to be a bit cheaper, because the wires just go straight in without the need for foil.*

Auxiliary lights should be wired in using their own fused supply from the battery via relays that are linked to the auxiliary or ignition feed from the key switch. To do this, one method is to have the relay coil connected to power via the key switch and earth via the lamp switch. Spot and driving lights should be linked to the main beam signal via relay so that on dipped beam they are off.

Auxiliary lights were available from Land Rover as an option, fitted to a type-approved A-bar like this.

RECOVERY

ABOVE: It is easy to fit lots of heavy protection plates under the car, but these make it heavier and are not always necessary. However, I have found that a steering guard like this one does save the steering linkages from damage on rocks. It also provides a useful front recovery point.

Even if you do not have a winch, if you need to get recovered then you need something sturdy on the car to attach the rope to. The trouble is that the standard bumpers are a bit weak, so suitable towing points need to be attached securely to the car.

One way is to fit heavy-duty bumpers with integrated recovery points. Another option is to fit specialist rings to the chassis rails, such as Jate rings. The advantage with these is that they put the force of recovery straight into the chassis; the drawback is that as they are slightly under the car they can be difficult to access if you have just sunk in mud.

Never use the standard lashing points on the chassis for recovery: these are designed for tying the car down in transport and are nowhere near strong enough for the huge forces involved in recovering a stuck car.

RIGHT: This is a Jate ring, which bolts to a standard bolt location on the chassis (where the steering box would bolt on for other markets) and provides a sturdy point for recovery and winching.

An adjustable tow hitch allows a variety of different trailers to be used. The trailer can be kept level and safe.

TOWING

These Land Rovers make fantastic tow cars, and luckily the provision of a towing bracket was thought of from the start. Land Rover offer original-equipment brackets, and so do many other companies, but this has not stopped some people fabricating their own systems from inadequate materials. For this reason check that any towing equipment you buy has a manufacturer's mark and is up to the job.

One of the problems is that the top of the bracket mounts onto the rear cross member, which is a traditional rot trap on all three models, so it is a good idea to inspect this area thoroughly before use. The bracket is stabilized with two links onto the chassis rails. Before fitting a bracket, the bolts and chassis mountings should be protected with spray grease or similar.

There are two types of trailer electrical socket: the light-coloured one is the '12S' for powering the internal devices in a caravan; the more important one is the black one '12N', which runs the lights and indicators.

12N wiring pin designations:

Pin	Wire colours	Function
1	Black/White	Left-hand indicator
2	White	Rear fog light
3	Brown	Earth
4	Black/Green	Right-hand indicator
5	Grey/Red	Side lights
6	Black/Red	Stop lights
7	Grey/Black	Side lights

The Discovery has a handy feature: there is an electrical connector in the load bed fitted as standard that simply plugs into the trailer socket lead, as long as you buy the genuine Land Rover item.

There are a few peculiarities to Land Rover towing brackets. First is that the car rides quite high so the bracket can easily end up too high for normal trailers. There are some off-road trailers available that ride equally high, but for most normal purposes the bracket needs some sort of drop plate to put the tow ball at the right height. Adjustable brackets are available with a range of holes and a heavy-duty pin arrangement to allow the height to be set up to suit whatever type of trailer you want.

This demountable arrangement is integral with a rear cross-member protection plate, and allows for a variety of couplings to be attached very securely.

One problem with a low-mounted tow bracket is that in off-road situations it can dig in and act like an anchor. For this reason there are a range of removable brackets, but even the standard Land Rover bracket can be loosened and swung up out of the way with a small tie-up plate. It is a little more work than a quick release bracket, but a lot cheaper.

LPG

Many V8s have been converted to run on liquefied petroleum gas (LPG), and unfortunately most of them will need some degree of mending due to the highly variable quality of installation. LPG has the potential to halve your fuel bills, but beware: there are many badly set up systems, which run very rich, resulting in significantly less saving than expected.

From a performance point of view, only gas injection, usually called 'sequential', is worth considering because the alternative 'mixer ring' venturi restricts air flow dramatically. However, if power is not your main concern then the cheaper and simpler mixer system may be acceptable.

Being a gas, LPG is not capable of lubricating the valve seats, and this can lead to higher seat wear than normal if the engine is regularly worked very hard, but if full throttle is rarely used then this may not be a problem. It is possible to fit an additional oiling system into the LPG system, such as Flashlube, but getting it to distribute evenly to all cylinders can be extremely difficult.

Finding space for the gas tanks is always tricky. LPG tanks have to be very rugged to cope with high pressures and also so they can survive in a heavy crash. Inside the tank there is a gas volume above the liquid fuel, so a 100-litre tank will actually only hold 80 litres of liquid fuel. Most dual-fuel conversions lose about 10 per cent on mpg on gas, so a 120-litre LPG tank should give a similar range to the standard 90-litre petrol tank. The simple option is to fit a large cylinder tank in the boot space, but this takes up most of the load area and renders folding rear seats a bit pointless. A common solution is to fit two small tanks between the chassis and sills, one on each side on a Discovery Series 1 but on a Series 2 car this space is smaller and occupied by other equipment so the only option is to remove the petrol tank.

On a Series 1 chassis a 35-litre tank is about the largest that can fit under the sill, so between the two of them a total of 70 litres can be achieved with a usable capacity of 56 litres. Some people add a third small tank in the boot space where one of the rear stowage bins are.

Another option is to remove the petrol tank and fit two cylinders in its place, then fit a smaller petrol tank in the rear wing area, which is obviously not the safest place for a petrol tank if the car is in a crash. By comparison LPG tanks have been known to survive being hit by a high-speed train.

Because LPG is stored under high pressure, from about 5 bar up to 25 bar depending on temperature, it is very easy for a small leak to be very serious. LPG is heavier than air so any leak will pool in the lowest area. During installation and testing, garages with pits should be avoided as should parking near drains. Any leak inside the car could be disastrous, so tanks have to have a leak-proof box fitted round

LPG systems need an ECU to turn injector pulses from the Land Rover ECU into signals suitable for the LPG injectors, adjusting for gas pressure and temperature etc.

Here I have two 35-litre cylinder LPG tanks in place of the original petrol tank, with the original tank guard in place. A small petrol tank is on the left of the picture behind the rear wheel arch.

Frontal protection bars may look good but are rarely needed although they give protection to the lights and radiator if you have to drive through hard vegetation etc. To work they must be strong and well mounted.

the valve gear with a generous vent pipe leading straight to the underside of the car. To help detect leaks a stenching agent is added to the gas during processing. If you can small gas from a converted car, other than when it is being refuelled, then there is a fault that must be repaired immediately.

LPG is a very good fuel, and when set up correctly can make the engine run smoother and more economically. In the years to come with increasing oil prices this fuel makes a lot of sense for old Land Rover petrol engines.

BULL BARS

Front protection bars, sometimes known as bull bars, brush bars, roo bars and even nerf or nudge bars, are probably the most contentious piece of equipment that can be fitted to a car. In many countries they are banned outright, so if you are planning an international trip then it is worth checking first. The law in the UK, at the time of writing, requires all bars made after 2005 to be tested for pedestrian safety (2005/66/EC), and that is why the official Land Rover items now come with a rubberized padding and will collapse if hit hard, which makes their usefulness as a protection system a bit questionable.

The main use of such bars is to reduce damage to the front of the car when driving past overgrown trees or bushes, and to protect the corners when manoeuvring in tight off-road situations. Additionally some bars extend under the front of the car to provide steering protection too. It is quite common for the bars to be used to mount extra lighting and to have extra protection for the headlight and indicator areas.

In other countries such as Australia they can provide protection from the larger wild animals that sometimes leap into the path of oncoming cars, and so have a slightly different design.

In some countries, where risk of damage is very high, bull bars are considered essential safety equipment, but because they are heavy and can pose increased risk to pedestrians it is best to avoid bull bars unless you really need them.

Unfortunately there are many bull bars on the market that are built for looks and perform very badly when used in earnest. Some are made from thin-walled tube, which crumples too easily and affords no real protection, and some have minimal mounting points that fail when loaded.

A good bar system should not reduce the beam of the headlights or obscure the indicators, and should allow easy cleaning of the light lens and bulb replacement.

Fitting them is usually quite easy as they use the existing bumper mounts at the front of the chassis, although lining the bumper and protection bars up at the same time can be a bit fiddly.

There is not much to hold all that metalwork on really, just those two flat plates at the bottom, which are bolted to the chassis. Any sizeable thump and they would buckle and effectively staple the bars to the bonnet.

Genuine parts may sometimes seem expensive, but beware of bargains that may be fakes. Some pattern parts are very good, but some are disastrous, so always buy from a reputable source.

10 where to buy parts and tools

Never has it been easier to buy car parts and tools. On the high street there are more tool shops and car accessory/part shops than ever before, but it's the internet where the availability of every conceivable car part has exploded. But as ever, as well as great opportunities there are also great traps awaiting the unwary DIY mechanic.

PARTS

Fake parts are not only deceptive but also potentially lethal. There is a vast quantity of fake parts that look identical to genuine parts and even have the right packaging with Land Rover holograms on. Fake parts are not made to the right standards, and are often badly made with inferior materials. They can be lethal. There are brake pads that peel off their backing plate in emergency stops, causing complete brake loss; there are ball joints that snap or disintegrate when cornering; there is even fake engine oil that will seize your engine on the motorway. If an offer looks too good to be true then it probably is.

Let us start with those 'safety critical' parts like suspension ball joints and brake pads. If these parts fail then the car could go out of control, and for this reason I always buy from a reputable car parts supplier who has high street shops as well as online shopping. These companies always use suppliers who can be traced, so if there is a problem

then the manufacturer of that part can be held to account. If a part does not fit or is faulty I can take it to the high street shop and show them, and then it is much quicker and simpler to get either a replacement or a refund. And because they know that customers can do this they work that little bit harder to make sure parts are up to the right standards in the first place.

By contrast some small online-only retailers may argue about returns, or even disappear without a trace. And more importantly there is no traceability of their supply chain, so you cannot be sure what you are getting.

Also, for safety-critical parts I would never buy second-hand, even from a reputable supplier. You never know the full history of the part. If it is a ball joint, you do not know if it has been stressed by kerbing or been in a crash. Never buy second-hand brake pads or discs. Discs could be warped or cracked, pads may be contaminated with oil or old enough for the bonding on the friction material to fail, but also you will never get second-hand brakes to fit without getting brake judder. Other parts to be wary of include seat belts, air bags and dampers (shock absorbers).

Tyres are a bit more complicated. Although they are clearly a safety-critical part, there can sometimes be a good argument for buying part-worn tyres. But you really need to have some idea of the history and the reason why they are for sale. One with a slow puncture may be hiding

Beware of 'New Old Stock' (NOS) bargains. Parts on a shelf age, albeit more slowly than on a car. Rubber perishes, some gaskets and seals harden, oils separate and glue becomes brittle.

internal damage, or one from a crashed car may be split inside and ready to burst. By contrast if the tyre is for sale because the owner upgraded their wheels, or because the car they came off failed its MOT test because of a rusty chassis, then they could be perfectly serviceable tyres with tens of thousands of miles left in them. Pulling tyres on and off rims stresses the beads, so if possible it is better to buy part-worn tyres on the rims they were originally fitted to.

Either way a tyre should be thoroughly inspected. Check the date code and avoid tyres over three years old. Small cracks are a sign of ageing and tyre performance and longevity will be reduced. A few nicks and scratches in the tread blocks may be okay, but if there is any damage to the sidewalls, bead or the base of the tread then just walk away. Do not take chances with tyres.

As well as safety-critical parts, perishable parts should always be bought new. Rubber parts such as hoses, window seals and suspension air springs generally only last about ten years before the ageing process makes them hard and prone to cracks.

Even 'New Old Stock' items that have never been used and just sat on the shelf for years will have aged to some extent, so I do not buy coolant hoses from auto jumble stalls that have loads of old dusty boxes.

Air conditioning hoses become very porous to the refrigerant at about the ten-year mark too, so new hoses are the way to go if you want the gas to stay in.

These parts can be bought from a high street retailer but can be cheaper on the internet. Check out the feedback of any online retailer first and ask on forums which one has

Sometimes it is more practical to buy a complete assembly than repair the one you have got. Big bits like this are okay to get second-hand.

provided good service to other Discovery owners. Again you want the parts to be new, but parts in this category could be safely bought from cheaper retailers as long as they are up to the right quality.

Some other sorts of parts are best bought second-hand, such as trim panels that can be difficult to find or very expensive to buy new, brackets and parts that do not really wear out. Things like window motors and lock solenoids do wear out but the second-hand price means it is usually cost effective as long as you get some sort of guarantee.

Big parts such as axles, gearbox and engines can also be sensibly bought second-hand, as new prices are very high compared to the value of the car. However, inspection is vital before buying, and it is also very much worth knowing the mileage and the reason that the parts are being sold. For instance if a donor car has had a front-end crash, the rear axle may be fine but the front axle should be avoided.

Oils and other fluids can seem costly and it can be tempting to buy cheaper brands, but remember that these items not only dictate how long the various parts of the car last but also they can have a significant effect on fuel consumption. For instance one of my cars was previously owned by someone who skimped on servicing to save money, but by just changing the engine oil and filter the fuel consumption on my regular commute went from 25 to 30mpg, and the saving in fuel cost paid for the service parts in just a few months.

Mineral engine oils do not last as long as synthetic ones; so although synthetic oils look expensive they do extend service intervals and can save time and money later, more so if you do high mileages. The very cheapest mineral oils break down very fast and are a false economy.

Most oils, and particularly engine oil, contain a vast array of additives. These can settle if the oil can is left on the shelf for years and significantly lower the oil's performance, so I avoid 'New Old Stock' and oils of unknown age in market stalls and auto jumbles.

I will not buy cheap internet filters and seals; this is one of those markets that is swamped by counterfeit parts that can fail or significantly underperform. These parts are usually so cheap that it is practical to buy from one of the more expensive shops that has a quality guarantee.

However, some parts are fine as pattern parts. For instance I have had good experience with buying new exhaust catalysts from an eBay supplier.

TOOLS

Finally, here are a few words on buying tools. Never buy cheap tools! For example, cheap spanners will flex more when pushed hard, increasing the chances of rounding off a bolt head and injuring yourself too. Your tools will outlast your car in all likelihood, so consider them as an investment and buy the best you can afford.

However, there are still bargains to be had. Wait for the sales and get full tool sets at much lower prices. Ask in your local tool shop about ex-display items too. But one way of getting good tools cheap is to buy second-hand. Look on internet auction sites for retiring mechanics selling their full tool box. Most professional mechanics have one set

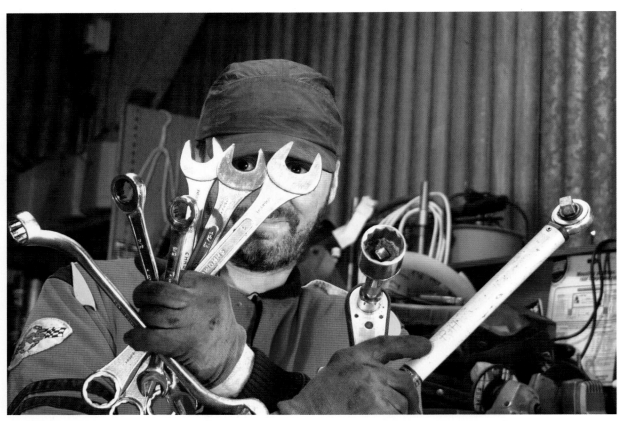

Good tools make the world of difference. I have never rounded a good nut off with a decent spanner, so buy the best you can afford.

Remember you only need to buy the tools you actually use. Big sets may not be the best buy.

of tools at work and another one at home, so when they retire they just keep the home one. Second-hand tools go for substantially lower prices than new ones, but most tools do not wear out. The few tools that do wear out should always be bought new, such as drills and files. And do not buy cheap files and drills either – good ones are heat treated, but cheap ones are not and will blunt almost immediately.

Do not buy tools you don't need. Massive socket sets may look good, but why spend money on sizes you will never use? The flip side of that argument is that it is vital to use the right tools. Do not try turning a ½in nut with a 13mm socket; buy the right size. But also get the special tools such as Torx bits for the seat bolts and the deep socket for the hub nuts, because if you try to get away with using the wrong tools then you will damage the car and yourself.

There is a simple rule that is vital to follow: if the job you are doing is far too hard then you are doing it wrong! For instance, if the force you need to apply to a spanner is hurting your hand and making the blood vessels in your neck burst then you need a longer spanner or a breaker bar on a socket. If you are struggling then you are more likely to make a mistake and have an accident, so buy the right tools including nut splitters, top quality hacksaw blades and effective penetrating oils.

There are a few very specialist Land Rover service tools that you may only need once, and these can be rented from tool shops, but increasingly you will find that one person within a Land Rover club or forum group will be willing to lend theirs out. So always ask on forums before you spend money.

One tool you could use a lot is a pressurized oil can. These have refillable bottles that are pressurized by a simple hand pump on top, then a flexible tube allows you to feed oil into tricky spaces. These are ideal for oil changes on differentials, the transfer box and the automatic gearbox.

DIAGNOSTICS

There are several jobs on the Discovery 2 that are best done using the dealer diagnostic computer system, but there are also cheaper diagnostic systems that can do the same job for you. One such job is bleeding air out of the ABS system, which needs the solenoids to be cycled repeatedly in a special operating mode. Systems such as Nanocom and HawkEye are reasonably priced if you do a lot of work on

Diagnostic aids are getting cheaper and more sophisticated. They can read and clear faults, change settings such as ride height or locking preferences, and they can operate systems so you can test them or repair them. This Nanocom cost less than a set of tyres.

these cars, but again clubs and forum groups usually contain at least one willing member who will happily lend you one for a day.

For simple fault-code reading and clearing, I use a cheap OBD-to-Bluetooth adapter from eBay and the rather excellent Torque Pro app for my smartphone. This can show how lambda sensors are performing, if any sensors are failing and even tell you if there is an exhaust leak (if the fuel adaptations are high, you have a leak). And it costs less than a can of decent engine oil.

There is an even cheaper option: the Torque Pro app is one of many smartphone programs that connect via Bluetooth to a remote OBD interface and allow you to see and clear faults as well as read current data such as lambda or engine temperature.

Discovery 1, 200 style.

specifications

Specifications varied over the years and by territory, but these seem to be the most common ones. All dimensions in millimetres (mm) unless otherwise stated.

DISCOVERY 1

Production	1989–1999
Wheelbase	2,540mm (100.0in)
Length	4,539mm to spare wheel, 4,581mm to tow hitch.
Width	1,793mm
Height	1,966mm
Weight	1,882kg (V8 3dr), 1,885kg (V8 5dr), 2,008kg (200Tdi 3dr), 2,053kg (200Tdi 5dr), 1,979kg (300 Series V8 5dr), 1,890kg (Mpi 3dr), 1,925kg (Mpi 5dr)
Turning circle kerb to kerb	11.9m
Min. ground clearance	214mm
Track front and rear	1,486mm

Production years	Engine	Maximum power	Maximum torque
1989–1997	2.0 Mpi Petrol	134bhp @ 6,000rpm	137lb ft @ 2,500rpm
1989–1990	3.5 V8 Petrol	144bhp @ 5,000rpm	192lb ft @ 2,800rpm
1990–1993	3.5 V8i Petrol	165bhp @ 4,750rpm	207lb ft @ 3,200rpm
1995–1998	3.9 V8i Petro	182bhp @ 4,750rpm	231lb ft @ 3,100rpm
1989–1994	2.5 200Tdi	111bhp @ 4,000rpm	195lb ft @ 1,800rpm
1994–1998	2.5 300Tdi	111bhp @ 4,000rpm	195lb ft @ 1,800rpm

The 300Tdi was also available with 129bhp on auto gearbox models.

Discovery 1 VIN codes

Example: SALLJGBV3GA012345

SAL	Manufacturer code (Rover Group)
LJ	Discovery
G	Territory and specification (A=100in wheelbase Japan, G=100in wheelbase all other markets)
B	Three-door body, M=Five-door body
V	3.5-litre V8 carburettor petrol engine, F=2.5-litre 200 or 300Tdi diesel engine, L=3.5-litre V8 injected petrol engine, M=3.9-litre V8 injected petrol engine, Y=2.0-litre four cylinder petrol engine
3	RHD with automatic gearbox, 4=LHD with automatic gearbox, 7=RHD with 5-speed manual gearbox, 8=LHD with 5-speed manual gearbox
G	Model year=1990, H=1991, J=1992, K=1993, L=1994, M=1995, T=1996, V=1997, W=1998
A	Assembled at Solihull, F=Shipped as knocked down for overseas assembly
012345	Serial number

Discovery 1 recalls and alerts

Land Rover constantly updated their designs and there have been many dealer bulletins over the years. Not every 'Service Action' is absolutely necessary, but it is worth noting some of the major ones:

1995 (VIN LJ163104 to LJ172980 and LJ501920 to LJ504252): check seat belts.
1997 (April '95–July '96: 22,723 vehicles): possibility of failure of RHS front door latch.
1998: (build Jan '94–Mar '97): airbag may go off involuntarily.
1998 TSB dated 25/3/98 warned dealers of timing-belt failure due to misalignment of belt and pulleys on 300TDi up to VIN WA748935 and gave procedures for repair under warranty if warranty conditions apply.
5/5/2005 Safety Recall R/2004/069: possibility of stress cracks in plastic fuel tank of V8 petrol models, build dates 15/4/1993 to 7/9/1998.

DISCOVERY 2

Production	1999–2005
Wheelbase	2,540mm (100.0in)
Length	4,705mm to spare wheel, 4,715mm to tow hitch
Width	1,793mm excluding mirrors, 1,890mm including mirrors
Height	1,884mm without roof bars, 1,940mm with roof bars
Weight	V8 2,095 to 2,235kg, TD5 2,150 to 2,280kg
Turning circle kerb to kerb	11.9m
Ground clearance	253mm
Track front	1,540mm
Track rear	1,560mm

Discovery 2, pre-facelift with Range Rover Sport wheels.

specifications

Production years	Engine	Maximum power	Maximum torque
1998–2005	4.0 V8 Petrol	185bhp @ 4,750rpm	251lb ft @ 2,600rpm
2003–2005	4.6 V8 Petrol	225bhp @ 4,750rpm	280lb ft @ 2,600rpm (NAS only)
1998–2005	2.5 TD5 diesel	137bhp @ 4,200rpm	220lb ft (manual)/250lb ft (auto) @ 1,950rpm

Discovery 2 VIN codes

There were two versions:

Territories except North America and Canada   Example: SALLJGB73WA012345

SAL	Manufacturer code (Rover Group)
LJ	Discovery
G	Standard (100in) wheelbase
B	Five-door body
1	Engine 1=4.0 V8 low compression with catalyst, 2=4.0 V8 high compression with catalyst, 3=4.0 V8 low compression without catalyst, 4=4.6 V8 low compression with catalyst, 5=4.6 V8 high compression with catalyst, 6=4.6 V8 low compression without catalyst, 7=TD5 ROW (Rest Of World spec), 8=TD5 with EGR and catalysts, 9=TD5 with EGR but no catalysts
3	Transmission 3=RHD with automatic gearbox, 4=LHD with automatic gearbox, 7=RHD with 5-speed manual gearbox, 8=LHD with 5-speed manual gearbox
W	Model year W=1998, X=1999, Y=2000, 1=2001, 2=2002, 3=2003, 4=2004, 5=2005
A	Assembled at Solihull, F=Shipped as knocked down for overseas assembly
012345	Serial number

North America and Canada   Example: SALTY124O012345

SAL	Manufacturer code (Rover Group)
T	Discovery
Y	Standard (100in) wheelbase NAS and Canada, N=Standard (100in) wheelbase California
1	Five-door body (four-door station wagon)
2	Engine 2=4.0 V8 high compression with catalyst, 5=4.6 V8 high compression with catalyst
4	Transmission 4=LHD with automatic gearbox
O	Check digit
W	Model year W=1998, X=1999, Y=2000, 1=2001, 2=2002, 3=2003, 4=2004, 5=2005
A	Assembled at Solihull, F= Shipped as knocked down for overseas assembly
012345	Serial number

Discovery 2 recalls and alerts

Land Rover constantly updated their designs and there have been many dealer bulletins over the years. Not every 'Service Action' is absolutely necessary, but it is worth noting some of the major ones:

26/8/2011: Alert over chafing of fuel pipe. The chafing issue on the plastic (neoprene) pipe routed/crimped under the rear subframe between the plastic tank and wears on the metal body edges.

21/1/2012: Warning: Stick to OEM (Girling) brake and clutch parts. 'Pattern' versions of these parts are often poor quality and frequently fail.

31/3/2004 Safety recall R/2003/180: (where ABS fitted) possible loss of braking, build dates 1/10/1998 to 1/12/2003.

31/3/2004 Safety Recall R/2003/179: on Discovery 2 V8 and TD5 possibility of under-bonnet fire, build dates 29/1/2000 to 30/9/2003.

11/8/2004 Safety Recall R/2004/093: on TD5 possibility that the rear fuel line may chafe against the harness, build dates 30/6/2001 to 19/4/2004.

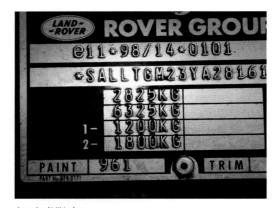

A typical VIN plate.

LAND ROVER AND OFF-ROAD PREPARATION SPECIALISTS

Devon 4x4
Southlea Service Station
South Molton
Devon
EX36 3QU
www.devon4x4.com
Tel: 01769 550900

Tomcat Motorsport
Old Wood
Skellingthorpe
Lincoln
LN6 5UA
Tel: 01522 683733
www.tomcatmotorsport.co.uk

Rakeway
Unit J Brookhouse Way
Brookhouse Industrial Estate
Cheadle
Stoke on Trent
Staffordshire
ST10 1SR
www.rakeway.co.uk
Tel: 01538 750500

Qt Services
Unit 11 B Miller Business Park
Station Road
Liskeard
PL14 4DA
www.qtservices.co.uk/partners
Tel: 01579 349688

PARTS SUPPLIERS

Dunsfold Land Rover
Alfold Road
Dunsfold
Surrey
GU8 4NP
Tel: 01483 200567
www.dunsfold.com

John Craddock Ltd
North Street
Bridgtown
Cannock
Staffordshire
WS11 0AZ
www.johncraddockltd.co.uk

Paddock Spares
The Showground
The Cliff
Matlock
Derbyshire
DE4 5EW
www.paddockspares.com

MM4x4
Droitwich Road
Martin Hussingtree
Worcester WR3 8TE
www.mm-4x4.com
Tel: 01905 451506

Rimmer Bros
Triumph House
Sleaford Road
Bracebridge Heath
Lincoln LN4 2NA
www.rimmerbros.co.uk
Tel: 01522 568000

ENGINES

RPi
Wayside Garage
Holt Road
Horsford
Norwich
Norfolk
NR10 3EE
Tel: 01603 891209
www.v8engines.com

Real Steel
Unit 9, Tomo Industrial Estate
Packet Boat Lane
Cowley
Middlesex
UB8 2JP
Tel: 01895 440505
www.realsteel.co.uk

TRANSMISSIONS

Ashcroft Transmissions Ltd
Units 5 & 6, Stadium Estate
Cradock Rd
Luton
Bedfordshire
LU4 0JF
www.ashcroft-transmissions.co.uk
Tel: 01582 496040

DIAGNOSTICS

Nanocom
info@nanocom.it
support@nanocom.it
www.nanocom.it

MUSEUMS

Heritage Motor Centre
Banbury Road
Gaydon
Warwickshire
CV35 0BJ
www.heritage-motor-centre.co.uk
Tel: 01926 641188

The Dunsfold Collection
Alfold Road
Dunsfold
Surrey
GU8 4NP
Tel: 01483 200567
www.dunsfoldcollection.co.uk

FOLLOW LAND ROVER

Web site: www.landrover.com
www.facebook.com/landrover.uk
www.landrover.co.uk
www.twitter.com/landrover_uk
www.youtube.com/landroveruk
www.flickr.com/photos/landroveruk

FOLLOW THE AUTHOR

twitter.com/RalphHosier

appendix i: Discovery 1 Technical Service Bulletins (TSB)

Here are the Technical Service Bulletins (TSBs) for the Discovery 1 including the original Land Rover spelling mistakes. To find out more use an internet search on the reference number at the end of each line.

You may notice that the first bulletins were issued years before the car was launched. That is because they were care points that were raised on the Range Rover Classic and carried over to the Discovery.

'A/C, Electrical – Rear Glass Defogger Element Repair', 'Jun 14, 2011', TECLTB003292

Suspension – Correct Ball Joint Splitter Usage, 'Dec 17, 2009', TECLTB00248

Audio System – Speaker Vibration/Rattle Noise Diagnosis, 'Sep 11, 2006', TECLRA415001

Body – Windshield Damage Diagnostic Aid, 'Jun 22, 2006', TECLRA501001

Maintenance – Fluid Specifications/Applications, 'Sep 28, 2005', TEC100105

Recall – Fuel Tank Replacement, 'Jun 17, 2005', RB1563

Recall – Fuel Tank Replacement (Canadian Vehicles), 'Jun 17, 2005', RB156C3

Body – Carbalflo XTR5(R) Lubricant Usage, 'Jun 10, 2005', TA057602

Recall 04V203000: Fuel Tank Stress Cracking, 'Apr 01, 2004', NHTSA04V203000

Emissions/Fuel Systems – Difficulty Filling Fuel Tank, 'Dec 05, 2003', TEC190403

M/T – Front Cover Oil Leaks, 'Jun 06, 2003', TEC370103

Keyless Entry – Remote Transmitter Button Splitting, 'Apr 25, 2003', TEC860303

Engine – Oil Leaks From Rear, 'Oct 11, 2002', TEC120202

Engine – Oil Leaks From Rear of Engine, 'Oct 11, 2002', TEC120102

A/T – ZF Transmission/Multiple Shift Concerns, 'Aug 16, 2002', TEC440102

Electrical – Intermittent Electrical/No Start Problems, 'Aug 09, 2002', TEC860502

Wheels – Difficult to Remove, 'Sep 11, 2001', TEC100101

Starter – Engine No-Start Condition, 'Jul 27, 2001', TEC860400

A/T – Fluid Leaks From Torque Converter, 'Jun 15, 2001', TEC4402002

Suspension – Coil Spring Installation Precautions, 'Mar 02, 2001', TEC540101

Fuel System – Fuel Pump Component Replacement, 'Dec 29, 2000', TEC1904963

Engine – Valve Guide Cleaning, 'Sep 29, 2000', TEC120100

Engine – Intake Manifold Fluid Leaks, 'Mar 24, 2000', TEC300100

Interior – Dash Pad Separation, 'Mar 24, 2000', TEC760100

Battery – Dead/Fails to Maintain A Charge, 'Mar 03, 2000', TEC860100

Drivetrain/Brakes – Brake Line Bracket Modification, 'Dec 10, 1999', TEC510299

Transfer Case – Output Seal Leakage, 'Nov 23, 1999', TEC4102973

A/T – Cooler Flushing, 'Oct 22, 1999', TEC440299

Ignition System – Hard Start/Rough Running/Misfire Codes, 'Jul 30, 1999', TEC190198

Engine – Excessive Noise/Vibration, 'Jul 09, 1999', TEC120399

Fuel System – Poor Throttle Response, 'Jun 18, 1999', TEC190299

Interior – Child Seat Tether Installation, 'Jun 04, 1999', TEC761599

M/T – Fluid Leaks, 'Mar 09, 1999', TEC370199

Battery – Intersate(R) Battery Retrofitting, 'Feb 26, 1999', TEC860299

Steering – Power Steering Hose Leaks, 'Feb 26, 1999', TEC570199

Drivetrain – Difficult Differential Lock Selection, 'Oct 23, 1998', TEC410298

Interior – Electric Front Seat Play Adjustments, 'Oct 16, 1998', TEC761898

Body – Sunroof Water Leaks, 'Oct 02, 1998', TEC761698

Engine Controls – MIL ON/Trailing Throttle Misfire, 'Oct 02, 1998', TEC190398

Paint – Plastic Component Refinishing Procedures, 'Oct 02, 1998', TEC761798

Multi-Function Unit – Wiring/Connector Information, 'Oct 02, 1998', TEC860498

Body – New A Pillar Replacement Trim, 'Sep 11, 1998', TEC761598

Drivetrain – Front Axle Swivel Seals Leaking, 'Aug 14, 1998', TEC6001973

Engine – Oil Pan Bolt Leakage, 'Jun 26, 1998', TEC120298

Drivetrain – Revised Pinion Assembly/Torque Values, 'May 29, 1998', TEC510298

Interior – Child Seat Tether Bracket Installation, 'May 01, 1998', TEC761198

Drivetrain – Rear Stub Axle Oil Seal Leakage, 'May 01, 1998', TEC5106963

Drivetrain – Front Stub Axle Oil Seal Leakage, 'Apr 24, 1998', TEC5402963

Recall – Inadvertent Air Bag Deployment, 'Mar 20, 1998', D488

A/T – Fluid Level Checking, 'Mar 06, 1998', TEC440198

A/C – Low Pressure Line Refrigerant Leaks, 'Mar 06, 1998', TEC820298

Body – Tailgate Rattles, 'Mar 06, 1998', TEC760298

Suspension – Vehicle Does Not Sit Level, 'Mar 06, 1998', TEC640198

Transfer Case – Input Seal Leakage, 'Mar 04, 1998', TEC4101982

Campaign – Oil Pressure Switch Replacement, 'Jan 30, 1998', H4832

Bulkhead – Water Leaks to Interior, 'Jan 16, 1998', TEC7622973

Sunroof – Popping/Clicking Noise On Opening, 'Jan 16, 1998', TEC7623972

Sunroof – Rattles on Rough Roads, 'Jan 16, 1998', TEC7616974

MIL ON DTC P0451 Stored in Memory, 'Dec 19, 1997', TEC1907972

'MIL ON DTC's P0130, P0150 Set', 'Dec 19, 1997', TEC1703973

Wiring – Header Junction Repair Kit, 'Dec 19, 1997', TEC8603973

Door Handle/Lock Button – Noise/Difficult Operation, 'Dec 19, 1997', TEC7617972

ECM Connectors – Water Contamination, 'Dec 05, 1997', TEC1910972

Heater Hose – Coolant Leaks, 'Dec 05, 1997', TEC1207972

ECU/ECM – Intermittent No Crank/No Start, 'Nov 26, 1997', TEC8616973

A/T – Evaluation Report (ATER), 'Nov 14, 1997', W97-011

A/T – Filter Replacement Interval, 'Oct 31, 1997', G97-028

A/T – Evaluation Report (ATER) Warranty Claim, 'Oct 24, 1997', W97-009

Front Crankshaft Seal – Oil Leaks, 'Oct 06, 1997', TEC120597

Front Wiper Blades – Poor Performance, 'Oct 06, 1997', TEC8402971

ECM – MIL ON DTC P0461 Set, 'Oct 06, 1997', TEC190897

Squeaks & Rattles – Diagnosis And Repair, 'Oct 06, 1997', TEC7618971

Sill Button – Too Low/Difficult to Operate, 'Sep 19, 1997', TEC7614971

Oil Pressure Switch – Oil Leakage, 'Aug 22, 1997', TEC1204972

Cruise Control – Intermittent Disengagement, 'Jul 11, 1997', TEC8618971

Temperature Gauge – Inaccurate/False DTC's Stored, 'Jul 11, 1997', TEC8610972

Wiring/Connectors – Troubleshooting & Repair, 'Jul 03, 1997', TEC861797

Warranty Claims – MIL Event Requirements, 'Jun 27, 1997', W97-007

'VSS – DTC P0500 Set, Engine Misfire', 'Jun 27, 1997', TEC190397

Seat Base Access Panel – Rattles, 'Jun 20, 1997', TEC7613971

Key Interlock – Service Procedure, 'Jun 20, 1997', TEC5702971

A/C System – Water Leaks to Interior, 'Jun 20, 1997', TEC8001972

Engine – Oil Change Recommendations (PDI), 'Jun 06, 1997', TEC100297

Security System – Engine No Start Condition, 'May 30, 1997', TEC8606972

Steering System – Fluid Leaks, 'May 30, 1997', TEC570197

Warranty – Daily Transaction Summary, 'Apr 21, 1997', W97-006

Sunroof – Jams During Tilt Operation, 'Apr 18, 1997', TEC760597

Front Axle – Swivel Seals Leaking Grease, 'Apr 18, 1997', TEC6001972

Front Brake – Squeal, 'Apr 18, 1997', TEC7001972

High Mount Stop Lamp – Modification, 'Apr 11, 1997', TEC860797

Squeaks And Rattles – Diagnosis/Repair, 'Mar 31, 1997', TEC860597

Door Mirror – Wind Noise/Dust Intrusion, 'Mar 21, 1997', TEC760397

Fuel Injection – Misfire Diagnostics, 'Mar 21, 1997', TEC190297

Air Bag – Safety Label Instruction, 'Mar 14, 1997', G97-05

Engine Oil Pan – Oil Leaks, 'Mar 07, 1997', TEC120896R

Replacement Battery – Installation, 'Feb 14, 1997', TEC860297

Inside/Outside Door Handle – Intermittent Operation, 'Jan 17, 1997', TEC760297

Central Locking System – Intermittent Locking, 'Jan 17, 1997', TEC760197

Recall – D456 NHTSA #96V247 Door Latch, 'Jan 17, 1997', R97-001

'Recall – Door Latch, Failure to Fully Latch', 'Jan 17, 1997', D456

Engine – Valve Cover Gasket Replacement, 'Dec 31, 1996', 35167

Front Hub Seal – Oil Leaks, 'Dec 31, 1996', TEC540396

HO2S – Handling and Diagnostic Procedures, 'Dec 31, 1996', 35081

Rear Stub Axle Seal – Leaks Oil, 'Dec 31, 1996', TEC510696

Bulb Holder – Improved Design, 'Dec 31, 1996', TEC861996

Crankshaft Position Sensor – Loose, 'Dec 31, 1996', TEC190596

Transfer Gearbox – Output Shaft Seal Leak, 'Dec 31, 1996', 41-02-96

Windshield – Water Leaks To The Interior, 'Dec 31, 1996', TEC762996R

Engine – Misfire Diagnosis, 'Dec 31, 1996', TEC120396

Engine – Hard Starting When Cold, 'Dec 31, 1996', TEC191396

Valve Cover – Oil Leak, 'Dec 31, 1996', TEC120496

CKP Sensor/Heat Shield – Revised Tightening Bolts, 'Dec 31, 1996', 35204

EVAP CANPV – Diagnosis, 'Dec 31, 1996', 35112

Front Stub Axle Seal – Leaks Oil, 'Dec 31, 1996', TEC540296

Oxygen Sensor – Handling and Diagnosis, 'Dec 31, 1996', TEC170196

Transfer Gearbox – Unable to Shift Out of Gear, 'Dec 31, 1996', 41-01-96

Speakers – Buzzing Noise From Front Tweeters, 'Dec 31, 1996', TEC862196

Transfer Gearbox – Will Not Shift Out of Gear, 'Dec 31, 1996', TEC410196

Rear Hub Seal – Oil Leaks, 'Dec 31, 1996', TEC510796

Transmission Input Seal – Leaks Oil, 'Dec 31, 1996', TEC370696

ECM – DTC's P0443 & P0441 Sert, 'Dec 31, 1996', TEC170296

Discovery 1 Technical Service Bulletins (TSB)

M/T – Input Shaft Seal Leaks, 'Dec 31, 1996', 37-06-96

Differential Pinion Oil Seal – Leaks Oil, 'Dec 31, 1996', TEC510596

Rear Brake Light/Rear Defogger – Short Circuit, 'Dec 31, 1996', TEC861396

Sunroof – Water Leaks to The Interior, 'Dec 20, 1996', TEC762696

Engine Oil Filler Neck – Oil Leaks, 'Dec 20, 1996', TEC120996

Engine – Oil Leaks at Valve Cover Vent Tubes, 'Dec 20, 1996', TEC121096

A/T Shift Lever – Locked/Will Not Move, 'Dec 20, 1996', TEC440296R

Hub Nut – Revised Torque Setting Procedure, 'Dec 13, 1996', TEC510496

Lower Radiator Hose – Incorrectly Routed, 'Dec 13, 1996', TEC260396

Alarm Remote Buttons – Wear Out Prematurely, 'Dec 13, 1996', TEC861696

'Security System – Antenna, Inadequate Range', 'Dec 13, 1996', TEC861496

Coolant System – Lower Radiator Hose Misrouted, 'Dec 13, 1996', 35150

Recall 96V247000: Right Front Door fails to Latch, 'Dec 11, 1996', NHTSA96V247000

'D' Post/Alpine Light – Water Leaks to Interior, 'Dec 06, 1996', TEC761796

ECM – DTC P0125 Set, 'Dec 06, 1996', TEC190896

GEMS Code P0125 Diagnosis, 'Dec 06, 1996', 35296

ECM – MIL ON DTC P1317 Set, 'Dec 06, 1996', TEC190996

Hub Bearing – Adjustment, 'Dec 01, 1996', TEC510196

Turn Signal Switch – Self Cancelling/`Fly Through', 'Dec 01, 1996', TEC860196

Engine Oil – Viscosity Recommendations, 'Oct 25, 1996', TEC120796

Engine Oil – Winter Driving Specification, 'Oct 25, 1996', 35258

Restraint System – Collision Repair Guidelines, 'Oct 18, 1996', G96-012

Seat Lumbar Knob – Falls Off, 'Sep 02, 1996', TEC760996

Driver Closure Plate – Fixing Stud Omitted, 'Sep 02, 1996', TEC760496

Steering – Lock Stop Setting Procedures, 'Aug 03, 1996', TEC5703962

Connector Housing Bracket – Vibration, 'Jul 26, 1996', H449

Cylinder Block – Applications/Interchangeability, 'Jul 26, 1996', TEC120296

Antifreeze – Protection Level, 'Jul 26, 1996', TEC260296

Coolant/Antifreeze – Checking Protection Level, 'Jul 26, 1996', 35121

M/T – Gearbox 5th Layshaft & Gear Retention, 'Jul 19, 1996', 37-04-96

M/T – Mod Improves Joint Between 5th Gear & Layshaft, 'Jul 19, 1996', TEC370496

GEMS – DTC Report HelpLine, 'Jul 12, 1996', G96-006

Technical Literature Corrections/Suggestions, 'Jun 24, 1996', G96-005

Warranty – Parts Handling Reimbursement, 'Jun 14, 1996', W96-010

Exchange Power Steering Boxes – Availability, 'Jun 10, 1996', W96-008

Hood Liner – Production Modifications, 'May 31, 1996', TEC761496

Lease Program – Warranty Extension Deletion, 'May 28, 1996', W96-009

Transfer Gearbox – Backlash/Clonk, 'May 24, 1996', TEC370296R

Warranty – Diagnostic Trouble Code Report, 'May 20, 1996', W96-007

Technical Manual – Updates, 'May 13, 1996', G96-003

Brakes – Squeal, 'May 04, 1996', 70-01-96

GEMS System – OBD II Diagnostic Information Document, 'Apr 24, 1996', G96-002

Steering – Lock Stop Settings, 'Apr 18, 1996', TEC570396R

No Obstacles Lease Program – Scheduled Maintenance, 'Apr 04, 1996', W96-006

M/T Mainshaft – Spline Wear Prevention, 'Mar 29, 1996', H415

Idle Air Control Valve – Stalling/Poor Idle/Surging, 'Mar 22, 1996', TEC190396

Paint – Codes & Types, 'Mar 22, 1996', TEC040296

Warranty Repair – Authorizations, 'Mar 15, 1996', W96-004

Goodwill Self-Authorization Program – Simplification, 'Mar 15, 1996', W96-003

Campaign – Crankshaft Timing Gear Replacement, 'Mar 08, 1996', H877R

Cruise Control – 'Set/Hold' Inoperative, 'Mar 01, 1996', TEC190296

Suspension – Vehicle Not Sitting Level, 'Feb 16, 1996', TEC640196

Rear Inward Facing Seats – Rattle, 'Jan 28, 1996', TEC760696

Side Door – Water Retention, 'Jan 26, 1996', TEC760796

Ignition Key Cylinder – Too Much Free Play, 'Dec 18, 1995', H878

Warranty Repair Authorization – Procedure, 'Dec 08, 1995', W95-005

Cell Phone – Radio Mute Function, 'Dec 01, 1995', TEC860795

Electrical Troubleshooting Manuals – New & Revised, 'Nov 28, 1995', G95019

'Engine – Hesitation, OBD Fault 17/DTC P0121 Set', 'Nov 17, 1995', TEC190295

Windshield/Dash – Creaking/Squeaking Noise, 'Nov 10, 1995', TEC763695

Dashboard – Torque Specifications, 'Nov 10, 1995', TEC040195

ABS – Fault Blink Code Diagnostic Procedure, 'Oct 27, 1995', TEC700195

Steering Column – Noise Diagnosis, 'Oct 27, 1995', TEC570295

Front/Rear Sunroofs – Rattle Noise, 'Oct 27, 1995', TEC763895

Factory Warranty Plus – Extended Warranty, 'Oct 11, 1995', W95004

Trailer Warning Light – Intermittent Operation, 'Oct 06, 1995', TEC860595

Passenger Seat Belt Stalk – Rattles, 'Oct 06, 1995', TEC763795

Security System Antenna – Reduced Range, 'Sep 22, 1995', TEC860395

SRS – Component Replacement Policy, 'Sep 15, 1995', W95003

Wipers-Washers – Rear Washer Nozzle Damaged/Broken, 'Sep 15, 1995', TEC840295

Drink Holder – Replacement Procedure, 'Sep 01, 1995', TEC763295

Rear Washer Jet – New Design, 'Sep 01, 1995', TEC763495

SRS Harness – Replacement Procedure, 'Sep 01, 1995', TEC762495

Center Console – Creak/Squeal, 'Aug 18, 1995', TEC762895

Front Seat Trim Cover – Loose/Rattles, 'Aug 11, 1995', TEC762595

Driveline – Vibration/Noise at Low or High Speeds, 'Aug 11, 1995', TEC470195

Rear Air Conditioning Duct – Residue Accumulation, 'Aug 11, 1995', TEC761195

Security System – Long Arming Light Indication, 'Aug 11, 1995', TEC860295

Body – Vibration/Noise & Harshness, 'Aug 11, 1995', TEC761595

Sunroof – Malfunction/Incomplete Operation, 'Jul 21, 1995', TEC761095

Rear Bumper Lamp – Cracking, 'Jul 07, 1995', TEC761295

Coolant – Incorrect Anti Freeze Mixture, 'Jun 09, 1995', HC865

Antifreeze/Coolant Mix – Incorrect, 'Jun 09, 1995', TECSAHC865

Brake Light Switch – Adjustment Procedure, 'Jun 01, 1995', 9590009

Recall – Driveshaft Nut/Bolt Replacement, 'May 31, 1995', RDC867

Oil Cooler Pipe – Oil Leaks, 'May 19, 1995', TEC120395

Underhood Fuse Box – Poor Connections/Driveability, 'May 19, 1995', TEC860195

Alloy Roadwheels – Retrofit Recommendations, 'May 05, 1995', TEC740195

Washer Pump – Updated/Conversion Link Lead, 'May 05, 1995', TEC840195

Rear Bumper Attachment Bolt – Torque, 'Apr 07, 1995', TEC760595

Exhaust Manifold/Header Pipe – Exhaust Leaks, 'Apr 07, 1995', TEC300195

Transmission Mount – Vibration Noise, 'Apr 07, 1995', TEC440195

Heater Plenum – Water Leaks to Interior, 'Mar 10, 1995', TEC760195

Vehicle – Lift Standards & Approved Suppliers, 'Feb 07, 1995', TE95002

Towing – Damage Reporting Procedure, 'Jan 13, 1995', G95-001

Engine – Oil Leaks From Rear of Cylinder Block, 'Jan 13, 1995', TEC120195

Rear Bumper Filler Strip – Cracking, 'Dec 09, 1994', TEC761694

Mass Air Flow Sensor – Gold Plated Connectors, 'Dec 09, 1994', TEC190394

Heated Oxygen Sensor – Unnecessary Replacement, 'Dec 02, 1994', W94-013

Drivers Heel Mat – Lifting/Loose, 'Dec 02, 1994', TEC762194

Rear Footwell Carpet – Loose Fit at Seat Plinth, 'Nov 07, 1994', TEC760994

Oxygen Sensor – Codes 44 & 45 Diagnosis, 'Nov 04, 1994', TEC190194

Cranks – No Start/Hesitation When Driving, 'Nov 04, 1994', TEC861194

Serpentine Drive Belt – Update, 'Nov 03, 1994', TEC120294

Windscreen Glass – Replacement, 'Oct 07, 1994', TEC761394

Rear Footwell Carpet – Poor Fit, 'Oct 07, 1994', TEC760894

Driver's Door – Rattles, 'Oct 07, 1994', TEC760494

Ignition System – Misfire at High Engine Speeds, 'Oct 07, 1994', TEC861094

Rear Side Door – Windnoise At D Post, 'Oct 07, 1994', TEC760594

Special Tool List – Updated, 'Sep 29, 1994', TE94003

Pioneer Audio System – Fault Diagnosis, 'Sep 16, 1994', TEC860994

Front Suspension – Bolts/Hardware Comes Loose, 'Sep 02, 1994', TEC600694

Ignition Module – Engine No Start/Poor Start, 'Sep 02, 1994', TEC860894

Ignition Timing – Poor Engine Performance, 'Sep 02, 1994', TEC860794

Idle Air Control Valve – Unnecessary Replacement, 'Aug 12, 1994', W94007

Rear Subwoofer – Thump or Pop Noises, 'Jul 29, 1994', TEC860694

Front Grille – Lower Corner Cracking, 'Jul 29, 1994', TEC761794

Windscreen Finisher A Post – Poor Fit, 'Jul 29, 1994', TEC760794

Engine/Drivetrain – Vibration at 30 to 40 Mph, 'Jul 22, 1994', TEC010594

Automatic Gear Selector – Graphic Film Torn, 'Jul 22, 1994', TEC440694

Audio System – Diagnosis & Troubleshooting, 'Jul 08, 1994', W94010

Radiator Bleed Hose – Deformation, 'Jul 01, 1994', TEC260194

Power Take Off Cover Plate – Oil Leaks, 'Jun 17, 1994', TEC410394

SRS – Parts Replacement Policy, 'Jun 17, 1994', TEC010494

A/C System – CFC Free Refrigerant (R134a), 'Jun 17, 1994', TEC820194

Center Plate/Extension Housing – Oil Leak, 'Jun 10, 1994', TEC370494

SRS – Fuse Repalcement, 'Jun 10, 1994', TEC761594

Warranty Labor Rate – Request Forms, 'Jun 03, 1994', W94-009

Spark Plugs – Recommendations/Service, 'May 24, 1994', W94008

Carpet – Fits Poorly at Front Seats, 'Apr 27, 1994', TEC761494

Windscreen – Water Leaks/Windnoise, 'Apr 20, 1994', TEC761294

SRS System – Questions & Answers, 'Apr 15, 1994', TEC761194

LT230T Transfer Gearbox – Oil Specification, 'Apr 13, 1994', TEC090394

SRS – Torx Head Retainers, 'Apr 06, 1994', TEC761094

Radio Speaker – Clicking/Cracking Noises, 'Mar 30, 1994', TEC860294

Cylinder Head Gasket – Revised Part, 'Mar 11, 1994', TEC120394

Engine Valley Cover Gasket – Revised Part, 'Mar 11, 1994', TEC120494

Steering Wheel -Misalignment, 'Mar 04, 1994', TEC570594

Power Steering Box – Replacement, 'Feb 18, 1994', TEC570394

Engine – No Start in Extreme Cold Conditions, 'Feb 11, 1994', TEC120794

Alloy Wheel Rims – Tire Installation & Removal, 'Jan 28, 1994', TEC740494

Clutch Slave Cylinder Heat Shield – Rattles, 'Jun 12, 1993', TEC300196

Front Suspension Bushings – Replacement, 'Nov 19, 1992', P92-016

Interior – Cold Air Drafts, 'Oct 19, 1992', P92-015

Sunroof – Water Leak, 'Aug 24, 1992', 232092

A/T – Intermediate Plate/Oil Pump Replacement, 'Jan 14, 1992', P92-002

Speedometer – Noise Diagnosis, 'Dec 13, 1988', P88-018

Warranty – Annual Corrosion Inspection, 'Jun 09, 1988', W88-006

Transfer Gearbox – Overhaul Recommendations, 'Apr 12, 1988', W88-003

Headlamp Wash System – Filter, 'Feb 08, 1988', P88-007

Paint – Standox Tinting Guide for Paint Matching, 'Jan 15, 1988', P88-002

Front Seats – Fore/AFT Movement, 'Jan 06, 1988', P88-001

Sandpaper – U.S. vs U.K. Abrasive Grades, 'Aug 25, 1987', P87-038

Fuel Gauge – Diagnostic Guidelines, 'May 04, 1987', P87-018

Preliminary Paint/Body Information, 'Mar 16, 1987', G87-001

appendix ii: Discovery 2 Technical Service Bulletins (TSB)

Here are the Technical Service Bulletins (TSBs) for the Discovery 2. To find out more type the reference number at the end of each line into your search engine. For the sake of correctness I have left the original Land Rover spelling mistakes.

'A/C, Electrical – Rear Glass Defogger Element Repair', 'Jun 14, 2011', TECLTB003292

Suspension – Correct Ball Joint Splitter Usage, 'Dec 17, 2009', TECLTB00248

Navigation System – Diagnostic Aid, 'May 24, 2007', TECLTB00020

Audio System – Speaker Vibration/Rattle Noise Diagnosis, 'Sep 11, 2006', TECLRA415001

Brakes – Labor Time Change for ABS Modulator, 'Aug 25, 2006', TEC700206

Suspension – Air Suspension Height Sensor Connector, 'Aug 07, 2006', TEC680106

Body – Windshield Damage Diagnostic Aid, 'Jun 22, 2006', TECLRA501001

A/T – Revised Removal & Installation Procedures, 'Jun 13, 2006', TEC440106

ABS/TCS – Warning Lamp ON/DTC's Set, 'Mar 17, 2006', TEC700106

Engine – Upper Intake Manifold Gasket Replacement, 'Nov 10, 2005', TEC300105

Recall – A/T Fluid Water Contamination, 'Oct 29, 2005', D2332

Maintenance – Fluid Specifications/Applications, 'Sep 28, 2005', TEC100105

Drivetrain – Front Differential Installation Procedure, 'Sep 26, 2005', TEC540305

Cooling System – Viscous Fan Replacement, 'Jul 18, 2005', TEC260405

ABS/TCS – Warning Lamps ON/HDC Lamp ON/DTC's Set, 'Jul 07, 2005', TEC700305

Brakes – ABS Harness Damage Repair, 'Jul 01, 2005', TEC700105

Body – Carbalflo XTR5(R) Lubricant Usage, 'Jun 10, 2005', TA057602

Recall – ABS Modulator Plate Reinforcement, 'Apr 25, 2005', RB1482

Suspension – Revised Front Shock Replacement, 'Mar 16, 2005', TEC600205

Steering – Revised Steering Box Installation, 'Mar 16, 2005', TEC570305

ABS/TCS – ACE System Diagnostics/Bleeding Procedure, 'Dec 20, 2004', TEC600204

Brakes – Handbrake Vibration Noise, 'Oct 28, 2004', TEC700604

Brakes – Front/Rear Brake Squeals/Noise, 'Jul 20, 2004', TEC7001022

Brakes – ABS Sensor Availibility/Replacement, 'Jun 04, 2004', TEC700204

Interior – Front Seat Heating Elements Inoperative, 'Jun 04, 2004', TEC760704

Lighting – Condensation Inside Headlamps, 'Jun 04, 2004', TEC860504

SRS – Overlay Harness Availability/Repair, 'Apr 30, 2004', TEC860304

Body – Water Leak At Headliner, 'Apr 30, 2004', TEC760404

Recall – Suspension ACE Pump Banjo Fitting Torque, 'Apr 23, 2004', RB149

Brakes – ABS Sensors Availability, 'Apr 20, 2004', TA037001

A/C – Control Knob Hard to Move, 'Jan 23, 2004', TEC800104

Recall 04V005000: ABS Modulator Valve Bolts Crack, 'Jan 01, 2004', NHTSA04V005000

Interior – Various Squeaks and Rattles, 'Oct 31, 2003', TEC762003

Interior – Poor Functioning of 3rd Row Seats, 'Oct 31, 2003', TEC7614032

Body – Hinge Lubrication Maintenance Revision, 'Oct 28, 2003', TA037605R

Fuel System/Body – Fuel Filler Flap Won't Stay Closed, 'Aug 22, 2003', TEC761703

Body/Frame – Knocking/Creaking Noise on Turns, 'May 23, 2003', TEC761303

Engine – Idler Pulley/Belt Noise, 'May 23, 2003', TEC8602033

A/T – Sport/Manual Lamps ON Without Mode Change, 'May 02, 2003', TEC860403

Active Cornering Enhancement (ACE) – Lamp ON, 'Apr 25, 2003', TEC600503

A/T – Shift Lever Selector Knob Installation, 'Apr 23, 2003', TA034401

Wipers/Washers – Front Washer Nozzles Leak Fluid, 'Apr 01, 2003', TEC840203

Body – Water Leaks In Rear of Vehicle, 'Jan 17, 2003', TEC760103

Engine – Oil Leaks From Rear, 'Oct 11, 2002', TEC120202

Engine – Oil Leaks From Rear of Engine, 'Oct 11, 2002', TEC120102

Recall – Abnormal ABS Operation, 'Oct 11, 2002', D2636

A/T – ZF Transmission/Multiple Shift Concerns, 'Aug 16, 2002', TEC440102

Brakes – Front/Rear Brake Squealing Noise, 'Aug 09, 2002', TEC700102

Electrical – Intermittent Electrical/No Start Problems, 'Aug 09, 2002', TEC860502

Drivetrain – Rear Differential Water Contamination, 'Aug 09, 2002', TEC510102

Interior – Tailgate Trim Panel Vibration, 'Jul 26, 2002', TEC760302

Lighting – High Mount Stop Lamp Loose, 'Apr 26, 2002', TEC860202

Recall – Throttle Cable Inspection/Replacement, 'Mar 05, 2002', D274

Navigation System – Non-Operational, 'Feb 05, 2002', TEC860102

Recall 02V022000: Inappropriate ABS Activation, 'Jan 01, 2002', NHTSA02V022000

Recall 02V028000: Accelerator Cable Damage, 'Jan 01, 2002', NHTSA02V028000

Wheels – Difficult to Remove, 'Sep 11, 2001', TEC100101

Steering – Steering Box Installation Precautions, 'Sep 07, 2001', TEC570201

Recall – Winch Solenoid Overheating, 'Aug 10, 2001', D255

Brakes – Grunting Noise in High Heat Conditions, 'Aug 03, 2001', TEC700101

Interior – Glove Box Won't Stay Closed, 'Jul 27, 2001', TEC760501

Starter – Engine No-Start Condition, 'Jul 27, 2001', TEC860400

Starter – Knocking Noise When Starting Engine, 'Jul 27, 2001', TEC860801

Engine Controls – MIL ON/MAF Multiple DTC's Set, 'Jul 13, 2001', TEC190301

A/T – Fluid Leaks From Torque Converter, 'Jun 15, 2001', TEC4402002

Instruments – Erratic Mirror Compass Readings, 'Jun 15, 2001', TEC860701

Keys/Locks – Key Shank Detaches from Handset, 'Jun 01, 2001', TEC570101

Body Control Unit – Replacement Procedure, 'Mar 23, 2001', TEC860301

Antitheft System – Engine No-Crank Condition, 'Mar 23, 2001', TEC860401

Suspension – Coil Spring Installation Precautions, 'Mar 02, 2001', TEC540101

Interior – Rear Center Seat Belt Jamming, 'Mar 02, 2001', TEC760201

Fuel System – Unable to Remove Fuel Filler Cap, 'Feb 23, 2001', TEC190101

Drivetrain – Revised Wheel Hub Service Procedures, 'Feb 23, 2001', TEC600101

Wipers/Washers – Wiper Arms Come loose, 'Feb 16, 2001', TEC840101

Engine – Tapping/Rattling Noises, 'Dec 22, 2000', TEC120200

Discovery 2 Technical Service Bulletins (TSB)

Recall – Engine Idler Pulley Replacement, 'Dec 08, 2000', D2163

Campaign – Throttle Body Heater Gasket Replacement, 'Dec 08, 2000', H230

Recall – A/T Breather Hose Repositioning, 'Nov 22, 2000', TA004402

Recall 00V377000: Transmission Park Lock Failure, 'Nov 16, 2000', NHTSA00V377000

Engine Controls – Bosch ECM Reprogramming, 'Nov 10, 2000', TB0100

Electrical – MIL ON/Multiple DTC's Set/Systems Inop., 'Oct 27, 2000', TEC860500

Recall 00V142001: Serpentine Belt Pulley Failure, 'Oct 13, 2000', NHTSA00V142001

Engine – Valve Guide Cleaning, 'Sep 29, 2000', TEC120100

Interior – Rear Seat Latch Strap Separation, 'Sep 22, 2000', TEC760400

Drivetrain – Rear Axle Clicking Noise, 'May 12, 2000', TEC510200

Recall 00V142000: Serpentine Belt Pulley Failure, 'May 12, 2000', NHTSA00V142000

Engine – MIL ON/Rough Running, 'Apr 21, 2000', TEC300200

Suspension – Knocking Sound From Suspension, 'Apr 21, 2000', TEC600100

Wipers/Washers – Washer Nozzle Corrosion, 'Apr 21, 2000', TEC840100

Exhaust System – Rattling Noises, 'Apr 21, 2000', TEC300300

Campaign – Engine Thermostat Canister Replacement, 'Apr 14, 2000', H2022

Body – Tightening Support Strut Fasteners, 'Apr 07, 2000', TEC760200

Starting System – Intermittent Failure to Start, 'Mar 06, 2000', TA0086012

Battery – Dead/Fails to Maintain A Charge, 'Mar 03, 2000', TEC860100

Engine – Excessively High/Low Oil Dipstick Readings, 'Feb 16, 2000', TA001201

Recall 00V036000: ACE Hydraulic Tubing Leaks, 'Feb 09, 2000', NHTSA00V036000

Campaign – Engine Idler Pulley Replacement, 'Feb 04, 2000', H3692

Brakes – ABS Warning Lamp Illumination, 'Dec 17, 1999', TEC700299

Transfer Case – Output Seal Leakage, 'Nov 23, 1999', TEC4102973

A/T – Cooler Flushing, 'Oct 22, 1999', TEC440299

Battery – Battery Cover Latch Failure, 'Oct 08, 1999', TEC860899

Campaign – Power Seat Binding, 'Sep 28, 1999', H384

Antitheft – No-Start Condition After Unlocking With Key, 'Sep 28, 1999', TEC860699

Campaign – Erratic Alarm System Activation, 'Sep 24, 1999', H366

Recall – ABS Relay Contacts Sticking, 'Sep 24, 1999', D380

Frame – Knocking/Pinging Sound, 'Sep 03, 1999', TEC762399

Differential – Oil Level Plug Damage Prevention, 'Aug 20, 1999', TEC100299

Driveline – High Speed Vibration, 'Aug 13, 1999', 03-02-99A

Interior – 2nd Row Seat Squeaking Sound, 'Jul 30, 1999', TEC762299

Body/Interior – Dashboard Creaking Noises, 'Jul 30, 1999', TEC7611994

Ignition System – Hard Start/Rough Running/Misfire Codes, 'Jul 30, 1999', TEC190198

Interior – Front Seat Trim Loose/Misaligned, 'Jul 16, 1999', TEC762199

Interior – 2nd Row Seat Rattles, 'Jul 09, 1999', TEC761999

Campaign – Brake Fluid Filter Replacement, 'Jul 02, 1999', H362

Suspension – ACE System Noise/Vibration, 'Jun 25, 1999', TEC6002992

Engine – Stalling/Hesitation/Poor Idle, 'Jun 18, 1999', TEC120299

Fuel System – Proper Fuel Line Quick Fit Connections, 'Jun 18, 1999', TEC190399

Keys – Replacement Key is Inoperative, 'Jun 18, 1999', TEC761699

Interior – Center Console Rattles, 'Jun 18, 1999', TEC761899

Body – Front Door Top Sill Rattles, 'Jun 04, 1999', TEC761499

ABS – Unintended Warning Lamp Illumination, 'Jun 04, 1999', TEC700199

Engine – Oil Leaks From Rear of Sump, 'Jun 04, 1999', TEC120992

Body – Erratic Fuel Door Operation, 'May 19, 1999', TEC761299

Interior – 2nd Row Seat Squeak, 'May 19, 1999', TEC7606992

Body/Interior – 'A'-Pillar Rattling, 'May 19, 1999', TEC7610992

Interior – Glove Box Area Rattle, 'May 19, 1999', TEC7608992

Interior – 3rd Row Seat Jamming, 'May 07, 1999', TEC761399

Body – Rear End Door Rattles, 'Apr 23, 1999', TEC760799

Interior – Cup Holder Squeaks, 'Apr 23, 1999', TEC760599

Interior – Front Seat Height Adjuster Binding, 'Apr 23, 1999', TEC760999

Interior – Front Seat Squeaks/Rattles, 'Apr 09, 1999', TEC760499

Instruments – Fuel Gauge Inoperative, 'Apr 07, 1999', TA991901

Electrical – Multiple Electrical Malfunctions, 'Mar 19, 1999', TEC860499

Engine – Oil Sump Bolt Leakage, 'Mar 18, 1999', TA991201

Interior – Seat Back Functions Inoperative, 'Mar 12, 1999', TEC860399

Interior – Seatbelt Adjustment Lubrication, 'Feb 19, 1999', TEC760199

A/T – ZF Transmission Fluid Level Checking, 'Feb 19, 1999', TEC440199

Heater Hose – Coolant Leaks, 'Dec 05, 1997', TEC1207972

A/T – Evaluation Report (ATER), 'Nov 14, 1997', W97-011

A/T – Evaluation Report (ATER) Warranty Claim, 'Oct 24, 1997', W97-009

Warranty Claims – MIL Event Requirements, 'Jun 27, 1997', W97-007

Warranty – Daily Transaction Summary, 'Apr 21, 1997', W97-006

High Mount Stop Lamp – Modification, 'Apr 11, 1997', TEC860797

Air Bag – Safety Label Instruction, 'Mar 14, 1997', G97-05

Warranty – Parts Handling Reimbursement, 'Jun 14, 1996', W96-010

Lease Program – Warranty Extension Deletion, 'May 28, 1996', W96-009

A   Amperes

A pillar   Bodywork joining the front corners of the roof to the side of the car, holds the windscreen up and is vital for rollover safety.

A/C   Air Conditioning

ABDC   After Bottom Dead Centre

ABS   Anti-lock Brake System, detects a wheel starting to lock up when braking and reduces brake pressure to maintain optimum traction and braking force.

ac   Alternating current

ACE   Active Cornering Enhancement

AFR   Air Fuel Ratio

After market   Parts not made by the original car manufacturer.

ATDC   After Top Dead Centre

B pillar   Bodywork joining the roof to the sill, holds the driver and front passenger seat belts. Vital for rollover and side impact safety.

BBDC   Before Bottom Dead Centre

BCM   Body Control Module. Controls locks, windows, lights, immobilizer and just about everything.

BDC   Bottom Dead Centre

bhp   Brake Horse Power

BTDC   Before Top Dead Centre

C   Celsius

CAN   Controller Area Network, a communications network in the car that lets the engine, gearbox and other systems share information.

Cant rail   The long bracing on the inside edge of the roof, above the doors. This gives the roof its rigidity.

cm   Centimetre

CO   Carbon Monoxide

CO$_2$ Carbon Dioxide

Damper   Also known as a shock absorber, damps out the bounce from the road springs and controls wheel movement and grip at speed.

dc   Direct current

deg.   Degree, angle or temperature

dia.   Diameter

Diagnostic tool   A device to read fault codes; most tools can also clear fault codes and some devices allow you to use special functions such as calibrating the ride height.

Diff   Differential, the big bit in the axle that lets the wheels go at different speeds so you can go round corners without skidding.

DMF   Dual Mass Flywheel, an engine flywheel having two parts separated by rubber or springs to aid refinement.

DTC   Device Trouble Code, and OBD code relating to specific faults.

DTI   Dial Test Indicator

EACV   Electronic Air Control Valve

ECM   Engine Control Module

ECU   Electronic Control Unit

EDC   Electronic Diesel Control

EGR   Exhaust Gas Recirculation, used to reduce NOx emissions by feeding small amounts of exhaust into the intake.

EKA   Emergency Key Access, used when the remote key fob stops working.

EOBD   European On Board Diagnostics, similar to the US OBDII.

ETC   Electronic Traction Control

EVAP   Evaporative Emission

EVR   Electronic Vacuum Regulator

HC   Hydrocarbons

HDC   Hill Descent Control, uses the ABS to prevent the vehicle going to fast down very steep off-road tracks.

HO2S   Heated Oxygen Sensor

IACV   Idle Air Control Valve

k   Thousand

kg   Kilogram

km   Kilometre

km/h   Kilometres per hour

l   Litre

Lambda sensor   Another word for oxygen sensor, used to control fuel mixture.

LCD   Liquid Crystal Display

LED   Light Emitting Diode

LH   Left Hand

LHD   Left-Hand Drive

LPG   Liquefied Petroleum Gas, a road fuel that is a mix of butane and propane which is often half the price of petrol.

m   Metre

MAF   Mass Air Flow, the sensors that measure the amount of air the engine is breathing in.

max.   Maximum

MIL   Malfunction Indicator Lamp, also known as Check Engine light.

min.   Minimum

mm   Millimetre

MPa   MegaPascal

mph   Miles per hour

Mpi   Multi-point injection

MY   Model Year

Nm   Newton metre

No.   Number

NOx   Oxides of Nitrogen

OAT   Organic Acid Technology, a type of coolant that has longer life than ethylene glycol.

OBD   On Board Diagnostics, the system where the engine management and other ECUs detect and communicate faults.

Oxygen sensor   Also known as a Lambda sensor, used to control fuel mixture

Panel gap   The gap between body panels, similar to shut lines but also includes panels that do not move.

PAS   Power Assisted Steering

PCV   Positive Crankcase Ventilation, a system for taking combustible vapours out of the engine block to burn them cleanly in the engine, and allowing clean air in.

Prop   Propshaft, a shaft that joins the gearbox to the differential.

PWM   Pulse Width Modulation, a way of controlling electrical devices to get a proportional action, such as variable speed fans.

ref   Reference

RF   Radio Frequency

RH   Right Hand

RHD   Right-Hand Drive

Rot   Corrosion, rust or degrading of a part or body panel.

rpm   Revolutions per minute

Shut lines   The gaps between the edge of the doors and the body when the door is closed.

Sill   The box structure at the sides of the car floor that gives the underside of the body its strength.

SLABS   Self Levelling and Anti-lock Brake System

SLS   Self Levelling Suspension

Shock absorber   *See* Damper.

SRS   Supplementary Restraint System, airbags.

std   Standard

TC   Traction Control, detects wheel spin using the ABS when accelerating and reduces engine power and applies the brakes to maintain traction.

TDC   Top Dead Centre, when the piston is at the very top of the cylinder bore.

Testbook   The official dealer diagnostic tool of the time.

Toe (in/out/angle)   The degree by which the wheels on an axle point inwards or splay out.

Trans   Transmission, usually refers to just the gearbox but technically also includes the propshaft and axles.

UJ   Universal Joint, part of the driveshafts near the front wheels that allows the shaft to move as the wheel is turned.

V   Volt

VIN   Vehicle Identification Number